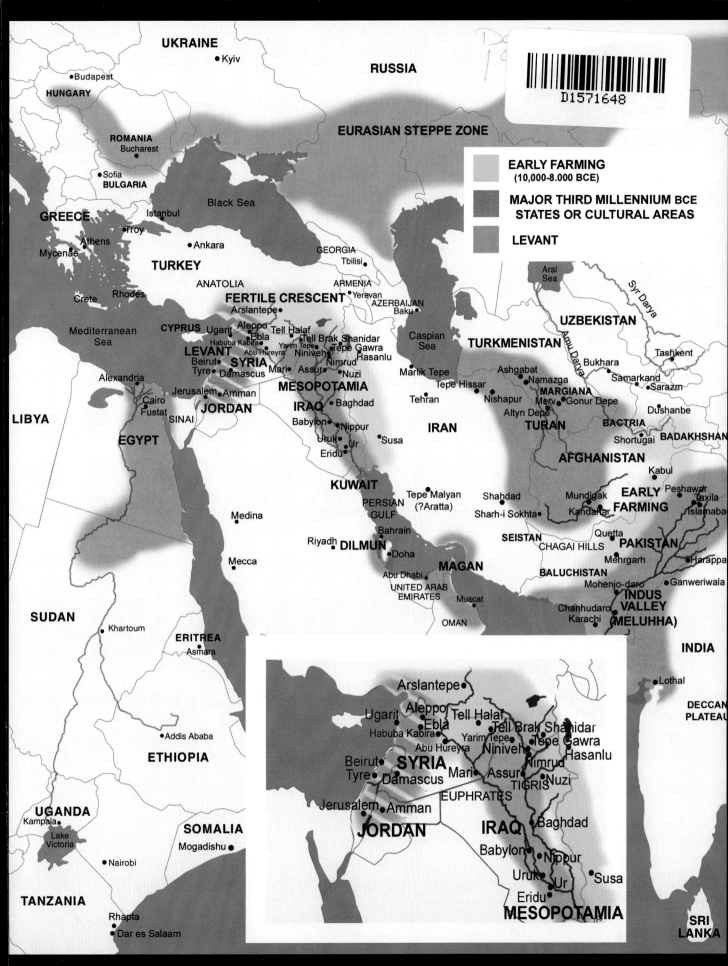

ACKNOWLEDGEMENTS

Our Bead Timeline concept was born when The Bead Society of Greater Washington (BSGW) dedicated the proceeds from its 1995 International Bead Conference to fund a bead museum in the nation's capital. Thanks to a generous $10,000 donation from The Bead Society in Los Angeles, California, we began planning a permanent exhibit to realize our mission — to study beads and disseminate the acquired knowledge. Lois Sherr Dubin's bead chart in her seminal *History of Beads* served as an inspiration and this format allowed an emphasis on the cultural and historical context of beads. To allow for continuous growth and display of the collection within the space strictures of our small museum, we designed seven plexiglass cases totalling 34 feet long by 24 inches wide, set atop canted storage cabinets.

Members and friends generously gave beads to start the Timeline collection. An anonymous grant enabled bead and jewelry historian Jamey D. Allen to work with us; he did a masterful job of laying out the beads and consulting with James W. Lankton on their identification, dating and classification. Allen's eye for spacing and layout is both meticulous and unerring, making the display an arrangement of great beauty. He and Lankton cataloged every Timeline bead or bead group, co-wrote a lectern catalog for visitors' use and co-curated the exhibition. Julia Lobotsky is our chief exhibit guide and volunteer trainer, intern Rebecca Price is a valued assistant and Kirsten Andersen and Ashton Douglass maintain the exhibit.

The Timeline has grown to over 5,000 beads donated or promised by Dan Adams, Jamey D. Allen, Christine A. Baker, Banares Beads Ltd., Betty D. Battle, The Bead Study Trust, Ellen Benson, Adel Boehm-Mabe, Jeanne M. Boskovich, Lucinda L. Brown, Susan M. Campbell, Susan Carlson, Judy and Thor Carlsson, Jo A.S. Carpenter, Oumar Cissé, Katrin Cittarns, Gisele Dahan-Hecht, Deanna G. Dove, Paula Eiblum, Joan C. Eppen, Leah Fairbanks, Brenda Forman, Leslie Fox, Noah Fox, George C. Gamache, Rajni Goel, Anita Gumpert, Carole Horn, J. Mark Kenoyer, Earl Kessler, Barbie Koncher, Margaret Kris Estate, James W. Lankton, Gabrielle Liese, Helene Lileikis, Jackie Little, Robert K. Liu, Kristina Logan, Eleanore Macnish, Maud McKalanos, Bruce St. John Maher, Polly Miller, Nan Mulville,

The current Bead Timeline exhibit at the Bead Museum, Washington, D.C.; this volume covers the beads of the left-hand and middle portions .

Cheryl Olkes Estate, Janet Olson, Howard and Marie José Opper, Kristen F. Orr, Theodora Pellet, Mirtha V. de Perea, Bob and Barabara Pringle, Paula Radke, Riverstone Bead Co., Jeannette and Jonathan Rosen, Bob Rubanowice, Barbara B. Simon, James Smircich, Ruth Smith, Cheryl Spence, Norma Sporn, Lisa St. Martin, Kirk Stanfield, J. M. Taggart, Louise E. Taggart, Kathleen Tilford, Stefany Tomalin, Cynthia Toops, Dorothy Trubacek, Ellen Vestergaard, Pier Voulkos, Edith A. Wachtel, Connie Walsh, Joan Weber, the Nathan Weissman Trust, Hilary Whittaker, Penelope Diamanti de Widt and Janet Wolery.

We deeply appreciate the contributions and collaborative efforts of those who made this book possible: for generous financial support which provided for book design, layout, prepress, film and photographic equipment rentals, we thank the Bead Society, Los Angeles; the Bead Society of Greater Chicago; Dr. James W. Lankton, The Rosen Foundation, Penelope Diamanti de Widt and the Portland Bead Society. Profound thanks are due author James W. Lankton, photographer and managing editor Robert K. Liu; associate editor Joyce Diamanti; assistant editor and indexer Penelope Diamanti de Widt; indexer Pat Diamanti; writers Joyce Diamanti, J. Mark Kenoyer, Robert K. Liu and Deborah Zinn, designer Caroline I. Carlson and Museum Consultant Christine O'Donnell for marketing assistance.

Hilary Whittaker, Timeline Coordinator

This book is published in conjunction with the exhibition, *The Bead Timeline of History*, on permanent exhibit at the Bead Museum in Washington, DC.; founded by the Bead Society of Greater Washington in 1995, opened 1997.
ISBN 0-97-25066-1-6
Copyright © 2003 The Bead Society of Greater Washington

All rights reserved. No part of this publication may be reproduced or transmitted in any form or by any means without the permission of the copyright owner. For permissions please contact: The Bead Museum, The Bead Society of Greater Washington, 400 Seventh St., N.W., Washington D.C. 20004.

Managing Editor: Robert K. Liu, Ph.D.
Associate Editor: Joyce Diamanti
Assistant Editor/Indexer: Penelope Diamanti de Widt
Writers: Joyce Diamanti, Jonathan M. Kenoyer, Ph.D., James W. Lankton, M.D., Robert K. Liu, Ph.D. and Deborah K. Zinn, Ph.D.
Photographer: Robert K. Liu, PhD.
Art Direction, Illustration and Design: Caroline I. Carlson
Typeface: AGaramond 10 pt.
Pre-press: Applied Graphics Technologies
Printer: Publishers Press, Inc.

A BEAD TIMELINE

VOLUME I: PREHISTORY to 1200 CE

A Resource for Identification, Classification and Dating.

BY JAMES W. LANKTON, M.D.

JOYCE DIAMANTI AND
JONATHAN M. KENOYER, PH.D.
PHOTOGRAPHY BY ROBERT K. LIU, PH.D.

The timeline is a well-known and widely used device to relate events or artifacts dispersed through time and geographic space. For small artifacts like beads and other perforated objects, timelines are ideal for showing such information as their age and place of origin, especially in a limited space. Their sizes, shapes, materials, technique of manufacture and variations in any of these characteristics are easily apparent to the viewer upon examination. When a timeline display is arranged so that chronological time is on the long axis and geographic regions are on the vertical axis, taking visual slices along either parameter yields much enlightening information about beads and their relationships through time and to different cultural or geographic areas.

The timeline in Lois Dubin's pivotal 1987 book, *The History of Beads*, was the first attempt to show the bead universe in one document. Her original bead chart was an eight-page foldout spanning from 30,000 BCE to about 1986. Individual photographs of some 1,300 beads and/or strands were photographically composited into a full color timeline, with all beads or pendants in approximate scale to each other. The examples shown were from individually or institutionally owned specimens. Thus this was a virtual timeline, since it did not represent an actual display. For the Second International Bead Conference of 1990, organized by the Bead Society of Greater Washington, Dubin's timeline was presented in an enlarged version as a poster, with the publisher's permission. An actual bead exhibition, set up along the format of a timeline but on tiered horizontal shelves, was also shown.

The first attempt to install an actual timeline of beads was during the 1997 Beaded Universe exhibition at the Mingei International Museum of Folk Art in San Diego. A lender and consultant to this show, Lois Dubin most likely recommended including a version of a bead timeline, which was then curated, designed and installed by Jamey D. Allen, utilizing some 800 loose beads (Liu 1997). Cases arranged linearly along a wall held the beads, while photographic enlargements of the printed timeline were shown above. The Bead Museum of Prescott, Arizona was the major lender of these specimens. In 1999 the second bead timeline was installed at The Bead Museum, which had by now moved to Glendale, Arizona. Again, Allen, their consultant, was responsible for the entire process; this measured sixteen linear feet and held some 1,000 beads. It will undoubtedly be re-installed on a larger scale when this museum moves in the near future. The third Bead Timeline, at The Bead Museum in Washington, D.C., was installed in 2000. Here, Jamey Allen, James Lankton and Hilary Whittaker all participated in various aspects of the specimen acquisition, curating, design, installation and funding. Configured in a U-shape, it is about thirty-four linear feet and contains some 5,000 beads, mounted primarily on rectangular, cloth-covered panels, which are numbered alphabetically. This is currently the most comprehensive extant Bead Timeline, with over 2,300 beads illustrated in this Catalog.

Both of these permanent displays have been revised since their initial installation. Like any collection or arrangement of objects that belong to distinct categories, a bead timeline faces some inherent disadvantages. As no bead collection is ever complete, the placement of new acquisitions in a fixed display or the movement of extant specimens to new positions when additional information becomes available requires revision. There arises the problem of how to insert these specimens into a limited space or prior arrangement. In addition, as examples of beads from a certain category or geographic area increases, there may be the need to expand the space both along the horizontal time axis and vertically in the cultural areas. Thus Dubin's timeline had constrictions or expansions along the vertical axis; this feature has been adapted to some degree in the revised Washington exhibit but the need for periodic major re-installations will continue for any bead timeline.

Because the actual timeline in Washington, on which this catalog is based, has two panels which fit into the corner cases as abutting triangles, Lankton decided to re-arrange these images electronically. Thus, the illustrations shown in Chapter 5 are a virtual display. Other panels were similarly modified as Lankton wrote his chapters in this catalog and noted the need for revision in the positioning of various beads. More beads were added to the panels since photography in August, 2002 and additional beads, such as those from the Rosen Collection, will also be included. Current and future visitors to The Bead Museum in Washington, D.C. will no doubt detect differences between the beads shown in this publication and the actual display. Still, the current convention of full-page photographs of full or partial panels and closeups will enable readers and viewers to transition between the two.

We hope that this Bead Timeline will prove a true heuristic device for all who utilize, collect or study beads, whether on a casual or professional level.

Map of Europe . . . . .inside front cover

Map of Near East . . . . .page 1

Acknowledgements by Hilary Whittaker . . . . .page 2

Title page . . . . .page 3

Foreword by Robert K. Liu . . . . .page 4

Introduction by James W. Lankton . . . . .page 6

Beads, Trade and Cultural Change by Joyce Diamanti . . .page 8

The Technology of Stone Beads by Jonathan M. Kenoyer . .page 14

Chapter 1 . . . . .page 20

Chapter 2 . . . . .page 24

Chapter 3 . . . . .page 30

Chapter 4 . . . . .page 38

Chapter 5 . . . . .page 44

Chapter 6 . . . . .page 52

Chapter 7 . . . . .page 62

Chapter 8 . . . . .page 74

Rosen Collection Beads . . . . .page 84

References . . . . .page 86

Index . . . . .page 92

Online Resources by Deborah Zinn . . . . .page 95

Map of Asia . . . . .page 96

Map of Trade of Beads and Bead Materials . . . .inside back cover

Welcome to the Bead Timeline collection at The Bead Museum in Washington D.C. We hope that this catalog will help you to learn from and enjoy our *Bead Timeline from Prehistory to the Present*, which now forms a permanent display at the Museum. We present this publication as a way to share what we have learned with a wider audience, and we hope that both novice and expert alike will find something of interest. We begin with an essay by Joyce Diamanti on the very earliest beads and the role of beads in trade, followed by J. Mark Kenoyer's discussion of the history and technology of stone beadmaking. This Volume 1 of our Bead Timeline covers the period from the beginning of the Paleolithic/Neolithic transition around 12,000 BCE, to the Early Islamic period leading up to 1200 CE. The main text is divided into eight chapters, each one devoted to the beads on a particular panel of the exhibit. Following these chapters, we have included two pages of highlights from the recent, most generous gift of Jeanette and Jonathan Rosen of New York City, and on the last page of text, Deborah Zinn, founding moderator of the online bead group Beads-L, will help us make sense of the incredible profusion of bead-related websites and discussion groups. The reference and bibliography section includes works cited in the text as well as additional works, both classic and recent, that we felt would be useful to the reader. Finally, the index will improve access to information in the catalog, and the four maps will help the reader follow the story of beads through space as well as time.

It is important to keep in mind that this catalog is the record of an exhibit of actual beads, which has both advantages and disadvantages compared to a photographic timeline, such as the one included with Lois Dubin's groundbreaking *The History of Beads*. Foremost among the advantages is the power of the physical presence of an object. There is no substitute for the experience of seeing and examining an actual bead, and although this particular advantage may be less for those able to see only this catalog, we hope that for most readers, the catalog will be the prelude to an actual visit to the Museum. Our Bead Timeline is beautiful, and for this we are deeply indebted to Jamey D. Allen, whose knowledge helped us arrange the beads so that we could tell their story, and whose wonderful artistic sense has allowed the beads to tell their own stories through their inherent beauty. Through inevitable changes and additions, we have tried to follow Jamey's original design. Robert K. Liu photographed the Timeline for this catalog, making a panoramic view of each of the exhibit panels, as well as closer shots of selected groupings. The eight chapters focus on succeeding panels, presented in the way a Museum visitor might tour the actual installation.

Another virtue of the Museum exhibit is that the interested visitor can seek the help of one of our volunteer docents for guidance and explanation. We would like this catalog to serve a similar purpose, helping the reader understand the beads and their contexts, and shedding light on the important, underlying ways these beads help us learn about and appreciate the people who made, traded, used, and ultimately disposed of them.

When we first arranged the Bead Timeline in 2000, we were surprised at how many of the beads were not represented on the "Bead Chart" from *The History of Beads*. Although we tried to maintain the numbering system used by

Dubin, we found it necessary to make several changes, which we hope will not prove too confusing for those trying to compare one timeline with another. Our intention has always been that the exhibit is a work in progress, with beads added or rearranged as our collection grows and our knowledge increases. Indeed, the preparation of this catalog has stimulated both, so that the placement of a number of the beads in the close-up photographs may no longer be precisely in line with current understanding. In the panoramic views we have adjusted arrangements to be as accurate as we could make them, and the few exceptions are noted in the text. Also, because of these adjustments some of the numbers may be out of sequence, which I am sure the attentive reader will be quick to discover.

One of the fundamental parts of any timeline is of course *time*, which superficially would seem quite straightforward. We are accustomed to seeing dates for the discovery of the wheel, or for the Egyptian New Kingdom, given as relatively discrete numbers. What we may not realize is that neither of these dates is precise. For such relatively early events as the use of the wheel in the 4th millennium BCE, we must first decide what evidence we will accept that wheels were actually used, and then hope to define a range of several hundred years. For the Egptian New Kingdom, there are several alternative chronologies, generally high, low, and middle, for each of which respected archaeologists can make very convincing arguments. In fact, for dates before the mid-1st millennium BCE, there is no general agreement among experts working in the areas of history and archaeology. For the purposes of this catalog, we have adopted the chronology used by the Metropolitan Museum of Art, as published

James W. Lankton

on the Timeline of Art History, www.metmuseum.org/toah/splash.htm. Although I'm sure few would agree with all of the dates used on the site, these dates are easily accessible and quite comprehensive, covering most areas of the world during our period of concern. I believe that the interested reader will find the many maps useful as well. We have, however, made at least one change to the metmuseum dates, which are expressed as BC and AD, by using the convention BCE and CE, standing for Before the Common Era, and Common Era, a system formulated by a group of scholars attempting to find a non-sectarian reference for biblical events. We chose it for our original Bead Timeline exhibit and for this catalog.

Most of us are familiar with radiocarbon dating, which can be used for samples up to about 45,000 years old. Dates are based on the principle that the radioactive carbon contained in all organic matter, largely because of constant exposure to low levels of cosmic radiation, will decay at a predictable rate following the death of the organism. Thus, a date may be calculated based on the ratio of radiocarbon (C-14) to non-radioactive carbon (C-12). Results have been expressed as 12,000 years bp, for example, where bp refers to before the present and the present is taken to be 1950, the approximate year that the method was developed. It turns out, however, that the level of cosmic radiation has not been constant over the years, so the radiocarbon dates must be calibrated for a given area and time period. There are now computer programs that do this, giving a range within which the true date is likely to fall. Unfortunately, the several programs in use arrive at different results, but all add from 1000 to 2000 years to a radiocarbon date of 10,000 bp, giving a calibrated date

between 10,000 and 9,000 cal BCE. More recent dates change less, so that 5,000 bp (uncalibrated) would be 3900 to 3700 cal BCE. For the discussion of West Asian (but not Chinese) beads in Chapters 1 and 2, we have attempted to find calibrated dates, and where this was not possible, in order to create some consistency in dating, we have performed our own rough calibrations based on published calibrations from similar sites (for discussion and examples see Moore *et al* 2000: 258-259; Wright and Ripley 2001: 100-119; Cauvin 2000: xviii).

We are very fortunate that so many generous individuals have donated beads for our Timeline exhibit, allowing us to include a broad range of cultures and time periods. Indeed, no small museum can build a collection without such donations. Because our beads have come largely from private collections, our ability to speak with certainty about any given bead is limited to those that so closely resemble excavated specimens that their identity is all but certain; we have emphasized these beads in the discussion. In other cases we have relied on our best educated guess as to the identity of a given bead, and we state that such-and-such a bead represents the type of beads that would have been found.

The original concept of the Timeline exhibit was to show how beads, arranged in chronologic and geographic sequence, could illustrate and punctuate cultural history. We have tried to follow that concept in the Catalog, with the result that much of the space is taken by reviews of the historical events and technological changes for which beads were important. We have discussed a great many of the over 2,000 illustrated, but we have inevitably ignored many as well. We sincerely hope that what we have written will be of sufficient interest to encourage

the reader to learn more. For those interested in a specific bead that is not discussed, the bead's placement on the large panels will give some idea of our current thoughts on chronology and geography, and we plan to produce, within six months of the publication of the catalog, a companion volume with a complete listing of all of the beads, to be available either as a CD-ROM or on our website www.beadmuseumdc.org. Such a listing is now available at the Museum—another encouragement for the prospective visitor.

A project like this catalog is the work of many people. Joyce, Penny, Robert, and Cara have been wonderful to work with and have provided just the right amount of help and encouragement. We all play our part, and none of us is indispensable, but I would have to say that the least dispensable of all would be Hilary Whittaker, without whose concept, tireless enthusiasm, and willingness to take on any job, large or small, neither the Museum nor the Timeline would have its present form. Many others have been most helpful with the preparation of this catalog, generously sharing their time and knowledge, and I would like to particularly thank the late Peter Francis, Jr., Jamey D. Allen, Derek Content, Robert K.Liu, Maud Spaer, Hansel de Sousa, Simon Kwan, Vita Shevchenko and J. Mark Kenoyer, who tried his best to rescue me when I was drowning in the confusing literature of the Neolithic period. The author, of course, takes full responsibility for any remaining errors, and I would like to dedicate these all, large and small, to the memory of Dr. Samuel Johnson's horse. This famous animal could count to ten, which made him a remarkable horse, but not, Dr. Johnson pointed out, a remarkable mathematician.

Joyce Diamanti

"It's not about beads, it's about people," the late Peter Francis, Jr., never ceased to remind us. Peter devoted his lifetime to learning about beads and sharing what he learned with others, always emphasizing that the focus of his research was people—the people who made beads and traded them, how people used beads, why people treasured them, and how people ultimately conserved or disposed of them. Peter's perspective parallels the current thinking of many paleoanthropologists, who believe that beads can tell us much about what makes us human.

What Makes Us Human

Homo habilis crafted the first crude tools around 2.5 million years ago. But as our hominid ancestors slowly evolved physically, they showed few outward signs of cognitive development; for hundreds of thousands of years they continued to make simple chipped or flaked stone tools and left little evidence of art or ornament. Beads first appear toward the end of the Old Stone Age, or Paleolithic period, when *Homo sapiens* began to exhibit culturally modern behavior, manifesting artistic and technological creativity and the capacity to communicate through abstract symbols, which is the basis of all art and science, as well as language, both spoken and written.

Some researchers believe this change in behavior was a gradual, evolutionary process that began in Africa soon after the advent of anatomically modern humans around 130,000 years ago. As evidence, they cite scattered finds of improved tools and early artistic expression, including beads that date to nearly 60,000 years ago. Others hold these examples to be too few and far between to be significant, and argue that while the capacity for abstract thinking may

have been present, it remained latent. They maintain that people began to act in a culturally modern way rather abruptly only 50,000 to 40,000 years ago, as *Homo sapiens* moved out of Africa and spread to far-flung regions of the world, displacing the Neanderthals in Europe and other archaic hominids in East and Southeast Asia.

Behavioral changes may have been triggered by the need to adapt to changing environments, or the need to meet challenges posed by expanding populations and increasing social interaction. Some anthropologists hypothesize that the sudden manifestation of modern human behavior may be due to a genetic mutation that enhanced the ability of our ancestors to use symbols and communicate, to create and innovate. Perhaps a combination of factors contributed to this cognitive transformation that marks the dawn of human culture.

The Creative Explosion

Beginning around 45,000 years ago, a creative explosion ensued in every sphere of human activity. The Late Paleolithic has been called the "big bang" of human culture. New types of tools blazed the way for technological advances. *Homo sapiens* expanded in numbers and range, exploring and exploiting new environments. New survival strategies brought innovations in food, clothing, and shelter. Evidence of ritual suggests that new ways of organizing society were emerging, and the first signs of status appear. Using a variety of tools to work new materials, people produced not only utilitarian artifacts, but articles of personal adornment and other forms of art that had no practical use but were a means of symbolic communication. Among the earliest evidence of abstract

thinking, beads also express other attributes that distinguish us as human—artistic creativity, technological inventiveness, and self-awareness.

At the beginning of the Late Paleolithic beads first appeared in quantity almost simultaneously in Asia, Africa, and Europe. In a world of accelerating cultural change, beads could convey information and would contribute to that change, transmitting technological knowledge, mediating social relations, playing a role in religious, political, and economic life. Almost as soon as beads appear we find evidence of long-distance trade in materials used to make them. In time, beads and bead materials would become not only important trade commodities but vehicles of cultural diffusion.

The first objects used as beads were probably found objects, such as seeds or shells, with natural perforations or profiles by which they could be strung or suspended. The first manually perforated ornaments may well have been organic materials, such as flowers, seeds, and berries, that were easy to pierce and string. Although few have come down to us, garlands appear to have been used for many millennia. A well-preserved specimen unearthed in the Valley of the Kings in Egypt is an exquisite floral broad collar of cornflowers, olive leaves, and berries that may have been worn by a guest at Tutankhamun's funerary banquet in the 13th century BCE.

The oldest extant beads that mark the early beadmaking traditions of *Homo sapiens* are made of more durable organic materials. In western Asia, cave dwellers near the Mediterranean gouged holes in the tips of small marine shells, then strung them in strands of mixed species. In Europe hunter-gatherers cut grooves in animal teeth to suspend them as pen-

Joyce Diamanti

dants. In a rock shelter in eastern Africa, early beadmakers painstakingly chipped out little disk beads from ostrich eggshell. Worldwide, freshwater and marine shells were the most important bead materials throughout the Late Paleolithic. Ostrich eggshell was also widely used in Africa and across Asia.

Striking pendants were fashioned from the teeth of bear, bison, and lion; reindeer and gazelle; wolf, hyena, beaver, and marmot. These pendants have been interpreted as amulets to bring success in the hunt. Studies have shown, however, that the species chosen for personal ornaments were often different from the species consumed in the daily diet. Similarly, many of the animals depicted in the cave art of the Late Paleolithic were rarely hunted. Thus these artistic expressions may symbolize a more complex relationship between the artists and the animals depicted than that between hunters and their prey. Beautiful ivory beads and pendants were carved from the tusks of mammoths, mastodons, and elephants. Paleolithic artisans also notched or pierced the bones of mammals and birds and strung fish vertebrae for use as personal ornaments.

Although most bead materials were found locally, some came from distant sources. Some of the earliest beads from sites in Russia, India, China, and North America were made of marine shells that came from hundreds of miles away. Whether these shells found their way inland through gift exchange or barter, by people trekking to the sea and back, or as part of the adornment of Ice Age migrants, we do not know. During the Paleolithic, many shells from the Mediterranean and the Atlantic made their way into the French interior. The distribution of find-sites of these shells

shows that the frequency of the different species decreases as the distance from their source increases. This falloff indicates that the shells traveled inland through down-the-line trade. That is, the shells were exchanged repeatedly from one group to next, with each group keeping some shells before passing the rest along.

Coral and amber are rare organic substances that come from restricted sources. Prized for making beads, they have been traded over long distances since prehistoric times. Archaeologists have found coral from the western Mediterranean at scattered sites in Central Europe dating to as early as 30,000 years ago. Traveling south, amber from the Baltic Sea region reached the Mediterranean around 15,000 years ago. By Roman times these coral and amber routes would expand into trade networks stretching to the farthest corners of the known world.

Minerals of various colors, both local and exotic, were also occasionally used for beads and pendants, but Old Stone Age tools were generally limited to working soft stones, such as talc, limestone, and serpentine. Broader use of minerals would begin with advances in tools and technology in the Neolithic period. In the Bronze Age, beginning around 3000 BCE, widespread exploitation of ornamental hardstones for beads and pendants would become of major economic and social importance.

The beauty as well as the symbolism of most early organic ornaments derives from the natural contours, texture, color, or other inherent properties of the material— glowing golden amber, sharp pointed teeth, lustrous mother-of-pearl, blood red coral. Some Paleolithic artisans enhanced these raw materials by polishing them, altering their color or engraving them with geometric designs or animal motifs.

Especially striking are anthropomorphic ornaments—beads of mammoth ivory carved in the shape of pendant breasts, jet beads with the contours of female buttocks. The sexual imagery of these ornaments suggests they were fertility amulets.

Other anthropomorphic representations are more complex and, again, may involve more complex symbolism. Small voluptuous female figurines are found from southwestern France to Siberia. Carved of ivory, bone, and stone, many are pierced or grooved, suggesting they may have been worn on a cord. These figurines clearly refer to pregnancy and motherhood. Some anthropologists have extended that interpretation to the concept of a mother or fertility goddess. Others see them as "Venus" figurines representing ideals of womanhood, associate them with the mating game or call them "paleopornography." Some researchers see the shared imagery of these figures across so wide a territory as evidence of shared beliefs. Others point to regional variations as evidence of a sense of ethnic identity.

Recent studies suggest that these small portable sculptures were personal amulets intended to protect a woman through pregnancy, and that they may have been passed down from mother to daughter, increasing in power with age. Such heirlooming would imply a capacity to envision the future. These interpretations are not mutually exclusive. Most agree these figurines were used as a symbolic means to control unseen forces.

By 40,000 years ago, *Homo sapiens* had spread through Africa, migrated across Asia, colonized Australia, and expanded throughout Europe, and possibly 10,000 years later, migrants would cross over from Asia and begin to populate the Americas. Long-distance travel would pave the way for long-distance trade. Adapting to environments ranging from equatorial savannah to subarctic tundra, these new arrivals competed with panthers and cave bears as well as with earlier hominids for shelter in caves, built sturdy tents of animal hides, and dug pit dwellings. They fashioned clothing from furs and animal skins for protection from the cold of the Ice Age. And when the glaciers began to retreat, they explored new ecological niches for food sources. As human populations grew and the herds of large animals dwindled, people broadened their diet. They hunted smaller prey, took up fishing, and exploited new plant resources.

These new survival strategies required new tools and equipment. Late Paleolithic campsites show evidence of storage pits and elaborate hearths. Fishing equipment, water carriers, and cooking vessels appear. While earlier toolmakers had painstakingly chipped and flaked a stone core to shape it into an implement for butchering large animals, a breakthrough in lithic technology now enabled stoneworkers to strike numerous blades from a single flint core. They then trimmed these blades to make a wide variety of efficient tools—scrapers and awls for working hides; spearheads and arrowheads; razor-sharp knives and daggers; and burins, versatile new tools with sharp points and thin, beveled edges that could cut, carve, gouge, chisel, plane, and incise abundant organic materials.

Burins were especially useful for working bone, ivory, and antler, materials that had previously been little used, to make a range of specialized tools, such as barbed harpoon heads, spear throwers, and sewing needles. These same materials were used to make human and animal figurines and personal ornaments. In Europe, mammoth ivory was the dominant material for beads and pendants during this period. The smooth, warm luster of materials such as mother-of-pearl and dental enamel, appealed to a Paleolithic sense of the aesthetic, it seems, for that visual and tactile quality was much sought after by beadmakers not only in shell and animal teeth but in ivory, bone, and certain soft stones, which were polished to produce that same soft luster. Replications of deer canines and marine shells in polished ivory suggest that the aesthetic criterion that drove the artists was luster, and the surface quality of those natural materials is what they wanted to replicate.

Fresh mammoth ivory is hard and Paleolithic ivory workers may have cured it before reducing it to workable splinters by wedging and splitting. The beadmaking process varied from region to region. In France, beadmakers first made long, pencil-thin rods that were scored and snapped into bead blanks of uniform diameter. These were then perforated, by gouging or drilling from both sides, and ground with coarse abrasives to make beads of uniform size and shape. The desired luster was achieved by polishing the beads with metallic abrasives, generally powdered hematite.

Experiments indicate that each mammoth ivory bead represents an investment of 45 minutes to two hours of labor. Sites of intensive bead production show that different stages of the manufacturing process were carried out at different places, with beads being completed through perforation in one area, then later ground and polished in an adjacent area. This serial production suggests a division of labor. Bead production sites that have yielded an unusual abundance of exotic mammoth ivory may have been gathering places where groups met and exchanged raw materials. These suggestions of organized production and exchange, along with the formation of larger, more cohesive bands, are evidence of increasing social interaction and emergent socio-economic structures.

The use of beads and pendants also offers clues to more complex behavior. Variations from region to region—in types and numbers of ornaments used, the ways in which they were used—may reflect increasing group identification, resulting from increased group size and/or increasing competition between groups. Variations within a group may reflect differentiation of roles or incipient stratification. Personal ornaments were a means of communicating individual status or group membership to others. Heavily beaded clothing or lavish bead assemblages may reflect developing disparities in wealth or social status.

Late Paleolithic burials also provide evidence of the beginning of inequality, a significant departure from the egalitarian tradition that has prevailed in hunter-gatherer societies from prehistory to the present. Burials become more common in the Late Paleolithic and are increasingly accompanied by grave goods implying reverence for the dead and perhaps belief in an afterlife. Elaborate arrays of ornaments and other decorative artifacts deposited in graves suggest that funerary rituals honored the dead, implying the existence of an incipient hierarchy.

Three burials at Sungir, an Ice Age site in Russia, were accompanied by rich grave offerings, striking symbols of the social rank these individuals probably enjoyed in life 25,000 years ago. A broad-shouldered man, aged 60 years or older, was covered with 2,936 mammoth ivory beads and bead fragments that had apparently been sewn onto clothing. His beaded

Joyce Diamanti

cap was further embellished with perforated arctic fox canines, and his biceps and forearms were encased in ivory armlets and bracelets.

Two children, usually reported as boys, one aged 7 to 9 and the other 12 or 13, were buried together. Both had been dressed from head to toe in beaded clothing, with a total of 4,903 ivory beads on the clothing of the adolescent and 5,274 on that of the younger child. Both wore ivory rings and bracelets and an ivory pin, which probably fastened their clothing. The adolescent's beaded cap was also decorated with arctic fox teeth, more than 250 canines hung from a belt round his waist, and a carved animal pendant lay on his chest. Surrounding the children lay an impressive array of grave goods, including a massive ivory spear.

Based on a conservative estimate of one hour of labor per bead and calculated in terms of 40-hour weeks, it would take almost a year and a half to make the beads for the funerary garments of the man, nearly two and half years for the ivory beads of the adolescent, and even more than that for those of the younger child, not counting the time it would take to sew the beads on the clothing and make the other grave goods.

Studies of these elaborate burials have led to the conclusion that Late Paleolithic people would expend so much time and effort only to honor very special persons. A closer look leads to a further conclusion. The man may have earned his status through his prowess as a hunter or skill as a shaman but the children were almost certainly too young to have proven themselves. Yet the labor that went into their burials was even greater than that invested in the adult's burial. It is possible that at Sungir a social system was emerging in which rank was ascribed

rather than achieved and the status of the children was hereditary.

Personal ornaments offer startling evidence that early on in the Late Paleolithic period, social as well as economic patterns were evolving that show surprising levels of complexity. Beads were intimately involved in these developments. Thanks to technological advances in toolmaking, beads were proliferating, and in turn, the demand for beads was driving organization of craft production. In terms of social development, personal ornaments became an early means of communicating individual and group identity, and with the first early signs of hierarchical social organization, beads became symbols of rank and prestige.

The Neolithic Revolution

From the Neolithic period on, cultural change would accelerate ever more rapidly, tools would become an increasingly important extension of human physical activity, and beads would become an increasingly important extension of human cognitive activity. Trade would expand to become not only a conduit for material goods but an avenue for cultural change.

Around 11,000 BCE, climatic changes at the end of the Ice Age ushered in environmental changes that disrupted the subsistence patterns of hunter-gatherers and brought revolutionary changes in human life styles. Around the world, people settled in villages and began to cultivate crops and raise animals; develop pottery, weaving, and other crafts; and trade resources they had for resources they lacked.

Obsidian, a volcanic glass, was much sought after to make chipped stone tools. Sources in seismically active regions of the Mediterranean and Anatolia were

among the earliest to be exploited, and by 7000 BCE obsidian was traded widely. Easy to knapp, it produced a razor-sharp edge for spearheads, sickles, and all kinds of blades. Decorative as well as durable, shiny black obsidian was used to make beads as well as beadmaking tools. The advent of ground stone technology and the bow drill also contributed to new and improved tools and facilitated stone bead production. Beadmakers could grind harder stones, like agate and carnelian, into beautiful new shapes.

Catalhöyük, a farming village in the shadow of the volcano Hasan Dag in Central Anatolia, prospered from the obsidian trade to become a thriving community of as many as 6,000 people by 6500 BCE, living in an agglomeration of more than 1000 dwellings packed so closely together that access was only by ladder from the roof. Practicing simple irrigation agriculture, they cultivated a range of crops and raised cattle, sheep, and goats. Aside from food and food by-products, however, along with mud, reeds, and, of course, obsidian, almost everything that went into making this community was brought from other areas in Anatolia or more distant regions.

For bead materials, local bone, tooth, tusk, and antler were used, but the most common bead material was marine shell from the Mediterranean, especially dentalium, which was cut into slices. Whelk-type shells were also sliced, and mother-of-pearl made beautiful pendants. Cowries came from the Red Sea, and the few coral beads found at Catalhöyük came from sources in the western Mediterranean. Beads made of native copper mark the beginning of metalworking. Also heralding things to come were rare beads of carnelian, rock crystal, turquoise, and other ornamental

Joyce Diamanti

stones from distant sources, which would become important trade commodities after social stratification created a demand for luxury goods. But the trade that sustained Catalhöyük was down-the-line trade confined largely to utilitarian products and raw materials, passing from group to group through face-to-face barter, and no doubt accompanied by the exchange of ideas and information.

The Rise of Cities

The first civilizations arose in three great river valleys—Sumer in Mesopotamia, between the Tigris and Euphrates; Old Kingdom Egypt in the Nile Valley; and Harappan civilization in the Indus Valley—where urban society was made possible by the development of large-scale agriculture. With state-level political and economic organization came social stratification and craft specialization. To meet the demands of the emerging elite and the needs of the craft industries, long-distance trade was organized around a central place where products and materials were brought and redistributed. Seals and tokens, used to identify commodities and record quantities, helped facilitate trade and may have led to writing. Often perforated, they also may have been worn.

Much of the trade between Sumer and Harappa involved luxury goods, notably lapis lazuli and carnelian, both as raw materials and finished products for personal adornment. The regalia that accompanied Queen Puabi to her tomb in the Royal Cemetery of Ur in Sumer testifies to the splendor of the rulers, the trade in rich materials, and the skill of the craftsmen of both Ur and Harappa. Fragile leaves and flowers of beaten gold quivered on her headdress. She wore gold earrings, rings, and garters, and three lapis seals with gold pins clasped a shawl on her shoulder. On her diadem, gold animals nestled amid gold shrubs, fruits, and flowers on a field of lapis beads. Her choker and spectacular cloak featured slender carnelian bicones as well as beads of lapis, agate, gold, and silver.

No culture has so striking a history of beadmaking as ancient Egypt, covering some 4,000 years from Predynastic times through the Ptolemaic period. Beads were worn by people in all walks of life, and were buried with them in death. Bead materials comprised a wide variety of stones and minerals, both local and exotic, which were often chosen not for their color but for the color's symbolic value; metals—first copper and, later, bronze, as well as silver, gold, and electrum; and man-made materials—faience and, especially after 1400 BCE, glass.

Paintings and reliefs in tombs bring to life the specialized jewelry workshops attached to temples and palaces in the 3rd and 2nd millennia BCE. A metalsmith weighs out gold on a balance scale; another melts metal in a brazier while fanning the coals with a blowpipe. Lapidaries perforate stone beads with bow drills and grind chips for inlaid pectorals. A beadstringer holds thread with his toes and twists it between his palms to make twine for stringing a multistrand broad collar. Another sucks the end of his thread before starting to string the beads set out in baskets. Other workers add drop pendants and counterpoises, and pull the strands taut before attaching falcon-headed terminals. An inspector checks a finished piece before placing it on a shelf stacked with other necklaces, diadems, and pectorals. Hieroglyphs accompanying these describe the action and even record the banter of the workers, often depicted as dwarfs. "Make haste and get it done," one urges his partner. Holding up a completed choker, another compliments his fellow, "It's very beautiful, mate."

Beads and other forms of jewelry were closely associated with Egypt's complex religion, especially with funerary ritual. Certain symbolic pieces were made expressly for burial with the dead. Amulets, usually in the form of pendants, endowed the deceased with functions associated with what was represented—a hand conferred dexterity, a leg mobility, a carpenter's square rectitude, and a plummet equilibrium. Most important was the heart scarab, which ensured passage to paradise.

Bronze Age Commerce

Simple exchange between neighbors had developed into serial group-to-group exchange, which marked the down-the-line trade in obsidian and connected distant sources in Neolithic times. Urbanization had brought central place redistribution involving bilateral trade with multiple sources. As new technologies spread among the many cultures ringing the eastern Mediterranean and materials flowed in from their hinterlands, crafts proliferated and a vast network of multilateral trade developed, with Phoenicians often serving as middlemen.

In Byblos, Tyre, and other Canaanite cities on the Levantine coast, the Phoenicians produced a dazzling array of trade goods of carved ivory, engraved silver, and granulated gold, elaborate textiles, and glass beads and perfume vials. Also skilled shipwrights and enterprising seafarers, they would carry their own wares and goods of their neighbors throughout the Mediterranean and, by the 5th century BCE, would sail beyond Gibraltar north toward Britain in quest of tin and south along the African coast in search of gold.

A ship that went down at Uluburun off southern Anatolia in about 1300 BCE encapsulates the trade of the period. Thought to be out of Phoenicia, the trading vessel was plying a circuit of the eastern Mediterranean that would touch port in Cyprus and southern Anatolia, on the island of Rhodes, the Greek mainland, and Crete, then cross the open sea to North Africa, Egypt, and back to the Levant.

Its cargo consisted of products from seven different cultures. The main cargo was ten tons of "oxhide" copper ingots from Cyprus plus nearly a ton of tin ingots from Anatolia. Melted together these would make bronze tools and weapons like those on board: knives, daggers, and swords; axes, hoes, chisels, tongs, and drill bits; balance pans and weights. From tropical Africa came ebony logs, ostrich eggshells, and ivory, in the form hippo teeth as well as elephant tusks.

Luxury goods included gold and silver jewelry, Egyptian scarabs, and cylinder seals of gold, amethyst, jasper, and steatite. A hematite seal that had been cut with a religious theme in Mesopotamia around 1750 BCE had been carved over with a warlike image by an Assyrian artisan 400 years later. Thousands of beads retrieved from the wreck include: amber beads from the Baltic; agate, carnelian, steatite, and quartz beads; tiny faience disk beads and fluted bicones; lentil-shaped chalcedony beads; Mycenaean-type blue glass relief spacers and other glass beads packed in amphorae. Discoid glass ingots were found in shades of dark blue, with cobalt as the coloring agent, and light blue, colored with copper. Writing boards remind us that Phoenician traders spread the Phoenician alphabet around the Mediterranean, most notably to the Greeks, who in turn would sire the Roman alphabet used by modern European languages.

Trade and Empire

Beginning around 500 BCE, trade went global. As a series of empires extended their reign over the known world, they stitched their far-flung provinces together with trade routes. The Persian Empire under Darius stretched from the Indus to the Aegean. Less than 200 years later Alexander conquered it all and then some, ushering in the Hellenistic period. While smaller powers succeeded one another on the eastern margins, Rome rose in the west, reaching its greatest extent early in the 2nd century CE. But Rome's economic dominion extended far beyond its political frontiers, especially in the trade between the Mediterranean and Asia.

The overland route would become known as the Silk Road as this lustrous new textile became the rage in Rome. Equally sophisticated merchandise traveled eastward, including glass and amber beads. The caravan route traversed the northern rim of Southwest Asia to the ancient trading cities of Bukhara and Samarkand, then skirted the Taklamakan desert, and followed the well-beaten path of Buddhism to China.

The maritime route eastward was controlled by Rome through Egypt. From Alexandria, it followed the Nile southward, then crossed overland by camel train to the Red Sea, and continued south to the Indian Ocean where Rome maintained a fleet of merchant ships to vie with the Indians and Arabs for the African and Asian trade. Rome's trade was mainly with India, exchanging amber, coral, and payment in gold for great quantities of pearls, precious stones, and other luxury goods.

Beyond India, Asian mariners controlled the routes to Southeast Asia and northward to China and Korea. The fulcrum of this trade was the southern tip of India. From there, beginning in the 4th century BCE, Indo-Pacific beads out of Arikamedu would pour over the Indian Ocean and beyond for more than a thousand years to become the "greatest little trade bead of all time" as Peter Francis fondly called it. With the rise of Islam and Arab conquests, trade networks would expand to carry beads south across the Sahara into Africa and north into Scandinavia via the Vikings.

East Meets West

In the Americas marine shells traveled hundreds and even thousands of miles inland during the hunter-gatherer period. dentalium shells have been traded from the Pacific Northwest to the Central Plains for millennia. In the Southwest, as early as 500 CE the Hohokam trekked from their home along the Gila River in Arizona to the Pacific Ocean to bring back abalone and *Glycymeris* shell to make beads and pendants. Less than a thousand years later, other ornaments would come from the Atlantic, when Columbus stepped ashore in the Bahamas and offered the islanders strings of beads— the first symbolic exchange between the Old World and the New.

Jonathan M. Kenoyer

The large number and great variety of stone beads on the Bead Timeline make their origins and manufacture of special interest. Two factors define the process: the characteristics of the raw material being used, and the effort that a beadmaker wishes to expend. Soft stones, such as talc or soapstone, can easily be carved, drilled and polished to produce a bead or pendant. Harder stones require different techniques, worked out over many thousands of years. In addition, the surface of the stone can be painted, incised or glazed to modify its natural appearance. The nature of the raw material and the processes of manufacture often contribute to the longevity of a bead and its overall cultural or economic value.

Raw Material Origins

Each region of the world has distinct types of natural raw materials which could be used to create objects of value for local as well as external trade. Human communities have experimented with all varieties of rock to make beads or to use as tools in the processing of stone beads. Grinding and polishing stones, as well as drills, are made from specific types of rock that are hard enough to modify the surface of other rocks. The Mohs' hardness scale can be used to give an idea of the relative hardness of various rocks, with values ranging from 1(talc) to 10(diamond). A variety of raw materials commonly used for stone beadmaking is shown in Figure 1.

Selecting an appropriate raw material for making a bead is the first of many stages where decisions are made by a beadmaker. Many stone beads are made from rocks that have natural features that make them attractive, including specific colors, distinctive patterns, or the ease with which the stone can be modified and perforated. From the very earliest

FIGURE 1: RAW MATERIALS FOR BEADS AND BEADS ILLUSTRATING MATERIALS, in order of their numbers: limestone, fossiliferous limestone, orbicular jasper, carnelian, banded agate, dyed agate, onyx, chalcedony, sardonyx, moss agate, grey steatite, talc, bloodstone, malachite, lapis lazuli, sodalite, aventurine, serpentine, amethyst, rock crystal, smoky and rose quartz, ruby, jade, basalt, basalt with quartz bands, coral and turquoise. *Photographs: J. Mark Kenoyer.*

times, human communities have shown a preference for materials that are rare and exotic. Generally speaking, rare materials have more value than objects made from commonly available stones, except in situations where the common materials have been modified through complex technologies.

Each species of rock is formed through very specific geological processes that occur in distinct areas of the landscape or the earth's mantle. Plate tectonics create zones of tremendous pressure and heat, transforming the surrounding sedimentary and igneous rocks into their metamorphic counterparts. Rugged mountains form as these same forces push up layers of sediments and rock from the lowest levels of the earth's crust. Over the years, these mountain rocks erode to

expose a wide variety of exotic raw materials, many of which have been sought after for making beads.

Rocks themselves, which are composed of a number of constituent minerals, have been used to make beads; examples include basalt, a dark igneous rock; marble, the metamorphic form of limestone; and lapis lazuli, a rock composed of calcite, pyrite, and the blue mineral lazurite. More commonly, beadmakers have sought rocks with concentrations of minerals, such as steatite, serpentine, chlorite, calcite, nephrite, and jadeite, in order of increasing hardness. In order to obtain some crystalline gemstones, such as emerald, ruby, and sapphire, miners must blast through tons of the surrounding matrix to find crystal veins or inclusions. Volcanic eruptions produce obsidian,

Jonathan M. Kenoyer

a natural glass which comes in several colors and has often been used for making beads. Among the most popular bead-making materials are the various forms of crystalline quartz, ranging from rock crystal through the microcrystalline varieties of chalcedony and banded agate, which form in hollow pockets of massive volcanic lava flows. After millions of years these agate nodules or geodes erode and collect in stream beds as massive gravel deposits. Colored jaspers and chert are formed in limestone or other alluvial deposits that also eventually erode, exposing these very hard rocks for use as beads, or as will be discussed below, to make drills. Each variety of rock has specific features that a beadmaker must take into account as the bead is being processed.

Collecting and Mining

The collection of raw materials depends entirely on the type of rock being sought and the geological processes that have affected the landscape. In many regions of the world, the earliest beadmakers simply collected partially rounded pebbles from streams or beaches and then perforated them to produce a bead. Other rocks can be collected from eroding cliffs or from exposures where they can be broken from the parent rock. One of the early methods for obtaining lapis lazuli and other rocks from massive formations was to build a fire against the rock and throw water on the heated surface to make it crack apart. Through experimentation with fire, people gradually came to understand how to modify rock in other ways. When the surface rocks were depleted, mining was developed to follow a vein of desired rock deep into the earth. Today mining is the major method for obtaining materials such as carnelian, serpentine, talc, chert, jade, turquoise and fine gemstones.

Raw Material Preparation

After collection, rocks must be prepared for manufacture through various processes. Some rocks such as agate and chalcedony are dried in the sun for months to remove any moisture prior to heating. The nodules are then slowly heated to around 340° C to drive off the intercrystalline water, making them easier to flake. Heating also changes the color of the raw material. Rocks that are saturated with iron become reddish after heating in an oxidizing atmosphere. If a rock is heated in a smoky or reducing atmosphere it will turn darker and sometimes become black. Intentional coloring of rocks will be discussed below, but the coloring process actually begins right from the first heating. While some rocks become "softer" when heated properly, others can be made harder. Usually this is done after the bead is finished and the most common rock that is hardened by heating is talc or soapstone (steatite), which can change in hardness from Mohs' 3 to Mohs' 5.

Shaping Bead Roughouts

Some stone beads are made from naturally shaped pebbles without any further modification except to drill and sometimes polish the stone. However, most stone beads are made by selecting a large block of stone and breaking or sawing it into smaller pieces, referred to as blocklets or bead roughouts. Rocks such as agate and chert can be flaked relatively easily using a stone hammer or various sizes of metal hammers. In India, beadmakers use the technique of inverse indirect percussion, as shown in Figure 2. An iron stake is set into the ground at an angle and the bead chipper sits on the ground with one knee bracing the stake. In one hand he holds a bead roughout and the other wields a hammer made with water buffalo horn and a flexible bamboo handle. The bead roughout is placed against the stake and the soft hammer is used to strike the bead roughout against the stake to remove a flake without damaging the stone.

Materials such as nephrite and jadeite

FIGURE 2: Left-hand photographs show inverse indirect percussion technique of preparing bead blanks. Upper right shows sawing of agate with bronze saw and abrasives. Lower right shows preparation of material for microbeads, seen as strand. In middle are respectively from top to bottom: banded agate roughout, bead blank and pierced bead; carnelian roughout and finished bead.

do not break very easily and must be sawn or ground into smaller pieces. Sawing can be done with an abrasive sand and a copper blade, using water as a lubricant and coolant. In cultures that did not have metal tools, sawing was done with a string or even a piece of wood. The grains of hard quartz or emery in the sand become embedded in the soft copper or organic saw and gradually cut through the hard rocks.

Bead Blanks

Bead roughouts are often processed again to create various types of final bead shapes which are called bead blanks. Some rocks are initially processed by fine chipping using smaller punches and smaller hammers, but eventually most bead roughouts are ground or carved to achieve the final bead shape. Traditionally, grinding was done by hand using a hard quartzite or sandstone grinding stone. This process is extremely time consuming depending on the size and hardness of the bead material. A long barrel shaped carnelian bead can be hand ground in about four hours of continuous work by an expert, taking great care not to break the blank through excessive heat or pressure. Tiny beads that are too small to hold in the hand are held by a small wooden vise or attached to a wooden rod or dop stick using some form of adhesive. After grinding one side, the tiny bead is taken out of the vise and turned to allow the other portion to be shaped.

Another technique for shaping tiny beads is to cut thin sheets of the rock and break them into small squares or disks that are then drilled in the center. These drilled roughouts are strung on a cord or wire so that many beads can be ground and shaped at the same time. Neolithic microbeads of lapis lazuli and carnelian were prepared in this way, along with

as were the shell heishi beads produced in the American Southwest.

Even with modern grinding wheels, the preparation of stone beads requires considerable time and skill. Most beads are individually shaped by hand and only spherical beads can be produced with a minimum of handling.

There are many more techniques of preparing bead roughouts and bead blanks, some of them unique to specific cultures. Many cultures do not necessarily use the most efficient technique since the preparation of beads may be part of a larger social event, and careful hand grinding may be a ritual event undertaken for only a few hours a day.

Perforation or Attachment

The point at which a bead blank becomes a bead or pendant is defined by the grooving or drilling of the ornament to facilitate stringing. By taking a pointed object and turning it back and forth it is possible to gouge or drill into a stone and eventually perforate it. While much of the earliest drilling was done by hand, the use of the bow drill was widespread by the 4th millennium BCE, and is still one of the most efficient methods of drilling. Perforations were usually achieved by drilling from both ends, with the hole meeting at the center of the bead. If the drilling is properly centered, it will produce a smooth cylindrical or hourglass shaped perforation.

The actual drilling of the bead blank is one of the most difficult and critical steps in beadmaking, and the specific type of perforation used to make stone beads, whether by pecking or drilling, has turned out to be an informative detail of ancient lapidary that was never fully appreciated by earlier scholars. With the invention of high quality silicone based impression

materials, it is now possible to make extremely precise molds of bead perforations that can then be examined under the Scanning Electron Microscope. Experimental studies of perforation and drilling technology, using different types of tools or drill bits have made it possible to differentiate the various perforation techniques and correlate them to specific time periods and to cultural regions, as shown in Figures 3a, b.

Short disk shaped and biconical beads of carnelian and agate reveal the use of a pecking technique that results in a rough hour-glass shaped perforation. Although considerable effort has been made to replicate this process it has not been possible to reproduce the small carnelian beads that were made in the Neolithic of South and

FIGURE 3a: Chart of bead drills and resulting perforations. Lower left and right are respectively Scanning Electron Micrographs of silicon rubber casts of beads drilled by Indus and tubular drills.

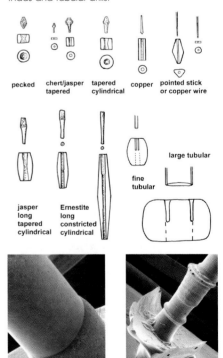

pecked   chert/jasper tapered   tapered cylindrical   copper   pointed stick or copper wire

jasper long tapered cylindrical   Ernestite long constricted cylindrical   fine tubular   large tubular

Jonathan M. Kenoyer

West Asia. In fact it was even difficult for ancient beadmakers since we find many beads that were broken in manufacture.

Long and short tapered drills, made by notching and steep retouch on chert microblades are found throughout the world, beginning in the earliest Neolithic period and continuing up through the Iron Age circa 1200 BCE in the Old World and much later in the New World. Some of these drills may have been used to perforate unfired steatite bead blanks, but most of them were probably used on shell, ivory or wood.

Some tapered stone drills made of chert or jasper bladelets were modified into a more specialized form referred to as a "tapered cylindrical drill". These drills were used to decorate and perforate softer stone, such as lapis lazuli, turquoise, or limestone, and to perforate short beads of harder stone such as agate or carnelian. This type of drill is found at sites throughout West Asia and the Indus valley, and has a long history of use that begins in the Copper-Bronze Age around 5500 BCE and continues through to the beginning of the Iron Age.

Constricted cylindrical drills have have only been reported from the Indus Valley during the Harappan period (2600-1900 BCE). They have a long cylndrical shape that is wide at the tip and constricted in the midsection. This shape was developed by the Indus artisans to facilitate the drilling of long slender beads of hard stone such as carnelian, agate and jasper. In contrast to tapered drills, these hard stone drills are made from a specific raw material called "ernestite," in honor of Ernest J.H.Mackay, who excavated the site of Chanhudaro, Pakistan where a carnelian bead workshop with large quantities of drills and drill manufacturing waste was found.

Microscopic examination of drilling striae on experimental and archaeological

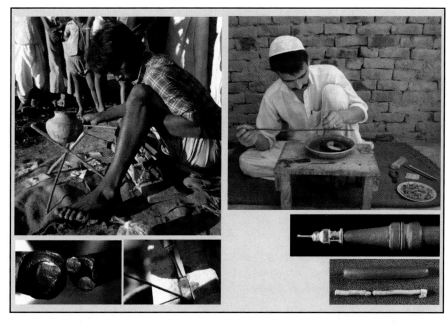

FIGURE 3b: Left-hand images show drilling with single and double diamond drills in Khambhat, India, and closeup of both types of drills. Right-hand images show drilling with single diamond drill in Peshawar, Pakistan. The diamond chip is held in a hyperdermic needle. Carnelian bead perforated with this type of drill and its silicon cast replicates the perforation.

samples of steatite suggest that long perforations were probably made using copper drills rather than with stone drills. The use of solid wood or copper drills with abrasive was the predominant form of drilling in East Asia and many parts of the New World.

Tubular drills made from a reed or bamboo have been documented in many regions of the world and represent a very efficient method of making a big hole with the minimum amount of effort. Instead of drilling out the entire center of a bead the tubular drill cuts a narrow ring and leaves the center of the bead a solid plug that can be removed by a light tap once the tube has been cut through the entire bead. This technique was also used with tubular metal drills beginning in the early Bronze Age, circa 2500 BCE.

The earliest use of hard gemstones for drilling is difficult to determine since much of the early abrasives may have had

some particles of garnet or corundum in them. In Africa and the Mediterranean many of the abrasive sands naturally contained the harder minerals. By the late 3rd millennium BCE the intentional use of corundum in western Asia greatly facilitated the perforation of hard stone beads.

The use of tiny diamond chips for drilling dates to around 600 BCE in western India. Although we do not know the precise form of the earliest diamond drills, they appear to have included two different styles. Some drills were made by using a single diamond chip that was crimped to the end of a narrow bronze or iron drill shaft. Anther type of drill was made by crimping two diamond chips at the tip of the drill. The single diamond drilling technique appears to have spread throughout the northern and western parts of Asia, while the double diamond technique appears to have been practiced only in South Asia, primarily in the western bead producing region of Gujarat.

Perforation of hard stone beads with stone drills or abrasive is extremely time consuming. Experimental studies have shown that chert or jasper drills can perforate agate at a rate of approximately 0.8 mm per hour. Ernestite drills are much more effective at 2.4 mm per hour, and the double diamond drill can perforate at the rate of 536.5 mm per hour. Without calculating the time involved in preparing the beads and the drills, the introduction of the diamond drill made it possible to drill beads at a rate 224 times faster than could be done with the most effective stone or abrasive hand drilling techniques. In fact, the introduction of diamond drilling so changed the value of hard stone beads such as carnelian and jasper, that elite consumers soon turned to beads made from rolled or faceted gemstones such as flawless rock crystal, emerald, ruby and diamond, as these were rare and more difficult to manufacture.

Finishing

Since many beads are broken during the drilling process, ancient beadmakers usually completed the final finishing after the successful drilling of the bead. The finishing includes polishing, heating or dyeing to enhance the color and decoration using various techniques of surface modification.

Polishing a stone bead usually involves repeated grinding with finer and finer abrasives to create a reflective surface. Throughout most of human history the polishing was done by hand, with initial polishing on fine quartzite or siltstone grinders, and final polishing on a wooden or leather surface with extra fine abrasive powder. The abrasive powder can be made from finely ground agate or even brick dust that has been carefully strained to remove all coarse particles.

Once stone beads could be produced in larger quantities using diamond drills the polishing of beads by hand was no longer economically viable and we see the introduction of mass polishing techniques. The earliest process was to place a large number of beads in a watertight leather bag along with water and powdered agate or corundum. The precise mixture of polishing powder was kept secret so that other people would not be able to replicate the process. By rolling or shaking the bag back and forth for around 15 days, the beads would attain a low luster polish. Bag polishing was eventually replaced with mechanized tumbling barrels using different grades of abrasive and this is the technique used for most common shapes of beads today. However, specially produced long bicones, carved beads and faceted stone beads are all still polished by hand.

The color of some stone beads was intentionally enhanced or modified by various processes as early as 5000 BCE. Nodules containing agate and jasper may erode into massive gravel beds that are then covered by other sediments that contain different types of minerals, including iron, in the form of hematite or limonite. As ground water percolates through the sediments it carries these iron minerals through the gravel beds, which become saturated with fine particles of iron. Agate and jasper are made up of multiple layers of silica that may have slightly different porosity due to density of crystal formation, which will affect the final appearance of the stone. Rocks with relatively uniform porosity will turn a uniform color, depending on the amount and type of iron found in the stone, as well as the degree to which it has been heated.

High quantities of hematite or limonite will turn the rock a deep reddish orange color which is called "carnelian", while smaller proportions of the mineral leave the agate a pale yellow, called "citrine". Agates with alternating bands of highly porous and non-porous silica result in banded red and white agates that are sometimes referred to as "sardonyx". If the rock is heated in a reducing atmosphere with very little oxygen reaching the iron, it can turn grey or black, resulting in black and white banded agate or onyx. Another way to make a stone blacker is to soak it in a sugar solution or honey and then basically caramelize the sugar which has saturated the porous stone. This process has been documented since the early Roman era and may have been practiced even earlier in South Asia. There are several examples on the Timeline of beautiful agate beads with intentionally enhanced banding, particularly in Chapter 3.

Many modern agate beads are colored with a wide range of chemicals to create blue, green, yellow, reddish orange and black colors. These processes were not used in antiquity, and the modern, dyed stones tend to be more uniform in color, without the luminosity of the ancient examples.

Another technique for coloring stone is to bleach the surface to turn it white. This can be done most efficiently by dipping the stone into an alkali solution or painting designs on the surface and then heating the bead over red hot charcoal. In ancient times the alkali solution or "potash" appears to have been made from a plant ash derived from burning certain desert plants, and then mixed with natural plant resin to improve adhesion. The ash contains potassium and sodium carbonate, and

Jonathan M. Kenoyer

is still produced throughout West and South Asia, where it is used as a flux for melting glass and as well as for producing a form of soap. The whitening appears to be the result of tiny microscopic fractures in the stone surface as well as a bleaching of any natural colors in the stone. After thousands of years the bleached surface often erodes, leaving a shallow etched design that led earlier scholars to refer to these beads as being "etched". The term "etched carnelian" is still used in the literature to describe red carnelian beads that have white designs painted on their surface. Etched carnelian beads from the Indus Valley have been found in Mesopotamia, most notably in the mid-3rd millennium BCE tombs at Ur. Examples on the Timeline in Chapter 7 are typical of beads from the Parthian and Sasanian periods, although decorated carnelian beads have been prodced into modern times. Beads that have a white surface and black lines appear to be the result of improper firing where the overall surface of the bead was whitened from heating; the painted lines became saturated with carbon, since they are more porous than the other surface areas.

Another technique of coloring was to blacken the bead and decorate it with white lines. Several different techniques may have been used to achieve this effect, but the most common process was probably to blacken the entire bead using the carbonizing process described above and then to use the alkali technique to create the white lines. The famous Tibetan Zi (dZi) beads are made with this technique.

Soft talc or steatite beads were usually heated to around 1000° C to harden the talc by transforming it into another set of minerals called cristobalite and enstatite, and many of the earliest high-quality

FIGURE 4: Left-hand images show hand polished canelian beads, hand polishing with bow-turned wheel and other polished agate beads. Middle image of two men engaged in leather bag polishing. Upper right is a wooden drum polisher, lower replication of bleached carnelians, with three ancient bleached carnelian beads, often called etched carnelians.

beads and stamp seals, such as those in Chapter 1, were formed by this technique. At times, the surface of the stone was bleached using some form of alkali solution. Large numbers of small black and white (often called "burnt," but probably including some sort of bleaching technique) steatite beads have been found at ancient sites, and are shown on the Timeline in Chapter 2.

Glazed steatite or quartz beads were made by coating the surface of the beads with finely ground silica colored with copper or azurite, and then heating under controlled conditions. This very early pyrotechnology was particularly well developed in Egypt as early as the last quarter of the 5th millennium BCE, and predates Egyptian faience, glass, and glazed pottery. Some soapstone beads were colored with an iron pigment to turn them red, and red and white beads were made using iron and the bleaching

process described previously.

Conclusion

Stone bead making is a fascinating topic that still has many unanswered questions. The creative abilities of early beadmakers and the continued use of stone in manufacturing modern beads have resulted in an almost unlimited combination of techniques and raw materials. With the global trade of beads it is almost impossible to be certain of where a bead comes from. In the markets of Africa, beads made in Europe, Asia and the New World can be found next to locally produced stone beads. The same situation exists in almost every corner of the world. It is only through the careful study of all aspects of stone bead manufacture that archaeologists and bead collectors will be able to associate specific beads to specific world regions and time periods.

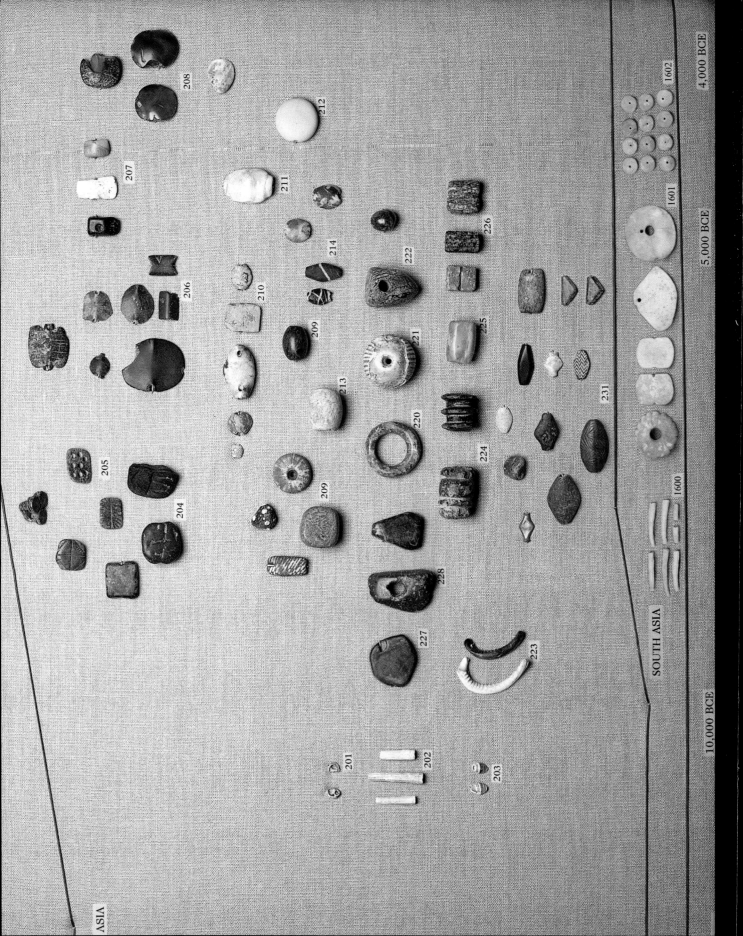

ASIA

208

207

212

211

214

222

226

206

210

209

221

225

231

205

213

220

224

204

209

228

227

223

201

202

203

SOUTH ASIA

1602

1601

1600

10,000 BCE

5,000 BCE

4,000 BCE

James W. Lankton

At Sungir in northern Russia, almost 25,000 years ago, two children were buried with 10,000 mammoth ivory beads, each one carefully shaped so that the beads could fit snugly together (White 1995: Figure 19). As discussed by Diamanti in this volume, the large numbers of beads found in graves from as early as 45,000 years ago suggest that people had begun to devote significant amounts of time to making beads from durable materials; those from Sungir would have required years of work. Most early beads were small, and painstakingly crafted from materials chosen for their lustrous finish: ivory, bone, shell, animal tooth, and certain soft stones—materials often gathered or traded from distant locations (Bahn and Vertut 1997: 87-89).

We begin our Timeline at 12,000 BCE, although we might just as well have said 20,000, since the *Nassarius*, *Dentalium*, and *Engina* species shown at 201, 202, and 203, Figure 1.0, had already been used for thousands of years. At some early sites, the small shells used for beads, sometimes up to fifty different species, may outnumber those used for food (Kuhn *et al* 2001: 7643). Around 12,000 BCE in the Levant, the land bordering the eastern Mediterranean Sea, now parts of Turkey, Syria, Jordan, Lebanon, and Israel, groups of hunter-gatherers began to settle in more permanent camps, some of them inhabited for most or all of the year. The same thing was happening at this time or slightly later in other parts of the world, including China,

coastal South America, and New Guinea, as well as in most of the Fertile Crescent (the homeland of wild forms of barley, wheat, sheep, and goats), which bordered the rivers, deserts, and steppes of West Asia, the source of many of the beads on our Timeline.

In some areas food became plentiful with the warm, wet climate near the end of the Pleistocene, the geological period which included the last Ice Age and led up to our own period, the Holocene. The increased carrying capacity of the land in specific regions made it possible for larger populations to emerge, either from natural population growth or from the joining together of different communities. Eventually we see evidence for more sedentary groups of hunter-gatherers, people who lived in the same settlement or locality for longer periods of time. As populations within these settlements grew larger, the social organization changed from egalitarian, relatively mobile band societies to more settled communities that were internally differentiated on the basis of social status or ethnic diversity (Renfrew and Bahn 2000: 175). During this time period, between 10,000 and 8000 BCE, we see the beginnings of plant domestication and animal husbandry in different parts of the Old World, with the most extensively researched area extending from the Mediterranean to the highlands of Afghanistan and the borders of the Indus Valley in Pakistan. People began cultivating wheat and barley, and herding animals such as sheep, goats, and cattle. These increasingly reliable sources

of food also allowed people to congregate in larger villages and eventually small towns (Moore *et al* 2000: 478). This change from hunting-gathering to food production is commonly referred to as the Neolithic Transition, named for the new forms of stone tools that were developed along with agriculture, and with the crafts required for processing grain and other domestic foods.

Beads play an important role in this period of transition. With food supplies more secure in these larger settlements, people had more time to develop ornaments, and also more need to have ways to distinguish themselves from others. Beads were used to reinforce social order because they could be worn as symbols of ethnic identity, status, and wealth. Some raw materials were undoubtedly viewed as highly valued materials or prestige goods (Hayden 1995: 259), while others may have been important for ritual purposes. Although today we may think of beads as having little practical use, in traditional societies a bead has power—either through the qualities of the raw material, or through the time and energy expended in producing it. The most highly prized beads were ones that were rare and difficult to procure, time-consuming to work, or bright and shiny so that everyone would notice. A quick glance at the beads in Figure 1.0 makes it clear that after 10,000 BCE, it was no longer just about shells and teeth. Bigger and better beads, often in unusual shapes and made from exotic stones traded over hundreds of miles,

FIGURE 1.0. Beads and pendants dating from 12,000 to 4000 BCE, corresponding to the Neolithic period (10,000-5500 BCE) and the first part of the Chalcolithic, or copper-using, period (5500-3300 BCE). Reflecting an increased stratification of society, the large size and varied materials of Neolithic beads are in stark contrast to the predominantly small beads of the Upper Paleolithic, which were made from shell, tooth, bone, and soft stone. The South Asian beads are similar to those found at Mehrgarh, an early farming community on the edge of the Indus Valley. Largest butterfly bead 4.7 cm.

were the products of specialized technology and trade. These beads reflect the increasing stratification of society, where privilege and power concentrate in elite groups, as well as the beginning of craft specialization, necessary in order to supply commodities to these emerging elites. Neolithic burials usually contain a wealth of rare and beautiful beads, often along with other signs of prestige and power. It is even possible that a leader's position could come from possessing certain types of beads, just as a shaman's power would come from his control over sacred objects believed important for the welfare of the village.

The beads at 206, Figure 1.1, represent some of the finest Neolithic stone working technology. Known as butterfly or double-axe beads because of their distinctive shapes, they may have been the most precious symbols of power between 8000 and 6000 BCE, the period of their greatest occurrence. But don't imagine that they were common—from the entire span of the ancient site of Abu Hureyra in Syria, lasting thousands of years, excavators found only a few of these butterfly beads; with one exception, in female graves (Moore *et al* 2000: 286-292).

Most butterfly beads were made from serpentine, a soft, green stone sometimes mistaken for jade, or from steatite. Also known as soapstone, steatite is a dense form of talc, which when heated is transformed into the much harder enstatite and cristobalite, as discussed by Kenoyer in this volume. Steatite has been one of the most popular beadmaking materials for just this reason—easily carved into delicate shapes, it becomes durable with heating. The large butterfly bead at the top of the photograph, marked with parallel and perpendicular lines, may be quite early—one of

a number of inscribed stones thought to precede the important group of beads to its left in Figure 1.0, at 204 and 205 (Fiandra 2000: Figure 4).

As settlements and populations increased in size and complexity during the 8th millennium BCE, some of these developing chiefdoms, to use the anthropological designation, turned toward an economic system based on delivering agricultural products to a central location and then redistributing them to the populace. These distributive centers, usually based in temple precincts, developed various ways to account for economic activity. We can assume that some individuals were able to keep track of trade activities based on memory, but symbolic objects such as seals and tokens soon came to be used as mechanisms for keeping track of ownership or exchange. Stamp seals such as those at 204 and 205, Figure 1.0. were pressed onto balls of soft clay that were used to identify and secure the gathered produce of an agricultural economy. It seems likely that stamp seals, which were almost always pierced to be worn, evolved from characteristic signs, including beads, that could identify individuals or groups. In this way, the beads and seals represent a developing information technology: data coded in visual symbols that served administrative needs for control and regulation. Some of the first stamp seals come from the early 7th millennium BCE Hassuna culture levels at Yarim Tepe I, an archeological site in the north of Mesopotamia, the land between the Euphrates and Tigris rivers, now part of Iraq and northern Syria (Merpert and Munchaev 1993a: 113). Processes of cultural change, possibly migration, but more

likely the adoption by local elites of new technologies, brought the Halaf culture, with its own stamp seals and intricately painted pottery, to Yarim Tepe and most of northern West Asia in the middle of the 7th millennium BCE.

Stamp seals are remarkable for their great variety in shape and size. At Yarim Tepe I, the rectangular forms seem to be earlier than the round, in both geometric and animal designs (Merpert and Munchaev 1993a: 113). Excavations at the Halaf period site of Yarim Tepe II revealed a number of seals, one of them quite similar to our seal at the upper left, with the design of a circle in a square. A seal from Tell Sabi Abyad, near Raqqa, a Syrian city along the Euphrates River, is one of several found with the drilled pattern of our seal at 205 (Roualt and Masetti-Roualt 1993: 248). Most of the early stamp seals were made from steatite or serpentine, as are ours, but they occur as well in marble and quartzite, diorite and rock crystal. While many stamp seals have been found in processing and storage areas, others were deposited as burial offerings, perhaps in the graves of individuals who grew powerful through their mastery of the new accounting systems. In the developing societies of the 7th to 5th millennia BCE, stamp seals symbolized increasing elite control of production and distribution, and were at the same time the medium by which this control was expressed—and all of this occurred four thousand years before the invention of writing.

The four beads at 209, Figure 1.0, were all made from fossils, three from fossilized coral, and one from a fossilized sea urchin. Similar beads have been found at Paleolithic sites in Europe

James W. Lankton

FIGURES 1.1 and 1.2. The six beads on the left are butterfly, or double-axe beads, and appear as early as the 9th millennium BCE in West Asia, continuing for up to 2000 years. Excavated examples from Abu Hureyra in northern Syria, found mainly in female graves, indicate the high status of the deceased. These butterfly beads represent the highest standards of early Neolithic technology. The 12 beads at 231 show some of the materials and forms of Neolithic beads, as well as the early predominance of red, black, and white (Boric 2002). The largest butterfly bead is 4.7 cm wide.

and occasionally appear mixed with Neolithic beads from Mali, West Africa (Oakley 1965: 117; Opper 2003: 10). Both Neanderthals and early modern humans collected interesting fossils, which they transported over long distances. Naturally perforated fossils, such as sections of sponge that had grown around a seaweed stem, or short lengths of crinoid, a fossilized sea-lily, were used as beads. In Britain, fossilized sea urchins, pierced for suspension, were called thunderstones from ancient times until as recently as the 19th century. These protective amulets were thought to fall from the sky following loud thunderclaps, and thus could protect the bearer against harm from lightning, a very real danger to early societies. Even today, when we say "lightning never strikes twice," we unconsciously echo ancient beliefs that had been expressed

through beads (Oakley 1965: 118).

Ancient turquoise is represented on the Timeline at 210, Figure 1.0. The raw material was traded over long distances from sources in northeastern Iran or the Kyzyl Kum desert of Central Asia. Often beige or green through weathering and dehydration, turquoise beads have been excavated at several sites dating from the 7th to 4th millennia BCE, after which they become less common in Syria and Mesopotamia. Our large rhomboid bead has been drilled at both ends rather than along the longitudinal axis, possibly to attach the bead to clothing or as some unique type of ornament. Turquoise was also quite common in ancient Egypt, with mines in the Sinai Peninsula.

Using flint drill bits and bow drills, perhaps as early as the 10th millennium BCE based on evidence from Zawi

Chemi Shanidar in Iraq (Francis 1988b: 75), Neolithic craftsmen transformed the available raw materials into magical jewels, important for the functioning of society. The twelve beads illustrated on this page show some of the beautiful variety of Neolithic beadmaking, including shapes, sizes, and colors well-attested at archaeological sites. The stones range from steatite to green chalcedony and carnelian, which are varieties of quartz, Mohs' hardness 7, one of the hardest beadmaking materials. Although still rare in the 7th and 6th millennia BCE, remarkably well-made quartz beads have been found from Syria to Pakistan. The large, inscribed red bead, possibly marble, is very similar to a bead excavated at Tell Kashkashok in northern Syria, dating to the 6th millennium BCE.

EASTERN ASIA
CHINA

James W. Lankton

For over 100 years, small objects, usually made from low-fired clay and sometimes perforated, had been found at excavation sites in West Asia. These simple artifacts, which have come to be called tokens, are thought to be evidence for a technique of keeping track of commodities and eventually accounting. The earliest tokens were usually cones or spheres, and appear as early as 9000 BCE in Syria and Iran, spreading within a few hundred years to the rest of western Asia. By the late 7th millennium BCE, more complex tokens in other materials, notably stone, are found as well. In the upper left corner of Figure 2.0, are ten small pendants that are the shape and size of these complex tokens; close-up views of several are shown in Figure 2.1. Since many tokens were perforated and were strung before being used, they can be classified as pendants or beads. Some of these tokens may have been used for accounting, and at the same time served as ornamentation. They have been found in a variety of contexts in ancient sites, from domestic areas to offerings in graves. These small beads may not be particularly impressive in appearance, but it is their potential message that is important (Schmandt-Besserat 1992: 195-199).

Some scholars think that each token represented a particular quantity of a particular commodity—one sack of grain or one unit of work, for example, in designs standardized across broad trading networks. When goods were packed for shipping, a round, hollow clay envelope would be filled with tokens corresponding to the

contents, and then sent along with the container or kept as a record of the transaction. In addition, the envelope would sometimes be impressed with a stamp seal in order to show origin or ownership. Near the middle of the 4th millennium BCE, a symbol of the token or commodity began to be pressed on the outside of the envelope, and the tokens were sealed inside with the rolled imprint of a cylinder seal. Eventually, the cumbersome and fragile clay envelopes were replaced entirely by solid clay tablets, marked with a symbol representing the commodity, and a number representing quantity. The marks on these tablets are the earliest forms of cuneiform writing, with both object and number represented by abstract signs. Because tokens persist in some contexts long after the emergence of cuneiform writing, it is possible that they continued to be used by illiterate communities, or they might have been reserved for unofficial trade. The emergence of writing in Mesopotamia around 3500 BCE appears to have been closely linked to accounting, and beads or pendants may have been an important stage in this process, in terms of both the use of symbols and the manipulation of numbers (Schmandt-Besserat 1992: 184).

During the 4th millennium BCE, with increasing population and trade between communities, we see the emergence of regional cultures organized as chiefdoms, with hereditary rulers and extensive kin-based networks for trade and politics. Similar processes were occurring in the settled areas of the ancient world, ranging

FIGURE 2.1. These small pendants, including a *hamsa*, or hand form, represent the tokens found at many ancient sites, and thought to be a precursor to writing. Largest 2.8 cm. long.

from Europe to China, and extending into Egypt and the Nile Valley. All of these regions were linked by overlapping trade networks that saw the movement of goods and people as well as ideas and technologies. By the end of the millennium, city-states, some with populations well above 20,000, began to dominate the landscape of the Middle East, with new models for social and political organization that involved the state, a political structure that was based on economic and political associations in addition to kinship ties. This new, urban society, often with a class-based hierarchy led by a king, brings with it monumental

FIGURE 2.0. The 4th millennium BCE was a period of tremendous change in social organization, as some of the first cities formed in northern and southern Mesopotamia, with new systems of accounting and the emergence of writing. At the same time, wheeled carts improved the efficiency of trade in beadmaking materials, and lapis lazuli began to become important, with examples at 233. In towns such as Habuba Kabira, an Uruk outpost along the Euphrates River, beadmakers turned steatite and carnelian into prized ornaments. The cylindrical jade bead at 800 is 7.3 cm long.

FIGURE 2.2. Red steatite beads in various forms, similar to those made at Habuba Kabira, a settlement on the Euphrates River in northern Syria. Habuba Kabira was a colony established in the second half of the 4th millennium BCE by settlers from Uruk in sourthern Mesopotamia, with evidence for beadmaking from gypsum, steatite, carnelian, and rock crystal. Largest bead is 2.6 cm long.

art and architecture, increased craft specialization, technological advances, including both the wagon wheel and the potter's wheel, literacy and numeracy. In a word: civilization.

Until the past few years, archaeologists agreed that most of these advances appeared first in southern Mesopotamia at the great Sumerian city of Uruk. Several urban centers along the Euphrates River in northern Syria were thought to have been Uruk colonies in the mid-4th millennium BCE, a period known as the Uruk Expansion. Recent excavations now suggest that some of the same structural changes in social organization that happened at Uruk were also happening in the north, perhaps through the influence of the preceding Ubaid culture. Uruk traders were indeed present at many of these northern sites, but the cities were not colonies, and in most cases the traders lived in discrete enclaves within an already established social structure (Schwartz 2001: 255).

In contrast, the major town of Habuba Kabira, along the Euphrates River in northern Syria, was founded by settlers from Uruk toward the end of the 4th millennium BCE, inhabited for 120 years, and then abandoned with the end of the Uruk Expansion. Living and working far from their homeland in southern Mesopotamia, the settlers took advantage of the river trade in raw materials, and made beads. German excavations at Habuba Kabira South, which includes the important industrial areas, have given us a good idea of the materials and the technology (Berlin 2000: *pers. obs.*). A number of the beads on our Timeline are similar to those excavated at mid- to late 4th millennium sites and can be used to illustrate the types of beads that were produced. Beads and ornaments very similar to those from Habuba Kabira were excavated at the southern city of Uruk as well, and it seems likely that they had

been shipped down the Euphrates to supply the capital, since there were few sources of raw material in southern Mesopotamia itself.

The red steatite beads at 232, Figure 2.2, are striking for their excellent condition and variety of shapes. The similar beads from Habuba Kabira give us a good picture of soft-stone beadmaking in the second half of the 4th millennium BCE. Both short flint drills and longer copper drills were excavated at Habuba Kabira, and it seems likely that the copper drills, along with abrasive powder, were used for at least the largest of the steatite beads. The square tabular beads at 234, Figure 2.0, made from red, black, and white steatite, are perforated in two directions and could have been strung as bracelet or necklace components. At Uruk, similar elements were attached to walls in decorative mosaic patterns; it is not clear from the excavation report whether or not the Uruk plaques were perforated. The small black and white beads at 264, Figure 2.0, are also steatite, and represent the most numerous beads from the 4th and possibly 3rd millennia BCE. Unfinished beads of black and white steatite were found at Habuba Kabira, along with the quartz drills that may have been used in their production. Unprocessed Mesopotamian steatite was dark in tone, although natural white steatite is thought to occur in the Indus Valley. In most archaeological reports, these small white beads are known as burnt steatite, and the stone was most likely treated with both alkali and heat to produce the white color, which seems to penetrate through the stone (Moorey 1994: 169-171).

We mentioned early quartz beads at the end of Chapter 1, and several, but not all, of the green beads shown are quartz as well. Green beads from softer stone may be listed as greenstone by archaeologists, although the actual materials could include serpentine, chlorite, amazonite, and, as if things were not confusing enough already, greenstone, thought to be a complex mixture of quartz, feldspars, and amphiboles, which may or may not be green, depending on the iron content (Moorey 1994: 83). Full identification requires laboratory analysis, but even without, we can certainly appreciate the beauty of these beads and the skill of the beadmakers.

Red beads are generally more straightforward, and those with a Mohs' hardness of 7 are usually carnelian, a color-enhanced chalcedony whose best known source is the Deccan Plateau in India. Heat treatment of flint as early as 20,000 years ago began a long tradition of altering stones to improve their working properties or appearance, and most carnelian was heated to bring out the red color, caused by iron contained within the stone. Both rock crystal and carnelian were worked into small disk beads at Habuba Kabira, similar to those shown at 354, Figure 2.0. A group of beads dated to 3500-3000 BCE on display in Leiden includes small carnelian, jasper, and rock crystal beads as well, along with a small banded agate bead much like that on the Timeline (Leiden 2002). Well-made carnelian beads were found at Susa, in Iranian Khuzistan, bordering southern Mesopotamia, as well as in northern Mesopotamia at such sites as Yarim Tepe and Tepe Gawra, all dating to the 4th millennium BCE or earlier. Both Mehrgarh, mentioned previously, and Mundigak, a town 35 km from Kandahar in Afghanistan, were making carnelian beads at this time, and Hiebert mentions early beadmaking from semiprecious

FIGURE 2.3. Nine beads made from various green stones, including quartz (1, 4, 5, and 6, clockwise from upper right), and serpentine. Although green stone beads were certainly appreciated in West Asia, they had nowhere near the importance of jade and the "social jades" in Central America. Even turquoise becomes rare during this period in West Asia. Longest bead in upper row is 3.2 cm.

stones at 4th millennium BCE sites in southern Turkmenistan (Hiebert 1994: 148), in the foothills of the Kopet Dag mountains. The conventional wisdom is that in most cases, hard stones like carnelian tended to be worked in a few major centers, often in Iran, India, Turkmenistan, and Pakistan, and then traded as finished beads. In contrast, such softer stones as lapis lazuli, Mohs' hardness 5 to 6, were traded as rough material, often in small blocklets, and then turned into beads through local industries. Unfinished carnelian disk beads at Habuba Kabira suggest that, at least for small beads, the reality may be more complex.

Over 300 whole or fragmentary ornaments were recovered from excavations at Mundigak and are now in the Musée Guimet in Paris (Barthelemy de Saizieu and Bouquillon 1995: 47), giving us a good idea of the types of stones being worked to the east of Mesopotamia.

Among the eight different groups of stones, 43% of the samples were either turquoise or lapis lazuli, in an approximate 50:50 ratio. Various forms of quartz, mainly carnelian, but also chalcedony and banded agate, made up almost 10% of the waste material. Most of these beads were small. In addition, veined calcite, as shown on the Timeline in the lower two beads at 246, Figure 2.0, was found along with white, yellow, and cream-colored forms of the same mineral. There was one piece of amazonite, as at 260, Figure 2.0, and about 6% steatite, chlorite, or serpentine, in a number of colors, including dark red, perhaps similar to our beads at 232, Figure 2.2. Glazed steatite beads, which we will consider in more detail in Chapter 5, made up a surprising 30% of the waste material, demonstrating the important contribution of synthetic bead materials during the 4th millennium BCE.

Figure 2.4 includes a number of small

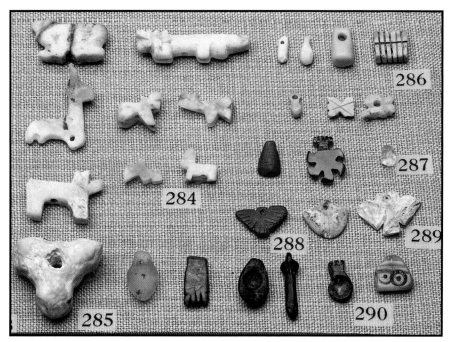

FIGURE 2.4. Small beads and pendants from the 4th and 3rd millennia BCE. The small animals and the triangular pendant at lower left are similar to figures from Habuba Kabira, dating to the late 4th millennium BCE, while the three eagle or Anzu pendants in lapis lazuli and shell are later, and resemble 3rd millennium BCE examples from northern Syria. Longest figure in upper row is 4.4 cm.

pendants dating to the 4th millennium BCE. In particular, the white alabaster animal beads at 284 are similar in shape to red steatite animals from Habuba Kabira and are among the most charming beads from the period. The large triangular bead at 285, of a type also made at Habuba Kabira, would have been carved with three human or animal faces. Of course, all of these beads may have had a more serious meaning to their original owners, and we can suspect that animal or human imagery was seldom purely decorative. We will return to the three small bird pendants in Chapter 3.

Fourth millennium BCE stamp seals were smaller and more likely to have animal images, compared to the early seals we discussed in Chapter 1. The four seals shown on the Timeline at 241 and 243,

Figure 2.0, all have counterparts at Tepe Gawra in northern Iraq, from levels dating to about 4000 BCE (Rothman 2002: Plates 29, 37, 56). During the second half of the 4th millennium, cylinder seals gradually replaced stamp seals, reflecting an increased complexity in administrative systems. These cylinder seals could be rolled onto soft clay to produce a larger and more distinctive image than would be possible with a stamp seal. After the development of writing at the end of the 4th millennium, the seal impressions could include short inscriptions as well, sometimes identifying the owner of the seal. We have included six early cylinder seals on the Timeline, at 261, 262 and 240, Figure 2.0. Cylinders from the Late Uruk and succeeding Jemdet Nasr periods were large and made from relatively soft stones. The pink marble and green

chlorite examples have both drilled and carved decoration and reveal an animal pattern when rolled out. Abstract brocade patterns are also common, as on the two seals to the right in the photograph. Early cylinder seals were more likely administrative than personal and, although perforated, may have been too large and heavy to wear (Collon 2001: 22). In later periods, an important official might have both an administrative and a personal seal, which could be worn around the neck or wrist, or suspended from a belt. Personal seals indicate high status and were often buried with the owner, while an administrative seal could be passed on for continued use.

During this period in Africa, local chiefdoms consolidated power along the Nile Valley in Egypt and Nubia, creating larger settlements and early cities. Although cultural developments paralleled those in Mesopotamia to such an extent that many scholars see a strong outside influence on Egyptian Predynastic culture, the earliest known example of writing may actually be from Egypt in the form of a recently discovered 46 cm x 51 cm carving on a limestone cliff overlooking an ancient trade route in the Egyptian desert west of Luxor (Wilford 2002). The panel shows the victorious Egyptian ruler, perhaps King Scorpion, leading a bound captive. Inscribed signs on the tableau appear to be related to later hieroglyphics, and preliminary dating to 3250 BCE indicates that writing in Egypt was emerging at about the same time as in Mesopotamia. No one has mentioned King Scorpion's beads, but beautiful stone beads from 4th millennium BCE Egypt and Nubia continue to impress us today. Glazed stone beads, usually steatite, begin as early as the 5th mil-

James W. Lankton

lennium BCE at Badarian sites, and the Egyptian faience industry was developing as well.

Stone symbolized culture in ancient China to such an extent that the formative period from 4000 to 2000 BCE has been called the Jade Age (Childs-Johnson 2001: 13). The earliest Chinese written sources compare the virtues of jade to the Confucian virtues of the just man, and the privileged place of jade in prehistoric cultures is clear from the many beautifully crafted jade artifacts found in prestige burials (Braghin 1998: 273; Forsyth 1995: 62). China's major jade-working Neolithic cultures were concentrated in the eastern and coastal regions, and included Hongshan, Liangzhu, and Shandong-Longshan. True jade may be either nephrite or jadeite, although the only variety used in ancient China was nephrite, with its major sources in far western Xinjiang Province. Ancient *yu*, the Chinese term for jade, refers more to the character of the stone than to its mineralogy, and can include a number of similar-looking decorative stones, not all of them nephrite, leading to confusion in both the early and the modern literature.

The beautiful Hongshan beads and pendants on this page are all nephrite, based on a Mohs' hardness between 6 and 6.5. They show the changes in appearance due to thousands of years of burial, particularly with exposure to moist conditions. The Hongshan culture (3500 to 2200 BCE) was based in present-day Liaoning Province and Inner Mongolia. The very earliest jade beads in China have been found at 6th millennium BCE Xinlongwa sites, also in Inner Mongolia, while the jade objects from Hongshan are remarkable for their variety and for the quality of the craftmanship. Because

FIGURE 2.5. Three Jade Age ornaments from the Hongshan culture (3500-2200 BCE), in Liaoning and Inner Mongolia provinces in China, The central nephrite eagle-owl has the typical "ox nose" perforation on the reverse, and would have been worn as a pendant. The righthand *zhulong*, or pig dragon, represents the earliest form of the Chinese dragon. The cylindrical bead is 7.3 cm long.

of extreme toughness secondary to its felted fibrous structure, nephrite was shaped by abrasion, rather than carving; such large beads as 800 on the Timeline could have required months of work. The middle pendant above is known as an eagle-type owl and is perforated on the reverse, while the pendant on the right, a C-shaped *zhulong*, or pig-dragon, may be the earliest Chinese representation of the dragon, a form that would continue to develop and resonate throughout Chinese culture. Hongshan jades appear to have been essential for religious ritual and have been found in tombs located in the sacred landscape of a large ceremonial center at Niuheliang in western Liaoning Province. Within the nearby semi-subterranean temple structure were a lifelike clay mask with inlaid jade eyes, and large clay figures, at least some of them female, suggesting the possibility of a matrilineal society (Lee

and Zhu 2001: 721-722).

The Liangzhu Neolithic culture (3400-2200 BCE), near the modern city of Shanghai, was contemporary with Hongshan, although there is little evidence for contact. The five Liangzhu beads to the lower right in Figure 2.0 are also jade, with the surface altered by burial deposit and the intentional burning thought to be part of Liangzhu funeral rites. Such important Chinese symbols as the *bi* (perforated disk) and the *cong* (a cylinder within a square box, symbolizing respectively heaven and earth) are first expressed in these jade beads. The beautiful *cong*-shaped bead at 812 is carved with characteristic Liangzhu animal and human masks, possible precursors to the *taotie* masks of later Chinese art.

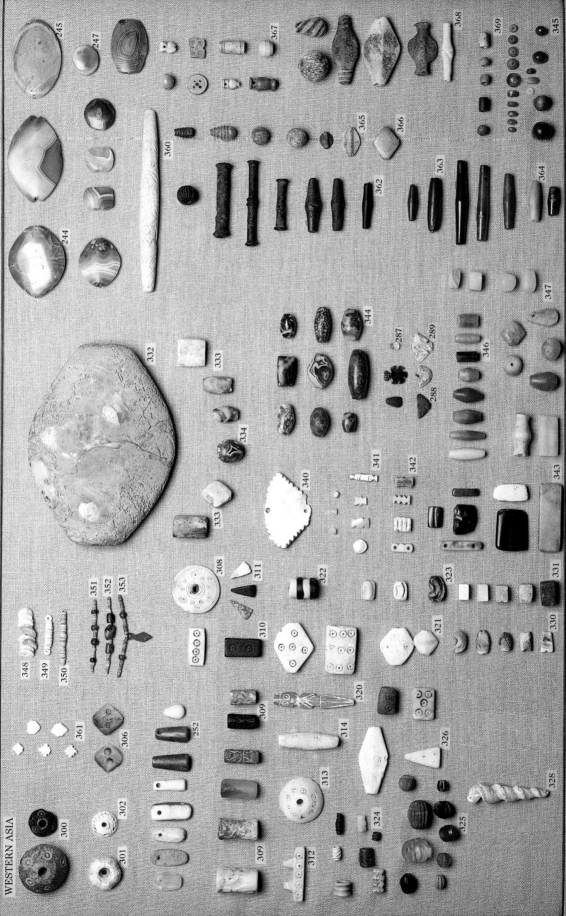

WESTERN ASIA

SOUTH ASIA

3,000 BCE

2,500 BCE

2,000 BCE

James W. Lankton

T he Three Age System, dividing early societies into Stone, Bronze, and Iron Ages, as suggested in 1836 by Danish scholar C.J. Thomsen, was an important breakthrough for the study of European and Middle Eastern prehistory. Today, most archaeologists prefer to use more specific chronologies tied to the culture being studied, particularly when written records become available, as occurs during the 3rd millennium BCE in West Asia and Egypt. While the terms Bronze or Iron Age can still be helpful in describing the broad sweep of cultural change, and will be used in that sense in this Catalog, we understand that the Three Age System is not applicable to many parts of the world, and we will consider these individually as they appear on the Bead Timeline.

The rise and fall of dynasties and empires throughout the Early Bronze Age, the time period of Chapter 3, created an extraordinary demand for luxury goods, both to demonstrate and to legitimize the power of emerging elites. This pattern would continue into the 2nd millennium BCE, leading to revolutionary developments in prestige technologies which remain important today. At the beginning of the 3rd millennium BCE, immediately following the collapse of the northward Uruk Expansion, many cities in northern Mesopotamia and Syria, including Habuba Kabira, were abandoned. By mid-millennium, others rose to take their places, most importantly Ebla and Urkesh, in northern Syria, and Mari, along the Euphrates River. Tell Brak, ancient Nagar,

FIGURE 3.1. Eisen suggested that melon beads served amuletic purposes (Eisen 1930a:20-43), and the many burials with a single blue melon bead as the only funerary offering support his idea. Our melon beads represent some of the stones used during the 3rd millennium BCE, including calcite, rock crystal, chalcedony, carnelian, and lapis lazuli. Rock crystal melon bead 2.2 cm diameter.

was one of the few 4th millennium cities to continue into the 3rd. In southern Mesopotamia, the great Sumerian city-states struggled for dominance in the Early Dynastic Period, while in Egypt, unification of Upper and Lower Egypt allowed the Old Kingdom pharaohs to concentrate on massive building projects, including the great pyramids at Giza, now a suburb of Cairo.

The beads shown above in Figure 3.1, known generally as melon beads and characterized by longitudinal grooves or gadroons, illustrate some of the colorful variety from 3rd millennium BCE workshops, and include the two most important stones: carnelian and lapis lazuli. Melon-carved lapis lazuli beads were found in

Early Dynastic graves at the Royal Cemetery of Ur, dating to 2450 BCE, in southern Mesopotamia, where they were used to decorate the gold pins from which cylinder seals would be suspended (Pittman 1998: 118). The Treasure of Ur, a cache of gold, lapis lazuli, and carnelian found at Mari, from the same period, includes a deeply grooved lapis lazuli bead, quite similar to our example. It was combined with long biconical carnelian beads from the Indus Valley (Fortin 1999; 94).

Lapis lazuli was the defining jewel of the 3rd millennium BCE. Just as jade symbolized the enduring values of early Chinese culture, lapis lazuli symbolized

FIGURE 3.0. Stone, bone, and shell beads from the 3rd millennium BCE, the Early Bronze Age in western Asia. The beads on the left side of the panel, many of them marked with dot-in-circle designs, represent the Early Dynastic period in Mesopotamia. Across the top, stone and shell beads from Central Asia range from very small, at 351-353, to very large, at 332 and 360. These large beads mimic the shapes of smaller examples, but little is known about their function. The banded agate tabular beads at upper right may be from the Bactrian oases. The longest carnelian bead is 6.7 cm.

the beneficent forces of nature and the life force for the Sumerians. Lapis represented the power of the Sumerian gods, who spoke through the beauty of the stone (Casanova 2000: 179). The most common use of lapis lazuli was for beads, although amulets, inlays, and small vessels were important as well. Lapis beads were restricted to the most wealthy and powerful: Consider that for the entire Bronze Age, 74% of the total lapis lazuli recovered from archaeological sites anywhere came from the Royal Cemetery at Ur, even though only 21% of the graves there included any lapis at all. An incredible 55% of all excavated Bronze Age lapis lazuli has come from two graves, those of Queen Puabi and her king (Casanova 2000: 173).

The most important source of lapis lazuli in the ancient world was at Sar-i Sang above the valley of the Kokcha River in Badakhshan, northeast Afghanistan, with the possibility of a second source in the Chagai Hills along the southern Pakistan-Afghanistan border; both areas are at least 2000 km from the cities of Mesopotamia. At Sar-i Sang, the rich lapis veins at 3600 m elevation were accessible for only a few months each year, and in ancient times were broken apart by throwing cold water on the heated rock face. The resulting fragments were taken to camps at a lower elevation for sorting and possible preliminary working. Although the use of lapis lazuli certainly reached its peak during the 3rd millennium BCE, trading mechanisms for lapis had already been present for several thousand years. Lapis beads have been found in Pakistan at Mehrgarh from the 7th millennium BCE, and are reported from Tell Sotto in northern Syria as part of a "rich necklace made from stone beads, including marble and lapis lazuli" (Bader 1993: 69),

FIGURE 3.2. A variety of spacer beads in chalcedony, carnelian, shell, mother-of-pearl, and bone. Many of these forms persist for millennia, and are difficult to date. Lower left 3.5 cm.

dating to the early 7th millennium, which would be by far the earliest date for lapis in Syria or Mesopotamia. By the mid-5th millennium BCE, lapis was found as well, although still in small amounts, at Tepe Gawra in northern Iraq (Rothman 2002: 8). The earliest lapis lazuli beads at Mehrgarh were imported, but by the beginning of the 4th millennium BCE, there is evidence for lapis lazuli beadmaking at Merhgarh and at Mundigak, near Kandahar in southern Afghanistan. Several eastern workshops from the 3rd millennium BCE, including those at Sarazm and Shortughai in Central Asia, and at Tepe Hissar and Sharh-i Sokhta in Iran, are all either near the lapis sources or along trade routes leading to Mesopotamia. Excavations at Sharh-i Sokhta, not far from the Chagai Hills, suggest that lapis coming from the mines was usually in the form of small blocklets, which could be made into beads for

local use, or traded onward from these distribution sites (Foglini and Vidale 2000: 476)

Excavations at Ebla, the greatest city-state in northern Syria during the mid-3rd millennium BCE, demonstrate another stage in the lapis lazuli story. With a total population for the city and surrounding area of between 250,000 and 300,000, and an economy based on agriculture and trade in textiles and finished objects, Ebla dominated northern Syria, and its merchants jouneyed up to 1900 km in search of raw materials for the city's craft workshops. Pettinato gives us a good sense for the active trade in such valuable commodities as lapis lazuli, gold, silver, copper, lead, and exotic sea shells that were brought back to Ebla for working into finished products: "The entire Fertile Crescent was swarming with wagons, full of valuable goods and hauled by oxen, which slowly managed to reach the trade centers in the various cities. Once there, merchants would engage in business transactions amounting to millions of dollars in today's values" (Pettinato 1991: 113).

While beadmakers at such eastern sites as Sharh-i Sokhta used lapis of superior quality to make a limited range of beads, those at Ebla or Ur made maximum use of whatever raw material was available. Documents from the Ebla archives include manuals on various raw materials used in the city's workshops, and the section on lapis lazuli lists more than 55 distinctions of color and quality. The extent of the lapis lazuli industry is suggested by the 23 kg of raw lapis blocklets found during the excavation of the burned Palace G, dating to the 3rd millennium BCE (Casanova 2000: 178). Finished lapis lazuli beads from Ebla would have been traded throughout western Asia, and

James W. Lankton

perhaps our melon bead is one of them.

Both carnelian and lapis lazuli became more common in the 3rd millennium BCE, along with rock crystal, while turquoise was less so, as mentioned in Chapter 1. In general, Early Bronze Age beads show a greater variety of form, particularly in the first half of the millennium in Mesopotamia. Soft stone and shell remain important, along with an increasing variety of hard stones. These raw materials were traded by land, as at Ebla, or by sea, with developing trade links through the Persian Gulf to Dilmun (Bahrain), Magan (the Persian and Omani coast at the mouth of the Gulf), and Meluhha (the developing Indus Valley civilization). Many of the small shell beads on our Timeline are virtually identical to beads made at Lothal, an Indus bead manufacturing center in persent-day Gujarat, India, known as well for the production of shell cylinder seal blanks from the columella of *Turbinella pyrum*, the Indian Ocean chank shell (Lothal 1999: *pers. obs.*). The cylinder seal second from the left at 309, Figure 3.0, is a good example, common only in the first half of the 3rd millennium BCE.

The many beads decorated with dot-in-circle designs, illustrated in Figure 3.0, are remarkable for their sizes and shapes; they are generally made from alabaster and other soft stones. The precise circles suggest that a hollow drill was used for the pattern, which can be found as early as the 7th millennium BCE at Yarim Tepe II in northern Syria (Merpert and Munchaev 1993b: 142). The dot-in-circle motif is characteristic as well for Central Asian beads from the 3rd millennium BCE, and remains in use today. Many other cultures, some with no known connection to early West Asia, have used the dot-in-circle design as well. I have

FIGURE 3.3. All of these beads were made from calcite, showing the great variety found in this one material. Calcite, Mohs' 3 in hardness, was easy to shape into beads or vessels, and could be perforated with chert drills. Both monchrome and banded varieties were used for beads, which have been found at Ebla, in northern Syria, dating to 2400-2300 BCE. Longest bead on the left is 3.3 cm.

not seen a thorough archaeological or anthropological study of the dot-in-circle, but one can imagine that a form of such longevity and wide distribution would have a very powerful meaning, most likely related to protection from the evil eye, a malicious glance that can lead to many types of illness and misfortune, a belief very much alive today in a number of traditional cultures.

The small bone pendant at 320, Figure 3.0, is our only goddess figure, perhaps representing some version of Ishtar, the Babylonian goddess of love and war. Goddess theory, popularized by archaeologist Marija Gimbutas, emphasizes the important role of female imagery, including many female figures, in Neolithic cultures. The unifying concept of a single Great Goddess is somewhat out of favor now, but there are still many examples of the linking of female roles with fertility, and in many early cultures, women had high

status in the community, judging from the types and numbers of grave goods. Female figures in clay, stone, and, later, glass, which are often frankly sexual, appear in many Bronze Age cultures (Talalay 2000: 789-792).

The spacer beads shown opposite, and the group of calcite beads on this page, illustrate additional examples of the variety of 3rd millennium BCE beadmaking. The earliest spacer beads were found in Iraq at Zawi Chemi Shanidar, from the 10th millennium BCE, where green chrysocolla spacers were combined with pink and red calcite beads (Francis 1988b: 71). Further examples of spacer beads continue in the 6th and 5th millennia, but the greatest variety of spacer beads appears during the 3rd, when Casanova identifies 15 distinct types from Syria, Mesopotamia, and Iran (Casanova 2000: 175). Calcite, Mohs' hardness 3, continued to be popular for vessels and

James W. Lankton

FIGURE 3.4. Variegated jasper beads have been found at both Mesopotamian and Indus Valley sites. The non-quartz elements in jasper can make up to 20 % of the total mass, and account for the color and decorative patterns. Although jasper may have the same hardness as carnelian and rock crystal, its greater toughness makes it useful as a drilling material. Longest bead 3.9 cm.

beads during the 3rd millennium, both for ease of carving, and for colors that range from deep red to colorless, with an appearance similar to rock crystal.

Throughout the Early Bronze Age, one of the major preoccupations of Mesopotamian rulers was to secure the sources and supplies of lapis lazuli. The land and sea routes were dangerous and easily disrupted, and at least one war was fought over the lapis lazuli trade. An early Sumerian epic poem, one of the very first written works of literature, dating from the 3rd millennium BCE, tells the story of Enmerkar, the king of Uruk, who wished to reopen the eastern caravan routes that brought lapis lazuli to Mesopotamia, so that he could build and decorate the sanctuary of Inanna (the Sumerian name for Ishtar) in Uruk. Enmerkar laid seige to the fabled city of Aratta, so wealthy that

its very walls were made of lapis lazuli, thought now to have been located in southern Iran at Tall-i Malyan. Aratta was blocking supplies of this most precious stone and Enmerkar was determined to regain access. He prevailed, but only with the help of Anzu, the lion-headed eagle, which brings us back to our Bead Timeline. In Chapter 2 we mentioned the three small bird pendants, in lapis lazuli, stone, and shell, at 288 and 289 in Figure 2.2. Similar figures have been excavated at Mari and Tell Brak in Syria, and at Susa in Iran, all dating to the mid-3rd millennium BCE. While the features are not clear on our small examples, larger carvings would have had an attached lion's head of gold. Anzu, also known as Imdugud, was a common figure in Mesopotamian mythology, serving as the emblem for the god Ningirsu in south-

ern Mesopotamia, and appearing on the standard of Ebla, possibly as Rashap, the god of war and the underworld (Black and Green 1992: 107). Lugalbanda, the hero of this early Sumerian drama, accompanied his master Enmerkar to the battle, having a number of adventures along the way, including an encounter with the fearsome Anzu. Anzu had left his nest, leaving his one chick unguarded while he went out to hunt. Lugalbanda stumbled on the nest and fortunately, realizing what it was, treated the nestling with great care, feeding it cakes and honey, salt meat and sheep fat, while crowning the chick with sprigs of cedar and painting its eyes with kohl. He also redecorated the nest, all of which so pleased the great Anzu, now returned from the hunt with one bull in his talons and another slung across his back, that he offered to grant Lugalbanda his greatest wish, that he be able to run anywhere without feeling tired. Wish granted, Lugalbanda returned to the siege, and through his swiftness and the intervention of Inanna, helped Enmerkar conquer Aratta, and bring back to Uruk all of its precious metals and stones, along with the metalsmiths and stoneworkers (Lugalbanda 2003). This story of Enmerkar is important not only because it relates the first war fought over beads, but also because it provides an early example of craft workers as part of the bounty of victory; this theme replayed many times over subsequent millennia provides a mechanism for the spread of craft technology in the ancient world.

During the mid-3rd millennium BCE, two new varieties of beads are found with Mesopotamian lapis lazuli: etched carnelians decorated with white patterns

James W. Lankton

resulting from alkali treatment, and carnelian bicones up to 12 cm long, shown above 364, Figure 3.5. Both types demonstrate the mastery of stone beadmakers from the third great ancient literate civilization, that of the Indus Valley. Located in present-day Pakistan and India, it covered twice the area controlled by the Sumerian city-states or the Egyptian pharaohs. The 3rd millennium BCE maritime trade to Mesopotamia from Meluhha brought exotic shells and shell beads and bangles, along with quartz beads, primarily carnelian, but also jasper and possibly banded agate. At 1604-1607, Figure 3.0, are some shell and stone beads from the Indus civilization, along with one long carnelian imitation made from terracotta. The constricted cylindrical drills needed to perforate these long beads, along with beadmaking debris, have been found at the workshop city of Chanhudaro in the Indus Valley, and there is some evidence for similar industry at the great urban centers of Harappa and Mohenjo-daro. The actual period of production may have been limited to a few hundred years, from 2450 to 1900 BCE, at Chanhudaro, although similar long carnelian beads from Marlik Tepe, located along the southern shore of the Caspian Sea in Iran, suggest that at least some of these beads were used up to one thousand years later. Faceted long carnelian beads have not been found at Indus sites, although they are present in the Royal Tombs at Ur, suggesting local production in Mesopotamia, possibly by Indus Valley workers. There is good evidence for Indus immigrants at Ur, both in the Early Dynastic and in the Akkadian (2350-2150 BCE) periods, when Meluhhan ships docked at Akkadian ports, and

FIGURE 3.5. Group with two long carnelian bicones from the Indus Valley. These striking beads were produced for a relatively short period following 2450 BCE. Longest bead 6.7 cm.

long carnelian beads are found at Ur during both of these periods.

In the second half of the Early Bronze Age in southern Mesopotamia, the Semitic Akkadian dynasty, founded by Sargon of Akkad, formed the first true empire, which was followed by a Sumerian revival under the 3rd Dynasty of Ur (2100-2000 BCE). Both were periods of prosperity and relative stability, with continued emphasis on the importance of gold and precious stone ornaments, primarily beads. The beautifully formed variegated jasper beads on the facing page at 344, Figure 3.4, would be appropriate for this period, which is marked by continued innovation in the working of very hard stones, including jasper, carnelian, and banded agate. Without access to the constricted cylindrical drills perfected at Indus Valley sites, most beadmakers were using hard jasper drills

or possibly copper drills with abrasive powder, usually crushed quartz, Mohs' hardness 7. Finding a more efficient abrasive would greatly improve drilling efficiency. As early as 2650 BCE at Sharh-i Sokhta in Iran, pieces of a particular apple-green quartz with high corundum (Mohs' hardness 9) content, appear in beadmaking areas; not found as beads or roughouts, they may have been used in drilling. (Foglini and Vidale 2000: 474). In Mesopotamia, the story of a Revolt of the Stones from Ur III mentions a stone used to work carnelian, possibly referring to corundum, and samples of corundum have been found at Ur in levels dating to the second half of the 3rd millennium BCE. (Tallon 1995: 96). By the end of the millennium, corundum, often mixed with magnetite to make emery, was commonly used to drill both beads and seals (Gwinnett and Gorelick 1998-9: 54).

The only banded agate bead we have illustrated so far is the small example to the left at 354, Figure 2.0, from the mid-4th millennium BCE. The large banded beads at 246 on the same page are primarily softer stones, although large chalcedony beads, such as 303 in the upper right corner of Figure 2.0, have been found in both Syria and Iran from this early period (Leiden 2002: *pers.obs.*; Amiet 1966: 148). While the banded agate beads from the Early Dynastic period at Ur were also small, the fact that they were found exclusively in the grave of Queen Puabi suggests their great value. Much larger lenticular and bow-shaped banded agate beads, often with closely fitting gold caps, become more common at excavated Mesopotamian sites from the Akkadian and Ur III periods. The few published examples of earlier large banded agate beads include two beads from the first half of the 3rd millennium BCE excavated at Susa, which were found with typically Central Asia beads (Amiet 1966: 148), and a tantalizing reconstruction of one of Queen Puabi's attendants wearing a very large lenticular banded agate bead which was illustrated by Woolley in 1929 (Woolley 1982: 172), but has not been included with subsequent exhibitions (Zettler and Horne: 1998).

The sources of these 3rd millennium BCE banded agate beads in Mesopotamia are not certain. Agate beadmaking at Harappa was particularly prominent from 2200-1900 BCE, correllating well with the dates of Mesopotamian finds (Kenoyer *in press*), although the Harappan beads were generally barrel shaped and not lenticular. A linkage between the Akkadian period banded agate beads at Ur and the Indus Valley is further supported by the presence at Ur of a few very long banded agate beads similar in shape to long carnelian beads (Pittman 1998: 114), a shape not known to have been made at that time by other than Indus Valley technology. It is of course possible that these long banded agate beads were actually made-to-order in Mesopotamia—perhaps by descendants of Indus beadmakers thought to be present at Ur one hundred years earlier (Kenoyer 1997: 272)

To further complicate the banded agate bead story, a number of large lenticular banded agate beads have come to the antiquities market as Bactrian or Namazga, and are represented on our Timeline in the upper right corner of Figure 3.0. In order to make some order out of confusing archaeological evidence, Possehl and others postulate a 3rd millennium BCE Middle Asian Interaction Sphere, with poles in Mesopo-

tamia, Dilmun/Magan (the Persian Gulf region), Meluhha (the Indus Valley civilization), and Turan (northeastern Iran/Afghanistan and southern Turkmenistan). This Middle Asian Interaction Sphere is marked by both maritime and overland trade, resulting in the sharing of prestige objects and symbols. One is our friend Imdugud, the Anzu bird. Another would seem to be large banded agate beads, although these are not addressed in Possehl's discussion. (Possehl 2002: 216)

Developing urban centers in the foothills of the Kopet Dag mountains in southern Turkmenistan, such as Namazga and Altyn Depe, reveal evidence for beadmaking, although primarily in soft stones, such as steatite, by the middle of the 4th millennium BCE (Hiebert 1994; 148). At the same time, such decorative motifs as the stepped cross are found at both Indus and Central Asian sites, possibly inspired by painted pottery from Quetta in Baluchistan, Pakistan. By the 3rd millennium BCE, the stepped cross had become a recognizable Central Asian design, found both on copper stamp seals and on steatite or limestone beads, as shown on our Timeline at 361, Figure 3.0. Large lenticular banded agate beads at Altyn Depe from the late 3rd millennium BCE (Masson and Kiiatkina 1981: 123), whether imported or manufactured on site, further suggest the sharing of common cultural themes in the Middle Asian Interaction Sphere, although the exact relationship of the Altyn Depe banded agate beads with those from other areas remains unclear.

Toward the end of the 3rd millennium BCE, the foothill centers of

Altyn Depe and Namazga lost population and cultural complexity, while new settlements in the oases of Bactria and Margiana, today parts of Turkmenistan and Afghanistan, grew rapidly, with possible immigration from the now failing urban centers. Between 2100 and 2000 BCE, urban dwellers in the Central Asian oases developed a new, shared set of cultural elements, known as the Bactria Margiana Archaeological Complex (BMAC), including architectural and decorative patterns. The new cultural motifs include images of desert animals; human figures carved from chlorite and alabaster; images of narcotic plants, along with traces of ephedra and poppy; and stamp seals and mace heads decorated with endless knot patterns made up of interlaced snakes or dragons. Additional features include symbols interpreted as precursors to Indo-Iranian mythology, associated with later cultures in Iran, South Asia, and the eastern Mediterranean (Hiebert 1994: 139)— and beads.

The large banded agate beads thought to be from southern Bactrian cemeteries, presumably dating to between 2000 and 1800 BCE—the most likely dates for the burials— have been the collector's dream and the archaeologist's nightmare. To many, they are among the most beautiful stone beads from any period, yet by the 1970s, widespread looting had already made scientific investigation difficult, and there are still many unanswered questions regarding the Central Asian Bronze Age. Less beautiful but perhaps more curious are truly massive beads with similar lenticular shapes but made from chert/limestone rock, such as 332,

James W. Lankton

Figure 3.0, which are said to come from the same areas. Like Mesopotamian beads, the Bactrian banded agate beads may also be capped with gold, but usually with truncated concave cones, unlike the close-fitting Mesopotamian gold caps. Thirty years after their discovery, there is no question about the attraction of these dramatic Central Asian beads, but where, when, and by whom they were made remains a mystery.

The two groups of beads illustrated on this page bring us to the end of the Early Bronze Age. Copper beads, usually made from rolled sheets of hammered metal, have been found at excavation sites from Anatolia to Pakistan from the 7th millennium BCE, and perhaps earlier. Copper, like most other metals to follow, and certainly bronze, began as a product of prestige technology, with use limited to ornaments and other elite objects. In general, as more practical applications for these metals were found, their prestige value decreased sharply, and they were replaced with some other material. It seems likely that the use of copper drills in the 4th millennium BCE (as at Habuba Kabira) along with large production sites, such as the manufactory for unalloyed copper found in southern Jordan dating to the Early Bronze Age, dulled the luster of copper ornaments. Enter bronze, shiny gold- colored when new, and perfect for making small beads and decorative pins, sometimes by lost-wax casting (Squadrone 2002: 1545). By the end of the 3rd millennium BCE, the size and complexity of bronze beads increased considerably, resulting in beads of the type shown at 362 in Figure 3.6.

The large faience beads shown at 368 in Figure 3.7 and at 381, Figure

FIGURE 3.6. Bronze beads from the 3rd millennium BCE perhaps formed by lost-wax casting. The six upper beads on the right are lead, and more likely date to the Roman period, 3rd to 4th centuries. Longest bronze bead 6.7 cm.

FIGURE 3.7. These large faience beads retain some traces of their original blue-green glaze. Similar beads have been found at Syrian sites from the 2nd half of the 3rd millennium BCE, but are otherwise rare. Center bead 5.5 cm.

4.0, are very similar to at least two excavated groups, both from northern Syria, dating between 2350 and 2000 BCE (Roualt and Masetti-Roualt 1993: 327; Allard Pierson Museum, 2002). While exact counterparts to our bronze beads have been difficult to find, designs shared with some of the faience beads would support our suggested dating. The relationship between faience technology and metallurgy is not yet clear, but it seems reasonable that the similar mastery of heat required would create a natural alliance. The earliest use of faience was, of course, for small beads, introduced as early as 5400 BCE in Mesopotamia and Syria

(Fortin 1999: 152), but well after the earliest copper beads. In Egypt, where faience later found its highest artistic expression, the first faience beads date to the early 4th millennium BCE (Moorey 1994; 168). Faience in both cases was preceded by heat-treated steatite and, at least in Egypt, by glazed steatite from the middle of the 5th millennium BCE. We will return to ancient faience in Chapter 5, recalling the impressive faience beads on this page, which illustrate the well-developed faience technology before the end of the Early Bronze Age.

B2

EUROPE

WESTERN ASIA

EGYPT

NORTH AFRICA

CHINA
EASTERN ASIA

AMERICAS

AFRICA

1,500 BCE

1,000 BCE

800 BCE

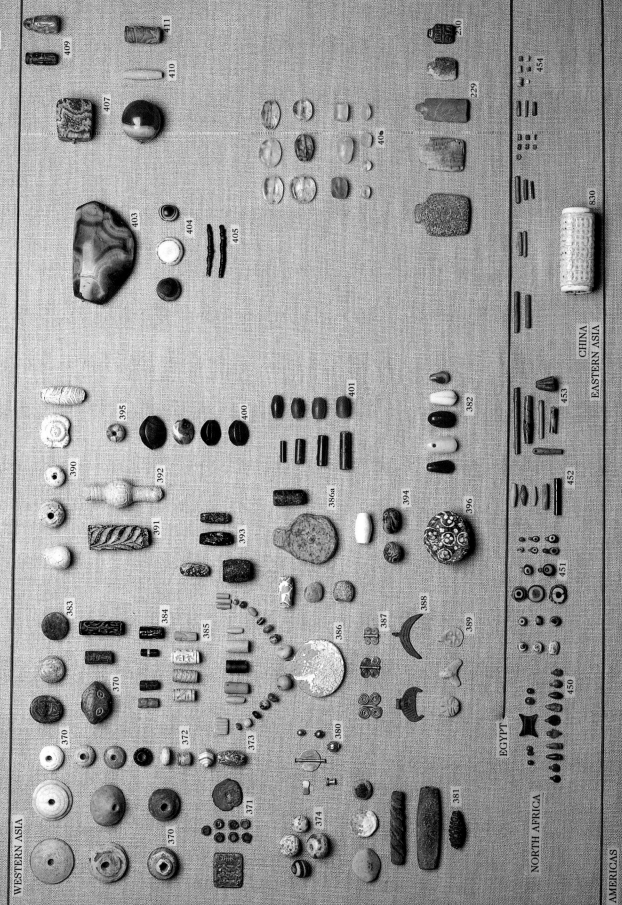

James W. Lankton

The 2nd millennium BCE opens with the sack of Ur. For the next 1500 years, empire follows empire in Mesopotamia as the Assyrians in the north and the Babylonians in the south trade control back and forth. During the Middle Bronze Age (2000-1600 BCE) city-states in Syria and along the Mediterranean coast become wealthy through trade, in part with Middle Kingdom Egypt, now a developing power with a greater international reach. Ebla regains prominence after its destruction toward the end of the 3rd millennium BCE, and Nagar (Tell Brak) remains important in the northeast. Along the coast of the Levant, Ugarit, Sidon, and Tyre become prominent centers, while to the north, the Hittites consolidate their control over Anatolia.

Powerful new groups, often taking control through force or treachery, created a constant demand for the symbolic objects that would reinforce their legitimacy to rule. Lapis lazuli remained the most precious material and was always mentioned in religious texts, but it becomes rare among the objects actually recovered from archaeological sites (Tallon 1995: 61). With an abrupt decline in maritime trade with the Indus Valley after 1900 BCE came a decrease in the variety of stone beads, now mainly agate and carnelian, often combined with gold. Turquoise continued to be rare, and the few lapis lazuli cylinder seals are smaller and appear to have been made from recycled supplies.

From the middle of the 3rd millennium

BCE, if not before, craft workers, most likely in northern Mesopotamia or Syria, had been experimenting with what would become the most important new prestige technology of the 2nd millennium: glass. It remains unclear exactly where glass-making started, and whether it built on faience or metal technology, or both. Evidence for early glass beads has been found in Egypt, Mesopotamia and the Indus Valley, and it is not unlikely that glass technologies emerged simultaneously in all three regions between 1700 and 1500 BCE.

The technologies needed for making glass had been around in all of these regions for thousands of years. By the middle of the 4th millennium BCE, metalworkers were smelting copper from ore and casting small ornaments in copper and bronze. The faience workers who made the large beads we saw in Chapter 3 had the benefit of over two thousand years of accumulated experience with

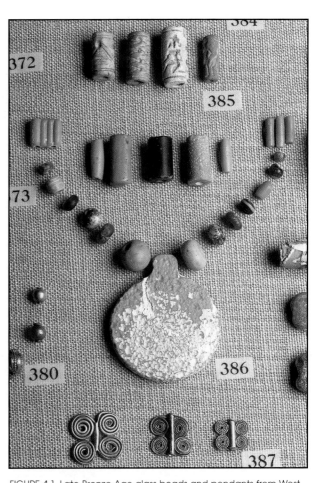

FIGURE 4.1. Late Bronze Age glass beads and pendants from West Asia, along with quadruple spiral gold beads. The Mitanni cylinder seals at 385 include faience and Egyptian blue (on the right), a calcium and copper double silicate. Blue glass pendant 4.6 cm diameter.

glazed silicate mixtures, albeit at a lower temperatures than needed for glass production. Two of the earliest well-dated glass beads were found in Akkadian levels at Nippur in southern Mesopotamia; one seems to be derived from metallurgical slag with sources in the Taurus Mountains of south-central

FIGURE 4.0. The Middle (2000-1600 BCE) and Late (1600-1200 BCE) Bronze Ages brought the development of great empires to West Asia and Egypt, with the Assyrians in northern Mesopotamia and the Babylonians in the south. By the 16th century BCE, the Mitanni kingdom dominated northern Syria, with eventual spread from the Mediterranean to northern Iraq. Mitanni kings exchanged gifts and letters with Egyptian pharaohs of the New Kingdom (1550-1070 BCE), and it was in Mitanni territory that many of the earliest glass objects have been found. Largest blue pendant 4.6 cm in diameter.

FIGURE 4.2. Second millennium BCE glass beads may lose alkali to the surrounding soil, leaving very thin shells of silica. The outer form of the bead remains, although most of the weight and strength is gone. The bead at 395 may be a very early example of mosaic glass, while the carnelian bead shows the carinated form typical of the Late bronze Age. The long spindle-shaped bead is 6.4 cm.

Anatolia, while the other, less well-crafted and with a compostion more like later glass, had alternating bands of white and olive green, perhaps an attempt to imitate the banded agate then becoming prominent (Vandiver *et al* 1995: 331). Just five hundred years after these apparently early efforts, glass beads and ornaments, now well-made and with uniform compositions, are found at a number of West Asian sites, most of which were related to the mid-2nd millennium BCE Mitanni kingdom. Within a short period of time, by the second half of the 16th century BCE, the beginning of the Late Bronze Age, blue glass spacer beads, along with disk-shaped and figural pendants, often in the likeness of a nude female, can be found from Iran to the Aegean.

The shortage of lapis lazuli, perhaps more than any other factor, transformed glass from a curiousity into a necessity—a substitute for the precious and semi-precious stones so important to the rulers of the emerging states. The quest for these materials drove the developing internationalism of the Late Bronze Age, resulting in a degree of contact and interaction unprecedented in the ancient world. Libraries of clay tablets found in the ruins of palaces from Egypt to Anatolia have preserved letters from one ruler to another asking for military help, wives, and beads and beadmaking materials.

Both the figural female pendants and the flat disks with an impressed eight-pointed star, shown at 386a, Figure 4.0, represent Ishtar, the goddess of love and war important in many West Asian cultures. Known also as Astarte, her name in Phoenicia, or Asherah, her biblical name, she was eventually incorprated into the Greek and Roman pantheon as Aphrodite and Venus. The female pendants, usually about 8 cm high and made in an open mold, show a nude woman with exag-gerated hips and abdomen, with her hands under her breasts (Grose 1989: 58). The disk pendants may be plain, as in Figure 4.1 at 386, or more rarely, impressed with Ishtar's symbolic star. They range from 5 to 8 cm in diameter, with the decorated disks generally smaller; most examples are heavily weathered. The doubly perforated spacer beads are also molded; some of these beads have additional longitudinal fold marks above the perforations (Cambridge 2001: *pers. obs.*). Our example above 373, Figure 4.1, has the characteristic four ribs on the upper surface. Most spacer beads are between 1 and 3.5 cm long; large examples may rarely have a sheaf-of-wheat design impressed on the surface (Spaer 2001: 58).

Spacer beads, disk pendants, and Ishtar pendants were all among the more than 11,000 glass ornaments excavated at Nuzi, a provincial agricultural town located near present-day Kirkuk in northern Iraq (Vandiver 1983: 239). In the 14th century BCE, Nuzi was a part of the small Hurrian kingdom of Arrapha, along the south-eastern edge of a large area controlled by the Mitanni. An important kingdom with a Hurrian population and a military aristocracy with Indo-Iranian names, the Mitanni seem to incorporate many of the characteristics of the BMAC culture. There are more questions than answers about the Mitanni kingdom, but between 1600 and 1350 BCE Mitanni, centered in northern Syria and dominating territory from the Mediterranean to northern Iraq, played an important role in the geo-politics of the ancient world.

The Hurrians, a group of people speaking a Caucasian language related to modern Georgian, had long been known for their metallurgical skill. All of the earliest glass vessels, which appear after 1500 BCE, come from sites controlled by the Hurrians, and many researchers have suggested an important role for the Hurrians in the development of early glass technology.

In addition to the characteristic spacers and pendants, there were many other types of 2nd millennium BCE glass beads. The tubular beads in Figure 4.1 could be cylinder seal blanks, although Mitanni seals are much more commonly made in faience, as shown at 385. The blue glass tubular beads, colored with either cobalt or copper, often weigh 40 g, the Babylonian unit corresponding to 0.1 gold *mina*, which suggests that trade in gold and glass may have been based on the same standard (Stern and Schlick-Nolte 1994: 128). The four beads at 374, Figure 4.0, include two glass beads, at the left and bottom positions, that are probably banded agate imitations, similar to beads excavated at Mumbaqa near the Euphrates River in northern Syria (Rouault and Masetti-Roualt 1993: 373). The two glass beads in Figure 4.2, 391 and 392, are both unusual, with 392 perhaps copying contemporaneous gold melon beads with extended collars (Spaer 2001: 57). The five beads at 390 are similar to beads found at Nuzi, with the exception of the bead second from the right, tabular with an impressed eye pattern not, to my knowledge, previously published. All of these beads show weathering typical of 2nd millennium BCE glass, resulting from three thousand years of wet and dry cycles, which leach alkali from the glass, leaving very thin shells of silica. These shells may

FIGURE 4.3. Banded agate eye beads begin toward the end of the 3rd millennium BCE, becoming more common in the 2nd, with glass and faience copies. Large bead 8.3 cm.

refract incoming light to create iridescence, or, more commonly for 2nd millennium glass, leave a white surface retaining decorative marks such as the combed trails on our example, but without the original color of the bead.

Mosaic glass vessels are known from several 2nd millennium BCE sites, and it would be surprising if a similar technique had not been applied to beads. We believe we have found such an example, shown on the Timeline at 395, Figure 4.2. The yellow and white flower petal design appears to have been cut from a mosaic cane, then laid onto the surface of a wound bead. Two very similar beads from Tell Brak are dated to 1300 BCE, and are described as having yellow inlay edged in white, but without reference to technique (Oates *et al* 1997: 246). A small white oblate bead from Nuzi has blue and white eyes, which may also have been cut from a mosaic cane; a larger bead from the Petrie Museum, dated to New Kingdom Egypt, has a similar structure (Lankton 2004: *in preparation*).

The large glass bead shown at 396, Figure 4.0, appears black in the pho-

tograph, but is a very dark translucent violet, most likely due to high concentrations of manganese and cobalt. The substantial body is perforated to be strung both up-and-down and crosswise, as if it were intended to be the centerpiece of a net-like structure. The twisted cane around the perimeter of the bead and the trailed eye designs are found on rare Mitanni-influenced glass vessels from the 2nd millennium BCE. To my knowledge, our bead is unique, although it appears to fit well within the 2nd millennium group.

Glass tabular eye beads made from fused layers of dark and light glass were found in significant numbers at Nuzi, some perforated, and some embedded in fragments of mud plaster, providing evidence that at least one use of the eye beads was to decorate the walls of the Ishtar temple in which they were found. Our example, centered above the large faience beads at 381, Figure 4.0, is heavily weathered, but enough remains to illustrate how the same forms could be produced in different materials, with similarity to beads in both faience (immediately to the right) and stone, shown above at 404.

Similar banded agate eye beads begin to appear during the last quarter of the 3rd millennium BCE, with an example from an Ur III grave in the Royal Cemetery (Tallon 1995: 62). In the early 2nd millennium BCE, tabular agate eye beads are associated with the BMAC culture in Central Asia, and become particularly important during the Kassite-dominated Middle Babylonian period of the second half of the 2nd millennium BCE, when they may be inscribed as temple dedications. In the Babylonian story of

FIGURE 4.4. Three stone amulets of the type used for protection against Lamashtu, the demoness who preyed on unborn and newborn babies. The two pendants to the left are apparently unfinished, and would be carved with an image of Lamashtu on one side, and a magical incantation on the other. The wedge shaped marks are nonsensical cuneiform. Largest example 4.3 cm high.

Ishtar's descent to the underworld, she wears a necklace of eye beads, powerful protection for her dangerous journey. The identity of the Kassites is not well understood, but it seems possible that their interest in banded agate eye beads could be a clue to their origins.

The large patterned agate bead in Figure 4.3, at 403, is a variant of the bow-shaped banded agate beads first known during the Akkadian period (2350-2150 BCE). Although Horace Beck himself called such beads leech beads, bow-shaped seems a more appropriate name for such elegant forms. In addition, I've been exposed to a number of leeches, and can assure you that none of them looked like these beads. An example very similar to ours from Tepe Hissar in northern Iran, dating to the early 2nd millennium BCE, is shown combined with two agate eye beads from the same excavation (Musche 1992: Taf XLIX). Both bow- and eye-shaped banded agate beads remained popular in the 1st millennium BCE. Beautiful examples of the agate eye beads were found

with hundreds of gold objects in the recently published graves of three 8th century BCE Assyrian queens from Nimrud, in northern Iraq (Damerji 1999: Abb.25,30).

With origins in the 3rd millennium BCE, three types of gold beads become increasingly popular during the 2nd millennium: the collared melon beads previously mentioned; flat disk beads similar to our example at 380, Figure 4.0, although without the central tube; and the quadruple spiral beads illustrated in Figure 4.1. Metallic gold, whether mined or alluvial, was found in the mountains to the north and east of Mesopotamia, and the spiral form itself may have originated in Anatolia (Huot *et al* 1980: 128). There are at least three variations in manufacturing technique, with the earliest, 3rd millennium BCE examples similar to the bead at the left in the photograph, where the ends of the tube are slit, and then doubled back as spirals. Such beads have been found in silver at Tell Brak from the Akkadian period, and in gold at Troy

II, the Early Bronze Age city that guarded the entrance to the Black Sea, itself long associated with the early gold trade, and the setting for the story of Jason and the Argonauts. The second variant, shown as the middle example on the Timeline, also starts with a tube, but in this case, the spirals are formed by separate pieces of gold wire, wrapped around the tube at either end and then spiraled back. Similar beads have been found most often at sites in Syria and Iran, as well as at Lothal, the Harappan beadmaking city in present-day Gujarat. This second variation of the gold spiral dates from the 2nd into the 1st millennium BCE, with later examples showing the twisted wire of our example on the right at 387. The extreme longevity of the quadruple spiral design—they remain popular for almost two thousand years—and their imitation in less precious materials (see 389, Figure 4.0, for a faience bead inspired by the quadruple spiral), suggest that they were a powerful symbol, perhaps associated with Ninhursag, a Mesopotamian goddess of fertility (Maxwell-Hyslop 1971: 35).

Just below the quadruple spiral beads in Figure 4.0 are two silver crescents, another symbol first known from Mesopotamia, and one which remains important today. The crescent was the symbol of Sin, the moon god, and gold and silver crescent pendants, along with imitations in faience, as at 389, appear from the late 3rd millennium BCE, becoming most common in the mid-2nd millennium. Both the thick and thin varieties were found at Tell el-'Ajull in Palestine, possibly the capital city of the Asiatic Hyksos, who had ruled Egypt during the 2nd

James W. Lankton

Intermediate Period (1640-1550 BCE).

The three stone pendants at 229 and 230 in Figure 4.4 are part of a group of five, shown in Figure 4.0. Their characteristic shape identifies these as Lamashtu amulets, most common during the Neo-Assyrian period (1156-626 BCE). The demoness Lamashtu was the daughter of An, the Sumerian sky god (Black and Green 1992: 115). Her favorite victims were unborn and newborn babies, and miscarriages and crib deaths were often attributed to her. Pregnant women, particularly while in labor, would wear an amulet similar to ours, usually bearing the likeness of Lamashtu or of Pazuzu, another unsavory character whose main virtue was that he could drive Lamashtu back to the underworld. We know Pazuzu today as the head-turning demon from the film *The Exorcist*, and very rare Pazuzu heads in molded glass are contemporaneous with the better known Ishtar pendants. Lamashtu, with her lion head, donkey ears, and Anzu talons, stands suckling both a pig and a pup, while holding snakes in her stained hands: the image alone was apparently enough to turn away the demoness, thus protecting both mother and child, much as the image of Medusa was thought to protect the bearer from that monster's stony gaze during Greek and Roman times. Written on the reverse, often in very rough cuneiform, would be an incantation against Lamashtu. The nonsensical cuneiform signs carved on our example may have served as such a spell, since it was unlikely that either the mother or Lamashtu could actually read; the other examples appear to be

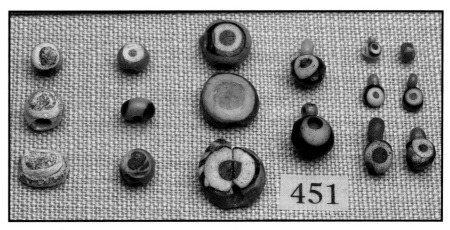

FIGURE 4.5. These Egyptian New Kingdom eye beads were most common in the late-18th and 19th Dynasties, the period of Thutankhamun and Ramesses II, and a possible setting for the Biblical Exodus. Moses himself could have seen these beads in Pharaoh's palace. Largest bead 1.5 cm.

unfinished. Typical materials for the excavated Lamashtu amulets from the Babylonian period, as reported from Uruk, were steatite, greenstone, white frit, and yellow alabaster, which correspond well with our examples (Becker 1993: Taf.1).

While the earliest glass beads in New Kingdom Egypt (1550-1070 BCE) may have been imported from Mesopotamia or were unintentional products of the well-developed faience industry, by the mid-15th century BCE, during the reign of Thutmosis III, palace-based production of glass beads and vessels was becoming established. We do not know whether Thutmosis, like Enmerkar one thousand years earlier, brought craft workers back home with him after his military campaigns in Syria and Palestine, but within one generation, Egyptian glass beads and vessels rivaled, and in some cases surpassed, those of West Asia. Among the treasures in New York at the Metropolitan Museum of Art are the beautifully preserved glass artifacts from Amenhotpe III's late 15th

century BCE Malkata palace near Thebes, which include several glass tubes with marked longitudinal striations, indicating that they had been drawn. Beck examined apparently similar tubes from Amarna, concluding that they were drawn from strips of glass folded around a wire, and suggested that small tubular beads from Abydos were simply broken-off lengths of such tubes (Beck 1928: 61), making these the earliest drawn beads. Eye beads became popular after the Amarna period (1350-1333 BCE); they are illustrated above in Figure 4.5.

The primacy of glassmaking appears to be settled in favor of West Asia, but there is little question that Egyptian craftsmen manufactured glass from raw materials at Akhenaten's capital of Amarna, where Flinders-Petrie excavated the only known second millenium BCE glassmaking furnace. Uluburun glass ingots match exactly Amarna ceramic crucibles in shape and size.

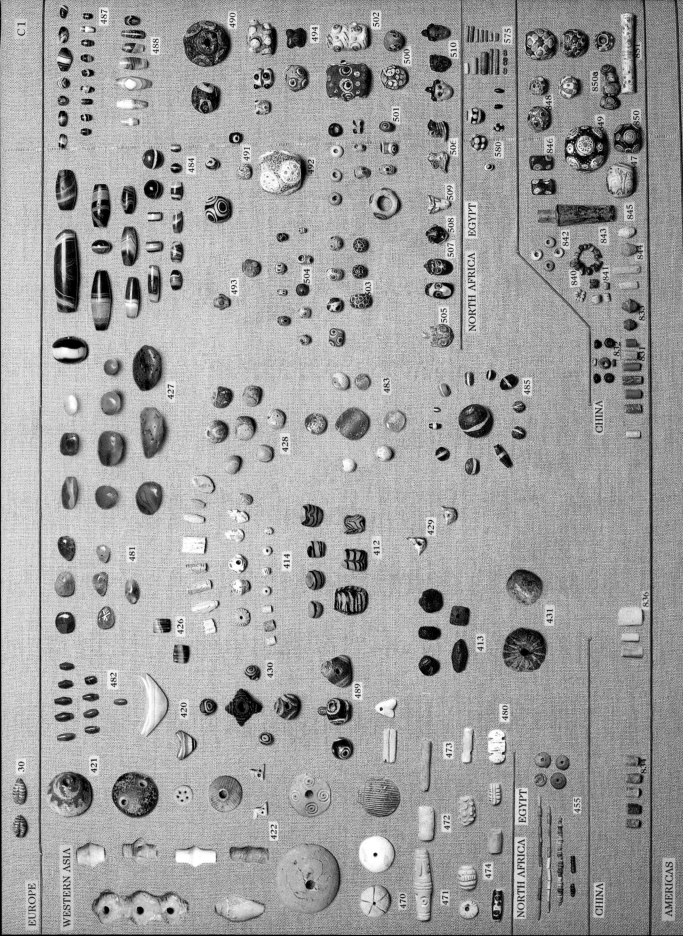

C1

EUROPE

WESTERN ASIA

NORTH AFRICA   EGYPT

CHINA

AMERICAS

AFRICA

NORTH AFRICA   EGYPT

CHINA

30
487
488
490
494
502
500
501
510
491
484
492
493
504
503
505
509
508
507
506
575
580
846
848
850a
831
851
850
849
847
845
843
842
844
841
840
835
832
851
836
485
483
427
428
481
414
412
426
430
489
429
431
413
420
421
422
482
470
471
472
473
480
474
155
834

500 BCE

600 BCE

700 BCE

James W. Lankton

In Chapter 4 we discussed the development of glass beads in the context of prestige technology. There are several lines of evidence that support this approach: the combination of glass and gold in fine jewelry; requests for glass materials from one Late Bronze Age king to another, as documented in preserved cuneiform tablets; the long-distance trade in luxury materials including ingots of glass colored with cobalt to resemble lapis lazuli, such as found in the 14th century BCE Uluburun shipwreck off the coast of Turkey. While glass becomes both abundant and inexpensive in later times, and could serve as a substitute for luxury materials for less affluent people, it appears that glass itself was precious during the 2nd millennium BCE.

One question lingers: Why is so much early glass turquoise colored? Turquoise itself became less common in Mesopotamia after the 4th millennium BCE, although it remained in use to the east and in Egypt, closer to the turquoise sources. It is difficult to link the decreased use of turquoise with the rise of lapis lazuli, since lapis did not become available in any quantity for almost another thousand years. Blue-green is one of the easiest glass colors to produce, simply by adding scrap bronze to the glass mix, and perhaps turquoise blue glass created its own market, along the theory that if you build it, they will come. There is, however, another major development that could provide a clue. Before the

end of the 5th millennium BCE, craft workers in West Asia, Egypt, and the Indus Valley region had begun to experiment with the heat treatment and glazing of stones, followed by the manufacture of faience—and almost all of this early material is colored with copper to produce a beautiful blue-green.

The terminlogy of the non-glass mixtures of alkali (sodium or potassium oxides), lime (calcium), and silica has confused generations of scholars. The two most commonly used terms—frit and faience—are both misnomers, but so ingrained by usage that they will be replaced only with difficulty. Both frit and faience are composed of closely compacted granules of mineral, usually quartz, which have partially fused, or sintered, with heating to between 800° and 1000° C, comparable to the temperature range needed for well-fired Bronze Age pottery. A thin layer of glass joins the particles together, and in the case of faience glazes the surface as well by one of several methods. Even weathered faience will retain at least microscopic traces of the surface glaze. On the other hand, frit is not glazed, and the surface color often extends through the body of the object. For this Catalog, we will use the term faience for the glazed material, and the term unglazed faience for material with no visible glassy phase on the surface. We recognize that unglazed faience is an oxymoron, but prefer to avoid the greater error of using frit, which has a different, specific

meaning in the context of glass technology. In practice, it can be very difficult to distinguish visually between the various silicates, and there seems little point in a more precise characterization without access to scientific analysis of the material in question.

The earliest faience beads were small oblates, found on almost all archaeological sites from the 4th millennium BCE on. Before the end of the 3rd millennium, large, well-made faience beads are found at Syrian sites, as illustrated in Figures 3.0 and 4.0. On the other hand, Egyptian faience from the same period and later, as shown in Figure 4.0 at 452-454 and in Figure 5.0 at 455 and 575, was used for small cylindrical and disk beads, which could be combined to produce the broad collars found in Egyptian tombs. In addition, Egyptian faience beads often copied plant and floral designs, which were uncommon in West Asia.

Indus Valley faience is unusual in many respects. Sometimes it was made from ground steatite rather than quartz. The powderlike substrate of most Indus faience produced a very dense material, much stronger than the usual Egyptian or West Asian faience, and the color of the glaze may continue into the faience body. At pre-Indus sites like Mehrgarh, just as faience and glazed steatite become important, the amount of turquoise declines, although not apparently because of decreased trading options, since the variety of other stones increases.

The many glazed and unglazed

FIGURE 5.0. Following a 200-year break at the end of the Late Bronze Age, glass and other luxury products reappear during Iron Age II (1000-586 BCE) in West Asia, Egypt, and the Aegean. Phoenician craftsmen help build and decorate the Assyrian palaces in Ashur and Nimrud with exquisite furniture inlaid with ivory and glass. The international trade in beads resumes, with the spread of glassmaking to Europe. Largest agate bead at 484 is 6.5 cm.

FIGURE 5.1. The three lower beads would have been similar to those in the upper row when new. While the original material was most likely glass, and the chocolate brown trailing supports this suggestion, highly weathered examples look more like faience than like weathered glass. Similar beads were excavated at Marlik, in Iran, dating ca. 10th century BCE. Largest bead is 2.6 cm long.

faience ornaments in Figure 5.0, at 414, 421-422, 470-474, and 480, come from West Asia and Iran. The white and yellow beads at 414 have close parallels from the mid-2nd millennium BCE in Syria, and yellow unglazed faience was found at both Tell Brak and at Nuzi, the important 2nd millennium BCE glass site in northern Iraq, where a well-developed silicate industry produced beads in blue, brick red, white, black, and yellow (Vandiver 1983: 241). The large beads on the left side of Figure 5.0 are more typical of the 1st millennium BCE, although some could be earlier as well. These striking ornaments, possibly from Iran, include beads with multiple perforations, shell imitations, large disks—one retaining its brilliant blue glaze—and even a small fly pendant, shown at the lower right of the group. Fly pendants had a profound meaning in Mesopotamian culture. They referred

to the Babylonian story of the great flood, the literary precursor to the biblical Old Testament flood. Ishtar herself wore a necklace of lapis lazuli flies that her father, the god Anu, had made for her; she swore to him that she would never forget the days of the flood, when men were, literally, dying like flies (Tallon 1995: 80).

In contrast to glass, it is more difficult to understand the emergence of faience, the "first high-tech ceramic" (Vandiver and Kingery 1986: 19), in terms of prestige technology, particularly in the context of West Asia. Much of the earliest faience would appear to be a substitute for turquoise, but there is little evidence that turquoise held anything like the importance of lapis lazuli. While luxury products, including vessels and figures, were certainly made with faience, the early faience beads are usually small and abundant, and do not appear to be

restricted to particular groups. Blanche Barthelemy de Saizeu (2000: 93) suggests that the production of glazed stones and faience during the 4th millennium BCE symbolized the domestication of the mineral world, which followed the domestication of the vegetal and animal worlds during the earlier mental Neolithic Revolution advocated by Jacques Cauvin (2000: 1-8); the principal force behind this domestication came from the innate human trait of curiosity—the need to know, and after that, the need to dominate. For the early 4th millennium BCE the tool was fire, and man's increasing control over and application of fire led to both faience and metallurgy. We haven't really answered the question of why so much early glass is turquoise blue; the explanation may be purely practical—blue green was easy to produce. On the other hand, turquoise blue glass may have been seen as a more luxurious form of faience, and not linked to turquoise at all.

The catastrophic end of the Late Bronze Age in 1200 BCE was accompanied by widespread destruction at the traditional centers in West Asia, and the disappearance of most luxury products, including glass, for the next two hundred years. At the same time, glass beadmaking did continue in Egypt, although at a lower level, and began in Europe, with several early sites dating to the 11th and 10th centuries BCE, including Hauterive-Champreveyres in Switzerland and Frattesina along the Po River Valley in Italy (Henderson 1995b: 71). European glassmakers used new and unusual formulas for their glass compositions, producing beads that may have been traded to the north. We know rela-

James W. Lankton

tively little about this earliest phase of European glass beadmaking, which is the subject of much active research.

In Iran luxury glass continued at Hasanlu, in the northwest, and at Marlik, on the slopes of the Elburz Mountains south of the Caspian Sea. The beads shown in Figure 5.1 are among the types reported from excavations at Marlik, which was apparently the royal cemetery for a group of Indo-Iranian speakers, and was in use from the 14th to the 9th centuries BCE (Negahban 1998: 43-55). These beads are commonly referred to as Marlik frit but are more likely glass, since only glass beads could have the chocolate-colored combed trails (Allen 2003a: *pers. comm.*). Similar beads were found in the later graves at Marlik, dating to the 10th to 9th centuries BCE (Musche 1992: Taf LXIII; Maxwell-Hyslop 1971: 194).

Small carvings, often portraying animals, are among the most distinctive early amber artifacts found in Denmark from the 8th millennium BCE. Large numbers of amber beads appear in Danish graves by the 4th millennium BCE, coincident with early agriculture, although both beads and carvings from Baltic amber have been found at late Paleolithic sites in France and Spain. Our amber beads shown above reflect the growth in long-distance trade in amber, which would become even more important as the Iron Age progresses to the Roman period. Excavated amber is often severely weathered and darkened, losing its translucency, as in the large bead in Figure 5.2, which is similar to beads found at Etruscan sites in northern Italy.

Both the Assyrians, in northern

FIGURE 5.2. By the 1st millennium BCE amber was widely traded throughout the ancient world, particularly from the 7th to the 4th centuries. In Italy, the Etruscans were particularly known for their large amber jewels, although amber was found as well in West Asia. These amber beads would have been translucent when new, but have weathered with burial. Largest bead 3.5 cm diameter.

Mesopotamia, and the Babylonians, in the south, shared in the general decline following the Late Bronze Age, but by the 9th century BCE, the Assyrians were in full recovery. Their demand for luxury objects of wood, ivory, and glass to fill newly built palaces stimulated the revival of these industries. Phoenician artisans from Tyre, Sidon, Byblos, and Arwad along the Syria/Lebanon coast provided the best quality workmanship, a fact recognized by Solomon when he asked Hiram of Tyre to build and embellish his new temple in Jerusalem.

Tyre was the leading city-state of the Phoenicians, who were culturally and linguistically related to the 2nd millennium BCE Canaanites. From the beginning of the 1st millennium BCE, Phoenician sailors and merchants began to establish colonies around the western Mediterranean basin, particularly in Tunisia, Sicily, and

Sardinia. Carthage, founded in 814 BCE by settlers from Tyre, became the most important colony, sponsoring its own outposts in Spain and Ibiza.

New varieties of glass beads provide some of the best evidence for the revival of international trade in the early 1st millennium BCE. Large triangular beads, with trailed eye designs over a brown or black opaque glass base, as shown at 489, Figure 5.0, have been found from Ireland to Iraq, at sites dating to the 9th century BCE (Haevernick 1987: 23). The triangular points may be applied separately, in the same color as the body of the bead (Spaer 2002: 80). Many of these early triangular eye beads have been found in the eastern Mediterranean area, particularly in Greece.

By the 9th century BCE the Greeks had begun to recover from a dark age of almost three hundred years, and to establish trade links with both West

James W. Lankton

Asia and Italy. Greek citizens, primarily from the Ionian Greek cities on the coast of Anatolia, started semi-independent colonies in Italy, Egypt, and the eastern Mediterranean by the 8th century BCE, moving into the Black Sea by 600 BCE, with important settlements at Olbia and Pantikapaion in the Ukraine.

Both the Phoenicians and the Greeks had important roles in glass beadmaking and trading during this period. Beadmaking at Tyre and Rhodes is suggested primarily by the large numbers of similar beads found, along with limited evidence for glass workshops. A second important type of glass bead which appears as early as the 8th century BCE is shown at 483, Figure 5.0. Up to three thousand of these highly translucent/transparent beads were found at Camiros, on Rhodes, with numerous other examples from northern Mesopotamia to northern Italy, where similar beads were mounted on bronze fibulas, a type of decorative garment pin (Spaer 2001: 63). While many of these beads may have been wound, several of our examples, as well as an excavated bead from Sardis (Saldern 1980: Plate 19, # 847), show characteristic seams at one end, suggesting that a warm pad of glass may have been pierced by a rod, and then folded around the rod to form the bead.

The dark brown glass beads at 430, Figure 5.0, follow the triangular eye beads by about one hundred years, although the distinctions may be rather subtle. The bead shape is less obviously triangular, and by the 7th century BCE, similar beads with four corners have a limited distribution in Europe, primarily in the Etruscan areas of north Italy, and in the south-

eastern Alps (Haevernick 1987: 25). The two beads at 30, in the upper left corner of Figure 5.0, are typically Etruscan, and were used as fibula beads. In fact, one of our beads still retains its bronze wire. Both large and small examples of these distinctive beads have been found in Etruscan tombs dating from the late 8th to the 7th centuries BCE (Meconcelli Notarianni 1999: 6).

While the traditional beadmaking centers of the eastern Mediterranean coast and the Aegean remained important, formerly peripheral areas became prominent as well during the mid-1st millennium BCE. Beadmaking at Carthage in North Africa, and along the Black Sea coast, is matched by new glassworking industries in Europe. Beginning in the 2nd millennium BCE, Indo-European tribes had been moving into Central Europe, and by the 8th century BCE the early Celtic Hallstatt culture had adopted both iron and glass technology. With wealth based on trade in tin and salt with Phoenician and Greek settlements to the south, the Celts provided a ready market for imported luxury goods. Some of the finest Greek bronzes and pottery have been found in Celtic burials, along with large numbers of glass beads and, in at least one case, silk cloth from China dating to the 7th century BCE, well before the start of the traditional Silk Road (Wilford 1993: B5). Imported glass beads found at Hallstatt sites resemble some of those from Etruscan areas and may be monochrome or decorated: blue beads with either a white equatorial wave design or with trailed eye rings in white or yellow. During the 6th century BCE Celtic craftsmen

began to make similar beads themselves. New forms of eye beads, now stratified, with eyes formed by successive layers of glass applied one on top of the other, are found at both Mediterranean and Central European sites from the 6th century BCE (Spaer 2001: 81).

These 6th century beads have a blue-green matrix and may have up to 20 layers in each eye, topped by a spot of darker blue glass. Often small, and very well made, they are associated with the Phoenician or Punic (Carthaginian) colonies, and possibly Egypt. The Central European beads tend to be larger, and the eyes rarely have more than six layers (Spaer 2001: 82). By the early 5th century, yellow beads with blue-and-white stratified eyes appear both north and south, becoming particularly important in Central Europe, where they continue well into the subsequent La Tène phase of Celtic culture, which began in the mid-5th century BCE.

Figure 5.3 on the facing page includes excellent examples of these early stratified eye beads. Sixth century beads of the Mediterranean type include the small beads with many-layered eyes toward the right in the second row from the bottom. One of our beads has 14 separate layers of glass, leading some to suggest that such complex eyes would have been made separately, and then applied to the bead (Spaer 2001: 82). The yellow beads with paired blue-and-white eyes show the characteristic orangey yellow color of many of these beads and could be either Mediterranean or Central European. It is not unusual to find two beads joined together as a doublet, although the mechanism for this is

James W. Lankton

not certain. While two beads could have fused during the preparation of sequential wound beads along an iron rod, at least one double bead on display at the Metropolitan Museum of Art in New York has a well-formed blue-and-white eye at the bottom of the crease between the two halves (New York 2002: *pers. obs.*), a situation that could only occur if one long bead were being separated into two after the eyes were applied. The blue-green beads with a single row of eyes, as shown in the third row from the bottom, were found as well at La Tène sites, as were the slightly later blue beads with ten or more eyes, usually placed in diagonal rows with three or more registers, illustrated by the lower beads at 503.

Among the most studied early glass ornaments are the human and animal figure pendants shown on this page. The earliest among these may be the ram's head pendant at 509, with very similar examples from the Late Bronze Age at Beth Shean in Israel (Spaer 2001: 160). All of the other pendants are of the 1st millennium BCE type that are commonly known as Phoenician and are found in the eastern and western Mediterranean area, with concentrations on the Phoenician coast and at Carthage. Examples from Celtic sites match those from the Mediterrranean while some of the examples found along the Black Sea coast may reflect local production. Woolley found a cache of 30 head pendants of various types at the Syrian port of Al Mina, suggesting a manufacturing site nearby, perhaps in one of the Phoenician cities (Seefried 1979: 23). The large numbers of 4th and 3rd century BCE pendants excavated at Carthage sup-

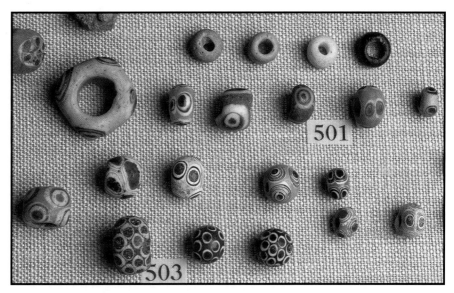

FIGURE 5.3. Stratified eye beads from the 6th to 3rd centuries BCE. Tabular eye beads composed of layers of glass were made in the 2nd millennium BCE, and the technique was rediscovered in the 7th century BCE, possibly in Egypt or the eastern Mediterranean. Many of the earliest beads are also the most detailed, as in the two beads below 501. Large ring bead 2.5 cm in diameter.

FIGURE 5.4. Small figurative pendants associated with Phoenician sites, but found also in Central Europe and along the northern Black Sea coast. The double-faced pendant to the left at 507 is early in the series, and the three examples at 510 are later. Central pendant at 507 is 1.7 cm high.

port the possibility of production there as well.

The earliest of the head pendants are represented in Figure 5.4, to the left at 507. With faces on both sides, these Janus-figure masks have been found in Egypt and could date to the early 7th century BCE. The slightly larger pendant at 507, classified as type B3 by Seefried (Seefried 1979: 19), has a smooth beard and bichrome wrap over the forehead, which is marked by a yellow dot, the meaning of which is unclear. Similar pendants from the mid-5th century have been found in Syria and throughout the Mediterranean. Large pendants with curly hair and beards are strongly associated with, and were probably made in, Carthage. The demonic face at 508, representing masks from the 6th and 5th centuries BCE, may be an extension of the Bronze Age Pazuzu masks, protecting the wearer from misfortune. The two bird pendants at 506 are slightly later in the series; many examples, some quite large, have been found in Scythian graves to the north of the Black Sea. Head pendants from the 3rd and 2nd centuries BCE, now molded rather than formed on a rod, are represented at 510. These beardless faces have applied eyes, but not separate eyebrows or forehead spots; two examples were found in the bead workshop debris on Rhodes. Whether they represent women or men is not certain, although they have traditionally been called female pendants.

Two other groups of glass beads dating from the 5th to the 3rd centuries BCE deserve comment. The cylindrical bead to the left at 502, on the right border of Figure 5.0, from the 4th to 3rd centuries BCE, appears to be related to both the Phoenician head pendants and the very similar head beads in which the eyes around the bead are separated by applied noses, making the resemblance to a face even stronger (Alekseeva 1978: plate 32, #71). The bead on the right at 502 is very similar to an example at the Corning Museum of Glass, dated to the 5th to 3rd centuries BCE, with a second published specimen reported by Fukai as having been found in Iran (Goldstein 1979: 112; Fukai 1985: Plate 18).

Compound stratified eye beads, rep-resented at 492 and 500, Figure 5.0, have been found at eastern and western Mediterranean sites, as well as in Europe, from as early as the 5th century BCE. Scythian graves on the north coast of the Black Sea, ranging in date from the 6th to the 3rd centuries BCE, contain both gold ornaments in a mixed Scythian/Greek style and large numbers of glass beads, including both compound and horned eye beads, similar to those shown at 94, Figure 5.0. Many of these, including a Black Sea style head bead, appear to be local products, most likely from the Greek cities along the coast (Odessa 1999: pers. obs.).

The Scythians were one of a number of semi-nomadic Indo-Iranian groups who dominated the great Eurasian steppe stretching from the Ordos Desert north of Xian in China to the Hungarian plain. North of the Black Sea, the rich farmland of the Ukraine was the main grain-producing area for Athens during its golden age in the 5th and 4th centuries BCE, and Scythian chiefs grew wealthy as middlemen in the grain trade.

By the 10th century BCE increasing evidence for exchange between China and the West includes new northern style bronzes along the Chinese frontier and Chinese silk decorating the hair of Egyptian mummies (Wilford 1993: B5). Also in the 10th century BCE, or even a little earlier, the first examples of faience are found in the tombs of the Western Zhou Dynasty, with its capital at Hao in Shaanxi Province, just to the south of the Ordos area. The tubular and oblate faience beads differ from West Asian or Egyptian faience in that their main alkali is potassium, rather than sodium.

Lead levels are low, but isotope studies done on one bead suggest a source not in China, and probably not in Egypt (Brill et al 1991: 116-118). Good examples of some of these early faience beads are at 836, Figure 5.0.

Although the details are far from clear, with conflicting lead isotope studies on other Western Zhou faience suggesting a Chinese source (Shixiong 1991: 152), by the 7th century BCE, faience beads containing more than 15% lead and 5% barium are found in even poor graves, suggesting that faience was not limited to particular groups. Such high lead and barium levels are found only in China during this early period.

The earliest glass beads, also without lead or barium, found in China are ascribed by Chinese archaeologists to the 6th to 5th centuries BCE (Kwan 2001: 117-121), and are virtually indistinguishable from the lowermost five beads in Figure 5.3, which would suggest a date no earlier than the 5th, and more likely the 4th century BCE. If in fact these beads were imported into China, the Scythian connection across the Eurasian steppe would seem to be a likely route, and further analysis of Central Asian faience may help answer the question of sources for the earliest faience beads in China. Also from the 6th to 5th centuries BCE are the earliest lead-containing glass beads in China, in either cylindrical or concave bicone shapes and colored with copper, shown at 831, 833, and 844, in Figure 5.0.

We mentioned that in China faience was not limited to wealthy graves. During the Warring States period (475-221 BCE), the situation is more complex, and rich tombs contain elaborate glass and faience beads, usually with some variation on a stratified eye design. Almost all of the eye beads, and all of the most elaborate designs, have high lead and barium levels. These Warring States eye beads entered the market in the mid-1930s, but so few have been scientifically excavated that building a satisfactory chronology has been difficult, and a well-founded idea of how they were used is just now emerging (Braghin 2002: 3-45). The beads are of two types: those of glass, and those referred to as *composite*, with an outer layer of glass "built up around fritted cores" that are "constructed around tubular terra cotta cores" (Brill 2001: 450). Both types have been found in the same tombs (Braghin 2002: 11).

On this page we illustrate some of the Warring States period beads from the Timeline collection. All are glass except for the two at 848, the three above 852, and bead 855, which are composite. Our beads display a great variety of form, perhaps too great, as we will consider in Chapter 6. The quadrangular shape of the eye beads at 846, dating to the 3rd century BCE, is rare outside China (Liu 1975: 11; Koch 1997: Taf. 5). But we have one further example on the Timeline in Chapter 8, Figure 8.1, upper right: a green and yellow eye bead from the Merovingian period. The two composite beads at 848 show an unusual trellis or snake design apparently uncommon on glass beads. The small bead at 855 shows the exquisite workmanship of many of the Warring States beads, with its small eyes of alternating green and white. The three beads above 852 show the most common composite design, with its pre-

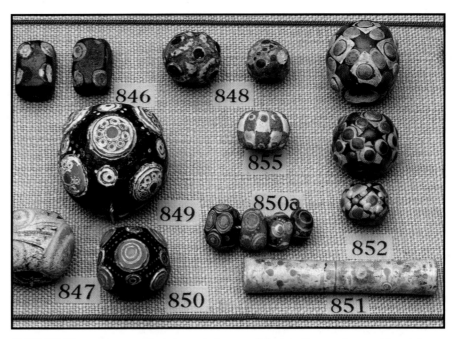

FIGURE 5.5. Glass and composite (a layer of glass over fritted and terra cotta cores) beads from the Warring States period (475-221 BCE) of the Eastern Zhou Dynasty (770-221 BCE). Most Warring States beads share some variation on a stratified eye design, which may have been imported into China by the steppe route from West Asia. Long concave cylindrical bead is 6.1 cm.

cise geometry of eyes and squares. Not all of the Warring States beads are large, and the four beads at 850a repeat familiar designs on a small scale. On the other hand, the impressively long glass bead at 851, with its persimmon calyx surface decoration, now weathered from brilliant blue to beige, recalls tubular shapes in jade from both earlier and later periods, as shown in Figure 6.0 at 853.

If we compare Chinese eye beads with those from West Asia and Europe, we can see a significant increase in complexity of design, even with our relatively simple Warring States examples. In many cases, the eye itself becomes a minor part of the surface decoration. Simon Kwan, who published his extensive collection of early Chinese glass in 2001, has suggested that because the Chinese did not share

the cultural tradition of the evil eye, the eye symbol was divorced from its original protective intent, and could be manipulated in ways unthinkable to the western beadmaker, for whom the apotropaic, or protective, value of the eye bead was always more important than its decorative quality (Kwan 2001: *pers. comm.*).

Further evidence for the luxurious quality of the Warring States period glass and composite eye beads comes from the use of both types as inlays in jade and bronze ornaments, including a gilt-bronze belt hook in the Arthur M. Sackler gallery, Smithsonian Institution, Washington, D.C. (Bunker 1995: 71). Both the Kwan and Miho Museum collections include additional examples (Kwan 2001: 189-195; Hajime 2001: 142-148).

C2

EUROPE

WESTERN ASIA

SOUTH ASIA

EGYPTO ROMAN

CHINA

SOUTHEAST ASIA

100 CE   1 BCE   100 BCE   200 BCE   300 BCE   400 BCE

James W. Lankton

The changing balance between the exploitation of established technology and the introduction of new technology is a recurrent theme in cultural history. Rather than trying to untie the Gordian knot—old technology—Alexander sliced it open—new technology. Chinese artisans transformed the stratified eye bead into precious gems unimagined in the west, just as western beadmakers abandoned the stratified eye concept entirely. New technology usually wins, although creative anachronists do make beautiful beads.

Alexander, the Macedonian general who in a few short years conquered most of the known world, ties these themes together and casts a broad shadow over the entire period covered by Chapter 6. We call the 300 years after Alexander's death the Hellenistic period—a short-cut name that does more to obfuscate than to clarify. Hellenes were Greeks, but the kingdoms were Persian or West Asian (Seleucids) and Egyptian (Ptolemies) as much as they were Macedonian or Greek; the cosmopolitan character of these kingdoms and their great cities was more important than the former nationality of the ruling dynasty. In the west, Alexandria surpassed Athens as a cultural and commercial capital, and became a center for eastern trade, with its inevitable mixing of Greek and Indian ideas. Berenike was one of the main Ptolemaic Egyptian ports on the Red Sea, and Indian influence

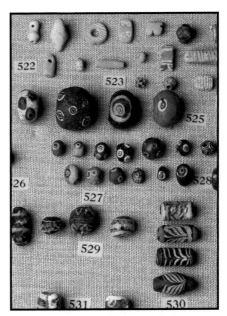

FIGURE 6.1. Glass beads from the 4th to the 1st century BCE, with a group of Egyptian blue and unglazed faience ornaments above. Large red mosaic eye bead is 2.6 cm diameter.

extends later to Indian ships, Indian sails, and Indian sailors (Wild and Wild 2001: 212).

Alexander's legacy brought the second, and last, great period of technological innovation in glass beadmaking. The first was, of course, the mid-2nd millennium BCE, when beadmakers experimented with every method of bead construction except complex folding. Glass artists of the Hellenistic period, perhaps stimulated by exposure to some of these new ideas, rediscovered and developed the techniques of making beads from drawn tubes, and combining glass of different colors into mosaic blocks or canes.

The eye beads that quickly replaced the stratified beads were made with just such canes, formed with bullseye designs and cut into short segments, then applied to the hot glass beads. A number of these mosaic cane eye beads can be seen on this page, at 525, 527, and 528. By the end of the 3rd century BCE it becomes difficult to find stratified eye beads in western Asia and around the Mediterranean basin. Only the Chinese and the Celts continued to make eye beads the old-fashioned way, and both of these groups quit making eye beads entirely by the end of the millennium.

Of course the great advantage to the mosaic eye cane technology was that once the eye cane was pulled, even moderately skilled beadmakers could turn out multiple beads, each having the same pattern, both quickly and efficiently, without the inevitable wastage of trying to center ever-smaller glass saucers one on top of the other. The earliest examples of this rediscovered mosaic-eye cane technology may go back to the 5th century BCE, as beads (Hencken 1978: 125) and as decoration for a core-formed vessel found on Cyprus (Grose 1989: 78), but the full exploitation of the mosaic cane eye bead was Hellenistic.

Another group of beads with a relationship to Mediterranean core-formed glass vessels is at 529, Figure 6.1. Our beads are closest in design and color to Grose's Group I vessels from the 6th to the 4th century BCE, with Rhodes a

FIGURE 6.0. The Hellenistic (331-64 BCE) and early Roman periods were a time of great innovation in glass technology, with the rediscovery of ways to combine glass of different colors into plaques and canes of mosaic glass. These were used to make beads in agate glass (533,568), mosaic cane eye beads (526, 527), and mosaic beads decorated with inlays (602) or an overall mosaic, or millefiori, pattern (544, 545). Much of our knowledge of bead production during this period comes from the rubble of a late-3rd century BCE glass workshop on Rhodes, which included both mosaic eye beads and gold-glass vessels and beads (early examples at 588, 589). Lowest Ban Chiang cylindrical bead, one of the longest glass beads known, is 13.8 cm.

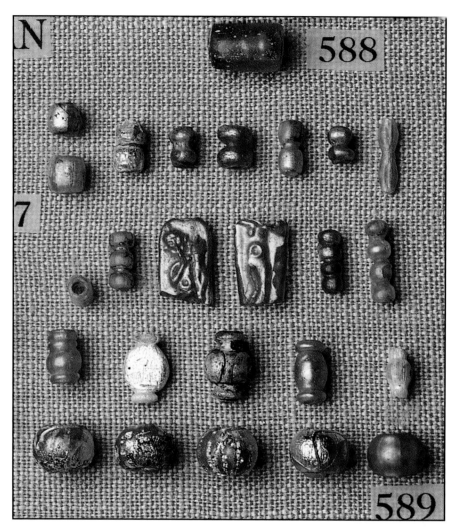

FIGURE 6.2. Gold-glass beads from the 3rd century BCE to the 1st century CE. One of the great innovations of Hellenistic glassworkers was to combine thin gold foil with clear, colorless glass to produce gold-glass beads. The earliest examples were finished bead by bead, with segmented beads later. Tabular beads 1st century BCE to 1st century CE. Center bead second row 1.3 cm long.

likely manufacturing site, at least for the vessels (Grose 1989: 110). What appear to be similar beads at the Corning Museum of Glass were given a possible 6th to 4th century BCE date as well (Goldstein 1979: 270).

The second great innovation of glassworkers from the Hellenistic period was to combine drawn tubes of colorless glass with gold foil to make gold-glass beads. The earliest well-doc-

umented examples were found in the city of Rhodes, in the debris from a glass workshop containing both beads and vessel fragments, dating to the late 3rd century BCE. The city itself had been founded in the 4th century and quickly became a commercial and artistic center to rival Alexandria. Glassworking had a long history on the island, particularly at Camiros, as mentioned in Chapter 5,

and evidence for both glassmaking and glassworking have been found in the city of Rhodes.

The distinction between *primary* glassworking, the manufacture of glass from its raw materials, and *secondary* glassworking, the manufacture of finished objects, most often beads or vessels, has become clearer in recent years, as archaeological investigations support the theory that the two were very different industries in the ancient world. We saw in Chapter 4 that even in the 2nd millennium BCE raw glass of various colors was traded as ingots, with examples from the Uluburun shipwreck and the glass workshop at Tell Brak. During the 1st millennium BCE the same system continues: Celtic bead-makers in Central Europe imported their glass from manufacturing centers to the south, most likely in Italy and the eastern Mediterranean (Zepezauer 1997: 61).

The glass workshop debris, discovered by chance in 1967, had been used as fill to raise the floor level of an ancient house; we don't really know exactly where the workshop was, or what it might have looked like. Even so, Weinberg's preliminary report from 1969 remains our best documentation of bead manufacturing for this critical period (Weinberg 1969: 143-151). More recent excavations a short distance west of the workshop area provide evidence for actual glassmaking, with underground rock tanks and chunks of colorless glass, supporting the idea of an extensive glass industry at Rhodes (Triantafyllidis 2000: 193). This colorless glass would have been used to draw the glass tubes needed for gold-glass beads, and supports the idea that secondary glassworkers would add their

James W. Lankton

own coloring agents. The early Hellenistic gold-glass beads reported by Weinberg are finished individually as short tubes or spheres. The unfinished tubes appear to be scored more than segmented; Spaer suggests that gold-glass beads finished by segmenting begin only in the Roman period (Spaer 2001: 131). Of the beads illustrated In Figure 6.2, the five beads in the bottom row could be early, while the cylindrical bead at 588 matches Weinberg's description of a similar bead with "an interior blue layer and a gold spiral beneath the colorless exterior layer" (Weinberg 1969: 146). The two fragmentary tabular beads with an impressed design of the Egyptian god Harpocrates are well dated to between the 1st century BCE and the 1st century CE, and were not found on Rhodes.

The third great contribution of Hellenistic glassworkers was to layer glass of contrasting colors in patterns that, when cut, would resemble banded agate. The term agate glass, as promoted by Francis, would seem to be a good description for this beautiful material used for both beads and vessels during the later Hellenistic period; an alternate description, ribbon mosaic, emphasizes the mosaic structure of the glass. While no agate glass was found at Rhodes, excavations at a slightly later site on the Aegean island of Delos suggest that beads and pendants were made from flat canes of mosaic glass (Nenna 1999). Beautiful glass imitations of banded agate, both in brown and white and in blue and white, were found at Amenhotpe III's Malkata palace near Thebes during the Egyptian New Kingdom, and Thebes is again suggested as a possible manufacturing site for agate glass in *The Periplus of the Erythraean Sea*, a 1st century CE mariner's guide to travel between Egypt and India which describes materials traded and stops along the way. The earliest agate glass bead from the 1st millennium BCE may be a large ellipsoidal bead found in Georgia as part of the 4th century to very early 3rd century BCE Akhalgori hoard. As illustrated, this bead looks very like the topmost of the five long beads shown on this page in Figure 6.4 (Lordkipanidze 2002: 151). Both

this bead and the one below it set with gold caps were lapidary worked from a mosaic block. Beads similar in appearance may be folded from a pad of agate glass, with a definite seam line along one side, or trailed with a design resembling agate glass, as in the upper right bead at 534.

We emphasized the importance of banded agate eye beads in Chapter 4; the group of glass beads below at 521, Figure 6.3, illustrate some of the glass imitations from the late Hellenistic period. The large oval beads on the left were cut from agate glass blanks with alternating layers of deep violet and white, while the four beads above appear to have applied white stripes, and may be slightly later. The tabular agate glass eye beads from this period are often highly iridescent, as is much other Hellenistic glass.

FIGURE 6.4. Glass imitations which may surpass the originals, these beads illustrate trailing, lapidary work, and transverse wave decoration. Longest bead, including caps, is 6.2 cm.

FIGURE 6.3. Several varieties of glass eye beads from the late Hellenistic period. The stratified eye beads with blue and red may be somewhat older, while the three beads at upper left may be later. Glass of contrasting colors combined as agate glass or ribbon mosaic could be worked by lapidary techniques to make beads as shown at lower left. Longest eye bead 2.7 cm.

FIGURE 6.5. With 593 you can double your luck with both phallic and eye imagery, two of the early Roman's favorite apotropaic symbols. The mosaic beads at 592 are similar to much later beads of the 9th century, although they differ in color choice, perforation diameter, and quality of fusion of the glass. The faience figures may be Roman or Parthian. Agate bead at 591 is 3.4 cm long.

FIGURE 6.6. These mosaic beads from the Roman period are among collectors' favorites. The upper beads in the two right hand columns may be the earliest, with a bead similar to that on the upper right found in a 4th-3rd century BCE Scythian tomb in the Ukraine. The mosaic bar above 600 could have been used to decorate a bead like the one above it. Longest bead at 601 is 3 cm.

The four lowest beads in Figure 6.4 were made by a different technique, and represent a second way to combine gold and glass, which was used for both vessels and beads. Known commonly as gold-band mosaic glass, the objects have a characteristic longitudinal wave or ribbon design (Spaer 2001: 109). The manufacturing method is not certain, but could have involved the application of colored stripes to an underlying bead or the formation of a bead from a pad of striped mosaic glass, in both cases with subsequent manipulation of the stripes. The name comes from the bands of gold foil covered by clear colorless glass, although yellow glass without the gold is sometimes used as a substitute. The earliest examples of these beautiful beads date to the 2nd century BCE, with few examples beyond the 1st century CE. Later beads with a similar manipulated stripe pattern, primarily in combinations of yellow with blue or green, tend to be smaller and less well-made. Most types of elaborate agate glass die out by the 2nd century CE, perhaps related to the replacement of molded glass vessels by the much more economical blown glass. Without the raw materials, which may have been manufactured primarily for the vessel industry, bead-makers may have been forced to quit making one of their most beautiful products.

The fourth contribution of glassworkers from the Hellenistic period was to revive or reinvent the techniques for making complex, decorative mosaic canes, and to use these canes to make beads. Although conceptually similar to making mosaic eye canes, the results are sufficiently different to

James W. Lankton

deserve separate recognition. Decorative glass inlays are associated with Phoenician craftsmen from the early 1st millennium BCE, but by the 6th century BCE the Egyptian industry had revived, and within two hundred years Egyptian glass plaques include precise checkerboard designs (Spaer 2001: 120). The earliest mosaic inlay beads on our Timeline are most likely the upper beads in the two righthand columns in Figure 6.6. The bead on the right closely resembles, even to the pattern of glass decay, one found in a late-4th to 3rd century BCE Scythian tomb near the Black Sea (Kyiv 2000: *pers. obs.*). Above 600 in the next column to the left, we have included a short segment of mosaic glass inlay with the same floral pattern as on the bead above it. One of the ways to make these beads with an equatorial mosaic stripe would have been to marver thin slices of such an inlay onto the basic wound bead. Another method would involve rolling a prepared mosaic pad around a mandrel. The uppermost bead on the right, along with the Ukrainian bead, has a dark core under an applied light grey and mosaic cover, suggesting a third method. Among the other beads in the righthand column, the three lowest beads, with a lotus blossom design, correspond to examples from the Black Sea area dating from the 2nd century BCE to the 1st century CE (Alekseeva 1982: Plate 48), and beads similar to the third bead from the top have been found in Danish graves from the 3rd century CE.

Checker mosaic beads are also associated with Egyptian manufacture, with evidence for checker inlays in the Nile delta at Hellenistic Gumaiyama during the 2nd century BCE (Spaer: 2001:

120). Even more impressive than their early origins may be the long duration of the checker mosaic beads. The four lower beads in the third column from the right in Figure 6.6 may be somewhat earlier, since the other five checker mosaic beads all have close parallels in 3rd century Denmark (Ethelberg 2000: 246, 284). Evidence for beadmaking with checker mosaic canes at 2nd to 4th century Tibiscum in Roman Dacia (now Romania) and in 8th century Ribe, Denmark, along with isolated beads from the centuries in between and even beyond, suggest that the production of checker mosaic beads continued for at least one thousand years, at one site or another. In Chapter 8, we will discuss some examples from the Islamic period.

In contrast to the long-lasting checkerboard beads, the mosaic face beads shown on this page were made for a short period of time around the 1st century CE, possibly in Egypt, although no manufacturing sites have yet been discovered. Probably the best provenanced examples come from Herculaneum and Pompeii, the two towns buried by the 79 CE eruption of Mount Vesuvius (Horicht 1989: 94; Gore 1984: 563). In both cases, only the tabular forms were found, although oblate face beads have been excavated near the Black Sea dating from the 1st century BCE to the 1st century CE (Alekseeva 1982: Plate 48). Our upper left example is unusual in that the mosaic canes were applied to an *aryballos*, or perfume bottle, form, while the lower righthand bead includes the shoulders and a miniature bead necklace in the cane design. Mosaic face beads were revived during the 4th century with a small group of beads, with various cane designs,

FIGURE 6.7. Tabular mosaic face beads were found at both Pompeii and Herculaneum, destroyed in 79 CE. The bead at upper left, with an *aryballos* shape, is rare; 1.7 cm high.

found in northern Europe (Stout 1986: 58). These beads have been interpreted as representing the family of Emperor Constantine, although they also resemble the faces on Egyptian Coptic textiles from the 4th and 5th centuries. We have four additional mosaic face beads on our Timeline, which we will discuss in Chapter 7.

The four capped millefiori beads at 601 in Figure 6.6 belong to another group of mosaic beads with a long period of production, extending from the 1st or 2nd century until at least the 10th. The end-caps are usually red, occasionally yellow, and rarely white, blue, or green (Callmer 1977: Colour Plate III). Although the better made beads appear to be earlier in the series, more complete study of well-dated examples

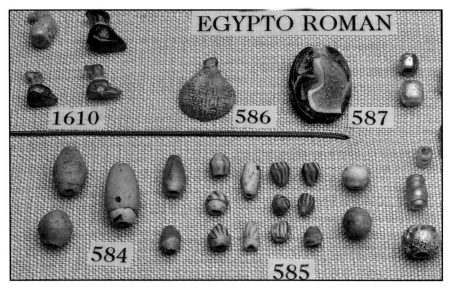

FIGURE 6.8. Roman period beads from Egypt and India. The glass beads at 584 and 585 are strongly associated with Egypt from the 2nd to 5th centuries, and were probably formed by rolling a pad of green and yellow glass around a wire, or mandrel. The four glass birds at upper left were found at Taxila, the ancient trading city near present-day Islamabad. Agate glass bead 2.6 cm.

would be helpful in establishing a reliable chronology for these distinctive beads.

The three groups pictured at 592, 593, and 594 in Figure 6.5 would all date to the first few centuries CE, early in the Roman period. The central pendant shows Harpocrates, the infant Horus, with his finger to his mouth. The unidentified lefthand figure is also found near the Black Sea (Alekseeva 1975: Plate 6), while the pose, but not the face, of the righthand figure is similar to an image of the Egyptian god Bes, also described by Alekseeva.

The three beads at 592, Figure 6.5, are characterized by relatively thin walls of preformed mosaic glass wrapped around a large mandrel. Francis described an oblate bead with a similar pattern found at Mantai, Sri Lanka, from the early centuries CE, providing evidence for at least indirect contact between Rome and Mantai, the great trading emporium and beadmaking center of

the early 1st millennium CE (Francis 1989a: 83). Cylindrical beads with mosaic stripes and eyes, usually in red, blue, white, and yellow, reappear in the 9th century, and have been found from Scandinavia to Thailand to Mauritania. Our example is at 696, Figure 8.0.

The glass pendant at 593 combines both eye and phallic imagery. Phallic symbolism in the Roman world had more to do with luck than with sex, and small rings and amulets were worn by infants and children to protect them from the evil eye (Puttock 2002: 95-97). Similar pendants in glass and bronze have been found at many Roman sites, and would date to the pre-Christian period.

We have mentioned Egypt as a beadmaking area on several occasions, suggesting an important Egyptian role in the revival and development of mosaic glass canes and of agate

glass. The geographer Strabo, writing in the early years of the 1st century in Book 16 of his *Geography*, mentions three regions known for glass production: Palestine near the mouth of the Belus River, Italy, and Egypt, particularly Alexandria. Other writers, including Cicero, mention Alexandrian glass; not surprisingly, there are few ancient references to beadmaking. Several primary glass production sites have now been excavated in Egypt, and Egyptian natron gradually replaced plant ash as the most important source of alkali for glass production throughout the ancient world, beginning as early as the 5th century BCE (Nenna *et al* 2000: 99). However, archaeological evidence for beadmaking is limited to two 4th to 7th century sites near the center of Alexandria, where Polish excavators found glass tubes in red, dark blue, and yellow, along with a variety of molds used to produce small segmented beads (Nenna *et al* 2000: 110). Francis (2002: *pers. comm.*) has suggested that one reason for the scarcity of evidence for beadmaking may be that only drawn beads and possibly mosaic canes may have been made at centralized locations. The mosaic canes in particular would then have been sold to beadmakers spread throughout the countryside. At least for the mosaic face beads, the great variation in quality of workmanship of the beads themselves would support the idea of multiple workshops using commercial canes. Until the Egyptian equivalent of the Rhodes beadmaking debris is discovered, such conjecture may be the best we can do in filling in the blank spaces in the contributions of Egyptian craftsmen during Hellenistic and Roman times.

James W. Lankton

The five green and yellow glass beads at 584, Figure 6.8, along with the associated yellow and striped beads to their right, have been found almost exclusively in Egypt, beginning as early as the 2nd century CE, and continuing for several hundred years. Petrie calls these beads Coptic, referring to the the cultural influence of this Egyptian form of Christianity, which by 450 would separate from the official church. Many of the green and yellow beads, known popularly as date beads in spite of their greater resemblance to unopened lotus buds, have a distinct longitudinal seam, suggesting that a small pad of warm yellow and green glass would have been folded around a mandrel (Spaer 2001: 111-112).

We promised in Chapter 5 to return to the Chinese Warring States beads, and Figure 6.9 on this page shows several more examples from the Timeline. The three glass beads in the bottom row show variations on the most common Warring States bead theme: stratified eyes of various complexity joined by lines of white dots, originally of white glass. The two beads to the right would have been almost identical when new, but the increased weathering on the righthand bead has obscured the decorative structure, which frequently is more affected than the basic bead.

Comparing the central bead at 856 with the similar bead at 850, Figure 5.5, we can see another pattern of change in the stratified eye design: the original eyes of bead 850 have been replaced with new green glass, which has been inscribed and filled to look like the original. The large bead at 849 has suffered a similar fate, and all of the eyes are modern replacements, while the dark bead itself may or may

FIGURE 6.9. Warring States period glass and jade beads. The two cylindrical jade beads have a surface pattern of raised spirals, known in Chinese as a *guwen* or grain motif. Similar cylindrical tubes have been found in Warring States period tombs, and probably formed parts of a pendant set (Boda 1994: 162). The two beads at 856 share one of the most familiar Warring States designs, with stratified eyes linked by lines of tiny white dots. The glass beads at 854 may be later. Longest 8.9 cm.

not be ancient. An additional clue that all is not well with this bead is the imaginative 8-plus-1 design of the compound eyes, instead of the more traditional 5- or 6-plus-1 pattern. Excellent reproductions of Warring States eye beads have become collectors' favorites, although not always knowingly. The challenge to sell these beads as ancient is one that many have been quick to accept, and every year the copies become more difficult to distinguish. On a trip to Hong Kong in 2001 I visited the antique shops of Hollywood Road looking for Warring States copies, and was not disappointed. My favorite was a very good-looking bead of classic form. My shock at seeing the dealer drop this bead onto the

glass countertop was surpassed only by my surprise when the bead bounced several inches into the air: the entire bead was made of plastic. Coming back to Figure 6.9, we can also doubt the lefthand bead at 856. The bead is very well-made, the color is beautiful and not un-Chinese, and two of the stratified eyes have popped out and not been replaced, all of which might give us some confidence for authenticity. However, the powdery white weathering is most likely not original. Kwan has suggested that such a surface deposit is produced by dipping the bead into plaster of Paris or white clay, often following an acid bath (Kwan 2001: *pers. comm.*). For genuine ancient glass, the weathering usually bites deep into the

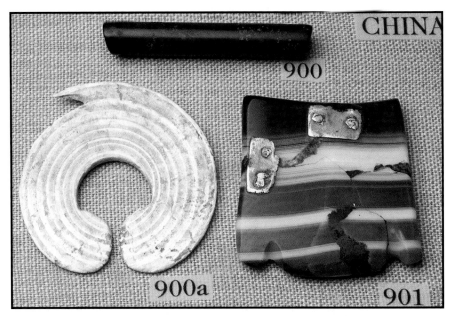

FIGURE 6.10. Thai ornaments from the Bronze Age to the Iron Age, ranging from the early 2nd millennium BCE to the first centuries CE. The large conus shell pendant and tubular stone bead represent the increased trade in luxury goods as regional chiefdoms developed in the Bronze Age. Notched agate pendants were perhaps made in India and modified locally. Tubular bead 6.2 cm.

surface, making it rough to the touch. New beads may be sand-blasted before the powder is applied to create the same effect. However, the sand-blasting will leave sharp edges visible at high magnificaton. With the exceptions discussed above, our other Warring States beads appear to be ancient, although the unusual design and rough surface of bead 847 suggest that further study is necessary.

The stone bead at 900 and the shell ornament at 900a, Figure 6.10, are well known from Thai Bronze Age cultures dating to the early 2nd millennium BCE (Higham and Thosarat 1998: 78-89). Similar tubular stone beads with beveled ends have been found in Vietnam from the same period (Frape 2000: 35), but in few other places (Francis 2002a: 133). Colors vary from black to white, with many shades of green in between, and most

of the stone is relatively soft. The perforations are drilled from both ends, and one of the surprising characteristics of these beads is the number of false drill passages, sometimes coming very close to the surface of the stone (*pers.obs.*). The large numbers of tubular stone beads in Thailand suggest that production continued well into the 1st millennium CE. The conus shell ornament belongs to a large family of slit rings found throughout Asia. Some of the earliest Neolithic jades in northern China were slit rings, and later materials include many other stones, plus shell, metal, and glass (Liu 2002: 38-39). While many of these rings were undoubtedly used as earrings, the size and weight of some examples also suggest use as pendants.

Large, notched, banded agate pendants similar to 901 have been found in the neck area in burials at Thai Iron Age

sites such as Noen U-Loke, from the 1st or early 2nd century (Higham and Thosarat 1998: 154). The original ornaments may have been made in south India by Pandukal beadmakers at Arikamedu (Francis 2000-1: 59). The fragile stone was drilled along the top edge, using double-tipped diamond drills. The pendants found in India are apparently not notched along the lower edge (Francis 2002: *pers. comm.*), and both the notching and the frequent repairs may represent local Thai work. The many broken and repaired examples are testimony to the high cultural value of these beautiful objects (Theunissen 1998: 8).

The three cylindrical glass beads shown at 902, Figure 6.11, are some of the longest glass beads known. They are associated with the late Iron Age phase of the Ban Chiang culture in northeast Thailand, with likely dates overlapping the Hellenistic and early Roman periods. Ban Chiang was the site of a Neolithic farming community, with a Bronze Age beginning between 1500 and 1000 BCE, and an Iron Age after 500 BCE. This last period at Ban Chiang is best known for the beautiful pottery decorated with curvilinear forms in reddish brown over a buff-colored slip, and for the several varieties of glass beads found in or near the village of Ban Chiang itself. Indo-Pacific drawn glass beads, from as early as the beginning of the 4th century BCE, have been excavated in Thailand at the site of Ban Don Ta Phet, and similar beads were found at Ban Chiang and many other sites (Glover and Henderson 1995: 148). In addition, three other types of glass beads are associated more exclusively with Ban Chiang: the long cylindrical beads

James W. Lankton

illustrated at 902, the small to large truncated bicones shown at 904, Figure 6.0, and the orange cylindrical beads at 903, which are actually glass, although sometimes mistaken for ceramic. In addition to the beads, large and small glass ornaments, apparently earrings, with some in a dramatic bufffalo horn shape, are thought to come from the Ban Chiang area.

The story of early glass in Southeast Asia is fascinating and developing. Ban Don Ta Phet, the oldest well-excavated site, was a reburial cemetery from the first quarter of the 4th century BCE (Glover 1990: 139-83). The many beads found there include both glass and stone, with a large bow-shaped Chung Zi (dZi) among the surprises—providing the earliest reliable dating for a bead with this design. The Indo-Pacific beads are similar in composition to those from Arikamedu, pushing back the beginnings of this great industry by at least 200 years. One bright blue small cornerless cube appears to have been colored with cobalt and may be related to Indian models. There are also glass beads which do not fit into the conventional categories, including large hexagonal barrel-shaped beads in pale blue-green glass with an unusual potash glass composition. Comma shaped glass earrings not found in India further support the existence of a Southeast Asian glass industry by this early date, and some of the Ban Chiang glass may be a part of the story.

The long cylindrical beads from Ban Chiang are also potash glass, and appear to have been manipulated into shape while the glass was warm. The beads often have a short seam at one end, shown on the lowest bead, as if they had been

FIGURE 6.11. These long cylindrical glass beads, typically in shades of blue and green, may have been formed by a technique involving folding a warm pad of glass around a mandrel. The left side of the middle bead shows evidence of a spiral twist in red, while the lowest bead has a characteristic notch at the lefthand perforation. All beads have asymmetric ends. Longest 13.8 cm.

folded. The surface is marked by striations, some twisting, but not actual evidence that the beads had been drawn as a tube (Francis 2002a: 129-134). The orange disk beads appear to have been sliced from glass tubes. The glass itself may be marbled with red, possibly relating to uneven control of the reducing atmosphere of the glass furnace. These beads are usually described as drawn, although the typical longitudinal striations are not always visible on the surface, perhaps because of subsequent lapidary work (Allen 2003d: *pers. comm.*). The orange glass disk beads may be even more characteristic for the Ban Chiang site itself than are the long tubular beads, which have been found rarely, if at all, in scientific excavations.

We close this chapter with consideration of the four glass birds at 1610, Figure 6.8, said to have been found near the ancient city of Taxila, now in northwest Pakistan. These small ornaments

bring us back to the man with whom we began the chapter: Alexander of Macedon. By 326 BCE, just three years before his death in Babylon at age 32, Alexander was near the end of his eastern campaign. One of his last great triumphs was the bloodless capture of Taxila, the greatest city between the Indus and the Jhelum River, the site of Alexander's last major battle (Green 1991: 386). Taxila was already a wealthy trading center, only to become more so during the Kushan empire from the 2nd century BCE to the 3rd century CE. Horace Beck reported on early glassworking at Taxila, finding evidence for drawn glass beads as early as 500 BCE, along with a blue glass cornerless cube bead from the 5th century BCE, perhaps the earliest known (Beck 1941: 27; Francis 2002a: 110). Our small birds are rod-formed, but serve as a reminder of the early development of glass bead technology in South Asia.

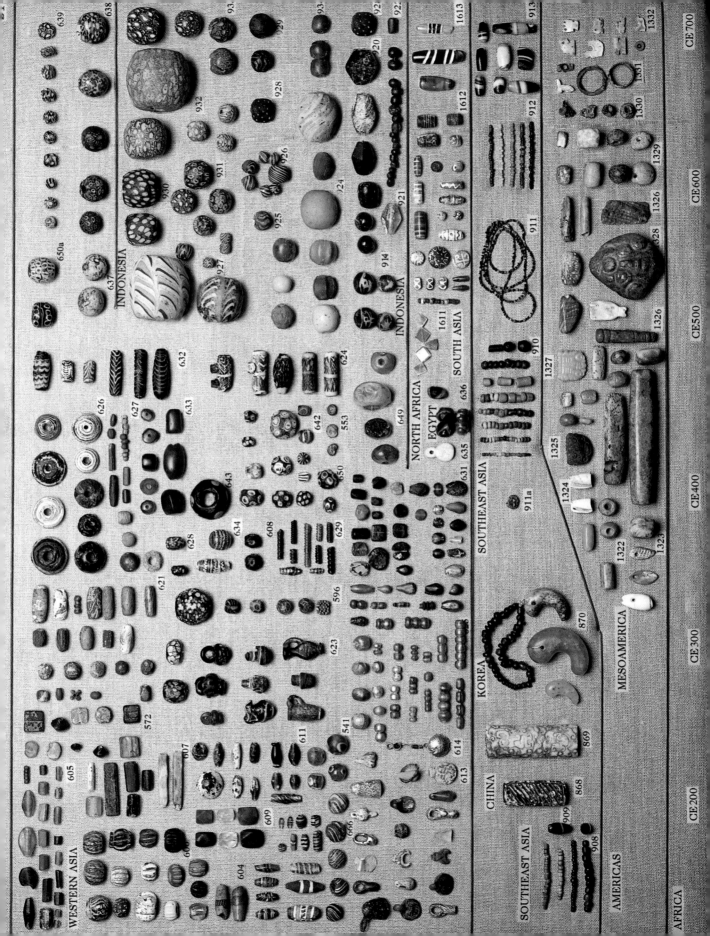

WESTERN ASIA

INDONESIA

INDONESIA

NORTH AFRICA

EGYPT

SOUTH ASIA

SOUTHEAST ASIA

KOREA

CHINA

SOUTHEAST ASIA

AMERICAS

MESOAMERICA

AFRICA

CE 200

CE 300

CE 400

CE 500

CE 600

CE 700

James W. Lankton

Peter Francis Jr. was fond of pointing out that not long ago, "nearly any complex glass bead was routinely called 'Roman'" (Francis 1999: 3). But what were Roman beads, and who, in fact, were the Romans? When Pompey the Great annexed the Seleucid Empire in 64 BCE, most of the eastern Mediterranean area came under Roman control—but the people continued to be Arab, Aramaic, Jewish, and Greek. Within a few years, Egypt also became Roman, much to the disappointment of Mark Antony and Cleopatra, the last of the Ptolemaic monarchs. But the people remained the same mix of Egyptian, Arab, and Jewish, and Alexandria was still a Greek city. The Roman provinces of Anatolia would become the richest in the empire, and from the beginning, the eastern empire far outshown the provincial west (Ball 2000: 1-4). Beyond the uneasy border of the Euphrates River was the Iranian Empire, Rome's great rival, and in many ways more wealthy and sophisticated than Rome itself. The Iranians, first under Parthian and then Sasanian leadership, would contest Roman hegemony in the eastern Mediterranean several times during the Roman imperial period (27 BCE-610 CE, taking Heraclius' reforms in Constantinople as the beginning of the Byzantine period in 610). In fact, the Parthians controlled Syria or Palestine at least twice during the mid-1st century BCE, the critical period for one of "Rome's" greatest inventions: the blowing of glass to make vessels. Of course the inventors

FIGURE 7.1. Glass melon beads, 4th century BCE to mid-1st millennium CE, along with 1st to 3rd century stone cornerless cubes, possibly South Indian. Large melon bead 2.3 cm in diameter.

were neither Roman nor Iranian, but rather the same eastern Mediterranean people who had been making and working glass since the 2nd millennium BCE—but their landlords may have been Iranian. Perhaps Herod best personifies the mixed nature of the Romans. After Mark Antony's defeat in 31 BCE, Herod traveled to Rhodes to meet the victorious Octavian. As Ball points out: "Thus, a plebeian, born half Idumaean half Nabataean, proclaimed king in a republican ceremony in a pagan temple,

armed with a Roman army, became King of the Jews" (Ball 2000:51).

Well before the 1st millennium CE, primary glassmaking and secondary glassworking had become separate industries. Glassmaking furnaces were set up near raw materials and fuel, and usually away from population centers. In contrast, the actual working of glass was in the industrial zones or markets of urban areas, where vessels or beads were produced for local use or trade (Gorin-Rosen 2000:50). Primary glassmaking centers in Egypt and the Levant could produce large amounts of raw glass, sometimes colored, but often nearly colorless. Each of the 17 furnaces at Bet Eli'ezer in Israel could produce up to ten tons of glass with each firing, and there were other installations up and down the coast (Gorin-Rosen 2000: 52). The comparison of glass compositions suggests that it was this glass that supplied the glasshouses of the west throughout the imperial period and for several hundred years afterward.

In contrast to the centralized primary glassmaking industry, the secondary industry—glass vessel making and particularly beadmaking—tended to be decentralized. We don't know to what extent blown glass vessel making and glass beadmaking overlapped, but certainly in Cairo today, glassworkers may do both, depending on commercial demand. Both vessels and beads were made at Sepphoris in Israel, throughout the 1st millennium (Fischer and McCray 1999:897), as well as in Alexandria, Tyre,

FIGURE 7.0. Chapter 7 takes us from the mid-2nd through 7th centuries, including the peak and decline of the western Roman empire. When the city of Rome fell in 476, it had not been the center of the empire for over a century, and the eastern empire continued with Constantinople as capital until 610, when the reforms of Heraclius marked the beginning of the Byzantine period. Early and late Roman beads show a remarkable continuity, with glassmaking centers in the east providing raw material for a decentralized beadmaking industry. Largest Precolumbian jade bead is 10.2 cm long.

FIGURE 7.2. These single strip folded beads represent the most basic folding technique, in this case using prepared pads of striped mosaic glass. A folded bead from 2nd millennium BCE Nuzi looks much like the 2nd bead from the right, lowest row, with a similar longitudinal seam. The single strip folding technique continues into the 1st millennium CE, and probably beyond. Longest 3.0 cm.

and Rhodes. In the western empire, Trier was a major glassworking site, making both vessels and beads, during the 3rd and 4th centuries (Welch 1999:5). The glass workshop at Tibiscum in Dacia, in and out of Roman control from the 2nd to the 4th century, "mainly produced" monochrome and mosaic beads (Benea 1997: 292). In Roman Britain, glass-works were located near both urban set-tlements and military installations from the 1st to the 3rd century, with glass vessels the apparent product (Price 1998:339). Glass beadmaking contin-ued in the west during the 5th through 7th century Merovingian period, still with glass imported from the same east-ern centers. Much of the production was very small scale—as few as four to six beads of a particular type produced at one time (Heck and Hoffman 2000: 344). During the days of empire, many easterners had traveled to western cities; there were Jewish settlements in every

major Mediterranean city, and Syrians or Arabs in Ravenna, Trier, Pannonia, and Britain (Ball 2000: 397-398). Many of these were glassworking centers, and perhaps some of the descendants of these migrants became itinerant glass beadmakers who, working with recycled glass and metal scrap for colorants, left only beads behind.

Many of our Roman period beads were found in Syria and may have been made both for local use and for trade. The Romans themselves were quite conser-vative in bead usage. Although such luxuries as spices and silk might cause alarm among conservative Romans, most of the wealthy preferred to invest their money in land, and much of the finest jewelry was relatively simple, mixing fine gold chains with imported pearls and emeralds (Haywood1998a:2.14). Large glass beads would have had no place in the wardrobe of the stylish Roman woman, who preferred well-made

stone beads, such as the lapis lazuli, carnelian, and rock crystal cornerless cubes in Figure 7.1, or the emerald-like stones at 570, Figure 6.0. Judging by the small translucent monochrome glass beads in the assemblages attributed to Roman settlers in Rhineland graves from the 3rd and 4th centuries (Siegmund 1995: 39-40), we might better change the maxim to say that any old, simple glass beads were Roman!

Because so few beads from modern archaeological excavations in West Asia and Egypt have been published that would date to the 1st millennium, we look to the provinces to identify our "Roman" beads. Long strands of beads, primarily in glass and amber, formed an important part of a woman's dress in the western empire and among the Germanic tribes of the *Barbaricum*, along the *Limes*, or borders of the empire. In addition, the use of jewelry as grave goods in inhumation burials was much more common than in the east, where cremation was the custom. Most women would wear two strands of beads: one, relatively short, with smaller beads, around the neck, and a second, longer strand with large beads, attached to bronze dress pins, or fibulas, placed near the shoulders (Ethelberg 1995: 93-94). While many glass beads had long periods of production, fibula styles changed often, making them ideal for dating the graves.

The glass melon beads shown at 606, Figure 7.1, are one of these long-lived forms. The shape itself is little changed from that of the stone melon beads we discussed in Chapter 3, and already by the 5th century BCE glass melon beads are found in both male and female graves in Italy (Erickson 1998: 836). In Roman Britain, glass melon beads may have had a special amuletic significance,

James W. Lankton

and single examples, often blue, are found in graves, particularly those of children (Puttock 2002: 94). Turquoise blue glass and faience melon beads similar to that at 583, Figure 7.0, were by far the most common beads at Pompeii, outnumbering mosaic beads by several hundred to one (Naples 1998: *pers. obs.*). Most of our melon beads are furnace-wound, the traditional method for making glass beads in the Levant, and still practiced in Cairo today, where the new melon beads are barely distinguishable from ancient beads in good condition.

The glass beads at 605, 607, and 572, Figure 7.0, along with melon beads, were among the types produced at Tibiscum from the 2nd to the 4th century. The emerald green hexagonal prism-shaped beads at 605, along with several examples from 607, were excellent imitations of the Indian beryl crystals used by the wealthy. The two lower beads at 607 were originally bright red in color but show the weathering typical for ancient red glass, changing from red to green, and then to beige.

The beads at 610, Figure 7.2, were made by wrapping a pad of striped glass around a mandrel, probably in the Levant or Egypt, beginning in the 1st or 2nd century. These strip-folded beads have a long history, and the second bead from the right on the lowest row is almost identical in form and color to a strip-folded bead from 2nd millennium BCE Nuzi. Early examples have been excavated on the north shore of the Black Sea (Alekseeva 1978: Plate 27), and similar beads, probably imports from the east, have been found from southwestern Germany to Britain progressing from the 5th to the 7th century. It is difficult to assign a time period to particular beads, but the lefthand bead in the

FIGURE 7.3. These small pendants range in date from the 4th century BCE (upper left) to the Islamic period (lower right). The simple loop pendants are most typically Roman, and may be as late as the 5th to 6th centuries. Eisen has suggested that these represent such Christian symbols as drops of blood or sacred nails of the Holy Cross. Largest unengraved seal pendant, upper right, is 2.4 cm.

lower row may be early, since most examples with this design are heavily weathered or iridescent, while the bead next to it, in the red, white, and blue of the later Union Jack, was particularly popular in Anglo-Saxon England in the 6th and 7th centuries (Guido 1999:72).

The small pendants grouped above at 613 range in date from the 4th century BCE to the 10th century, and demonstrate the continuing importance of small glass ornaments over a long period of time. The distribution was more in the east than the west, although particular forms, such as the abstract amphora shape fifth from the left in the upper row, were found from Hallstatt Iron Age sites in Slovenia (Hencken 1978: 182) to 4th century BCE Scythian tombs north of the Black Sea (Odessa 1999: *pers. obs.*). The sixth example from the left in the same row is also early, along with the

upper left pendant with a bronze ring, both of which are most likely uncarved stamp seals (Spaer 2001: 219). These early glass pendants could have been made at Hellenistic workshops on Rhodes, or in the Levant or Egypt . Slightly later, and more typically Roman, are the simple loop pendants with examples in the upper and lower rows, common in tombs in Israel from the 5th and 6th centuries, and perhaps earlier (Spaer 2001: 185). Early glass historian Gustavus Eisen suggested that these pendants represented Christian symbols such as drops of blood or sacred nails of the Holy Cross (Eisen 1927, quoted in Spaer 2001: 185).

More certainly religious were the glass amulets stamped with Christian or Jewish symbols and produced in the Levant in the 4th and 5th centuries. Barag has discussed these pendants and suggests Antioch as a production center. The

FIGURE 7.4. These miniature glass vessels, most likely from the 3rd and 4th centuries, may have symbolized the sacred or apotropaic quality of their contents. They employ typical beadmaking techniques, and would have been made in bead, rather than vessel, workshops. The beads to the right have no firm date, but may be as early as the 3rd to 4th centuries. Lowest bead on right 3.3 cm.

translucent brown, green, and blue glass of the Roman pendants contrasts with the opaque turquoise-colored glass more common in the early Islamic period, used both for coin weights and for pendants. Our example to the far right in the lower row at 613, with its distinctive endless or Solomon's knot design, would most likely fit in this later category (Rose 2002 for a discussion of the history of Solomon's knot). Of the two crescent-shaped pendants in our group, the type in the middle row was popular during the Roman period and is seen in 2nd century portraits (Tatton-Brown 1995: 41), while the crescent in the lowest row is lapis lazuli, and probably considerably older.

Miniature glass vessels were also used as pendants, and several examples are shown at 623 above. Three additional jugs, included at 623, Figure 7.0, with both trailed and crumb decoration, were made like glass beads and date from the

late-3rd to the late-4th century (Spaer 2001: 171). The glass matrix is usually very dark, and the fact that they are found mainly in the Levant makes local production there likely. These relatively closely dated pendants help us estimate the age of at least some of the similar, although larger, beads with the same colors and decorations, such as the crumb-decorated beads nearby on Figure 7.0 at 628. Like melon beads, beads with crumb decoration have a long history, beginning in the 2nd millennium BCE. Hellenistic examples from Rhodes and early Roman examples from the Black Sea coast show better workmanship, such as in the center, large bead at 628, while the 4th and 5th century beads are a little rougher (Alekseeva 1975: Plate 12; Spaer 2001: 127 for discussion).

Returning to Figure 7.4, the upper three vases, two with missing handles, all deserve some comment. The lefthand example looks more Greek than Roman,

and mimics the core-formed *oinochoi*, or pitchers, produced in the eastern Mediterranean before the advent of glass blowing. Whether from that period or simply in an anachronistic design, this vessel is the most carefully made of our collection. The center pendant is interesting for its resemblance to the Roman period glass cage cups, associated with German workshops. These tour de force vessels—with an inner cup surrounded by a raised lattice of freely carved glass that is attached at only a few points and thought to be carved from a single block—are among the rarest and most luxurious glass vessels from any period (Whitehouse 1997: 283-285). The three lower pendants also have counterparts in the 3rd and 4th centuries (Alekseeva 1978: Plate 31, #68), although I suspect that both of the outer examples have been repaired, if not reconstructed. The center blue jug in the lower row is similar to the black, red, and yellow example on the right in the upper row, which in turn is similar in color to the four beads at 624 in Figure 7.4.

These distinctive beads with combed red, black, and white trails and bright yellow bands vary greatly in precision of execution, and perhaps in age. Many are cylindrical and may have two upper applied loops to make a pendant. Although this form is most common from the Islamic period, when the lower cylinder may be closed off to hold a verse from the Koran, the form itself goes back to at least the 3rd millennium BCE, as we saw in Chapter 3. Stern finds parallels to the red, black, white, and yellow beads in Germanic graves from the 3rd and 4th centuries (Stern 2001: 388), with Spaer suggesting a later date (Spaer 2001: 117).

We moved these beads on the Exhibit

James W. Lankton

itself to make room for the five mosaic beads now at 596, to the right of the vase pendants in Figure 7.0. Checker mosaic beads, both tabular and oblate in form, were made at Tibiscum from the 2nd to the 4th century, and probably at many other small beadmaking sites as well. The checker canes appear to be imports, perhaps from centers in Egypt or the Levant, but by the 8th century the canes were likely being manufactured on site, as in the early Viking market town at Ribe, in Denmark. Beads very similar in color and design to our lower three examples have been found in Danish graves from the mid-3rd century (Ethelberg 2000: 246, 284). Such beads are not present in earlier Danish graves and their appearance could reflect manufacturing closer to the northern borders of the empire or simply a general increase in trade during the prosperous 3rd century. By the 3rd to 5th centuries, checker mosaic canes outlined in red were being combined with floral canes to produce the triple-register beads commonly called Viking, but which mostly predate the Viking period of the 8th to 10th centuries. The two upper beads at 596 were made by piercing a softened section of mosaic cane; both of these patterns were dated to the 2nd to 4th centuries by Alekseeva, based on beads found north of the Black Sea (Alekseeva 1982: Plate 49, # 21,24).

The segmented gold- and silver-glass beads above may have been made primarily in the eastern centers of Egypt and the Levant, with possible production in Constantinople after the Arab conquests of 640. The workshop at Tibiscum in Dacia may have made gold-glass beads, and the large concentration of gold-glass beads found near Gdansk in Poland (Guido 1999: 79) suggests possible pro-

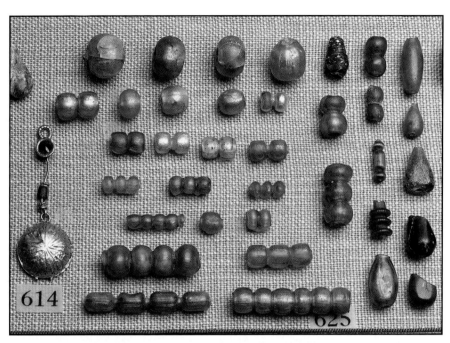

FIGURE 7.5. Gold-glass and blown glass beads from the Roman period. The five beads at right, and the lowest bead next-to-right were made by blowing, a technique usually reserved for vessels. Blown glass beads are quite unusual in the early periods; these examples were said to have been found in Syria, an important center for Roman glass. Longest gold-glass six-part segment is 3.7 cm.

duction along the trade routes going from the Black Sea toward the Baltic. In addition, Dussubieux and Gratuze have reported a possible bead workshop near Peshawar, Pakistan, dating between the 1st century BCE and the 1st century CE, with evidence for both gold-glass and mosaic bead manufacture (Dussubieux and Gratuze: 2001: 9). The actual archaeological evidence for later periods is slim, although two nearby sites in Alexandria, dating somewhere in the 4th to 7th centuries, produced other segmented beads (Nenna et al 2000: 110). We mentioned in Chapter 6 that the earliest gold-glass beads were finished one at a time, but by the Roman period most beads were segmented, perhaps using stone molds similar to those found in Alexandria, and several segments could be intentionally left together. Most of the gold-glass beads found

in Britain were from the late Roman period of the 4th to 5th centuries, although one necklace of 44 beads came from the 2nd century. In Denmark gold-glass beads become relatively common in the 3rd century, and by the 6th century, they are found all over northern Europe. Like other long-lasting bead forms, the gold-glass beads may have had special significance, and the deposit of just one bead, sometimes broken, in British graves suggests that they were important in life and in death (Guido 1999: 78). Gold-glass beads disappear in the north around 600, reflecting political distrbance in the eastern empire (Callmer 1995: 49), and providing indirect evidence that most of these beads did in fact come from the east.

This disturbance was of course the ongoing struggle for the control of West Asia between the eastern Roman empire

FIGURE 7.6. Mixed etched carnelian beads ranging from 4th century BCE beads from North India (the three small beads at left with infinity signs) to 5th to 11th century beads associated with Sasanian Iran, but continuing into the Islamic period. Many of our beads have South Indian designs; an exception is the lowest circular tabular bead. Longest striped barrel bead is 2.1 cm.

based in Constantinople and the Sasanian Empire of Iran. By the beginning of the 6th century, the Sasanians gained control of the valuable maritime trade routes, essentially shutting Rome out of trade with India. Nestorian Christians, persecuted in their Syrian homeland, found protection with the more tolerant Iranians and established communities along the Perisan Gulf and Indian Ocean, inculding in Kerala in southern India (Ball 2000: 130). The Nestorians were the seafarers, under the protection of Iran. Mantai in Sri Lanka was the main trading entrepot, and may even have been controlled by the Sasanians for part of the 6th century. Spices continued to be the main import from the east, along with pearls, precious woods and stones, ivory, and silk, which itself came from China by way of northwestern India, the Arabian Sea, and the Persian Gulf. While Red Sea trade between Rome and India was undoubtedly important during the 1st century, Ball takes the contrarian view that the Romans seldom if ever controlled the sea routes, and knew little about the sources of their imported goods. Further, he suggests that trade via the Persian Gulf,

dominated by the Palmyrenes, Arabs, Nestorians, and Iranians, was just as important, if not more so, pointing out that "archaeological evidence has a nasty habit of reflecting patterns of modern research opportunities rather than patterns of ancient trade" (Ball 2000: 132).

The same Sasanian King Khusrau I Anushirvan who may have controlled Mantai definitely captured Antioch and Apamea, the great Roman cities in Syria, in 540. The 6th century Byzantine historian Procopius, himself born in Caesarea, the city founded by Herod to honor Octavian, reports that these periodic changes of flag had little impact on the daily life of average Levantines, who "regarded it as stupid to undergo suffering for the sake of a foolish dogma" (Cameron 1985: 66). Things heated up again in the 7th century, as Khusrau II Parviz resumed the war against Rome, taking Jerusalem and then Alexandria, finally exorcising the ghost of Alexander, who had conquered Iran one thousand years before (Ball 2000: 28). Emperor Heraclius, one of Rome's greatest generals, proclaimed holy war against the Sasanians in 622, the same year that

Muhammad first articulated the Islamic concept of *jihad*. Heraclius defeated the Sasanians at Nineveh in 627, but within fifteen years had lost the provinces of Syria, Palestine, Libya, and Egypt to the advancing Arabs. The Sasanian defeat in 642 ended an Iranian empire which had existed with few interruptions for 1300 years.

The etched carnelian beads on this page may be the result of Iranian contact with India in the 5th and 6th centuries, the third great period of etched carnelian beadmaking proposed by Beck in 1933. Etching is of course a misnomer, since the surface of the stone is not carved, either by tools or by acid, but the name is so ingrained by use that it, too, seems to be etched in stone, and we reluctantly perpetuate the misinformation in this catalog. The South Indian stone beads differ from those of the better known western industry based in Gujurat. Francis has suggested that Pandukal craftsmen worked at Arikamedu, better known for the production of small drawn-glass Indo-Pacific beads (Francis 2000-1: 49-62). Pandukal products included onyx pendants, although without the notches peculiar to Thailand, as seen in Chapter 6, and faceted stone beads, perhaps similar to those on the Timeline at 609, page 62. In addition, certain styles of etched carnelian beads, including striped barrels and round tabular beads with partial ray designs, are typical for South India and similar to beads found at Sasanian sites (Francis 1980:24-27; Matabaev 1998: 292 for a group of 5th to 6th century beads excavated in Uzbekistan). The production of etched carnelian beads in Iran is also suggested by Francis (1980: 26-27), emphasizing specifically Sasanian designs and shapes which are rare in India. Our beads illustrate both Beck's

James W. Lankton

Type I, carnelian with a white design, and Type II, an overall white bead with a black design, perhaps intentional, or perhaps the result of overheating. The etching process itself is described by Kenoyer in this volume. Many ancient agate beads, including some of those shown in the photograph, are partially covered by a white film due to natural etching by alkali in the soil (see Allen 2002 for a more detailed discussion of the chemical decoration of stones). The darker red bead in the upper row of the photograph opposite is naturally banded, although the contrast has been enhanced by heating, and may be the type of stone the banded etched carnelian beads would imitate.

The small monochrome glass beads shown at 910 on this page may not look like much, but these are in fact the beads which launched a thousands ships, nearly as many articles, and at least one excellent book: *Asia's Maritime Bead Trade*, one of the last major contributions of Peter Francis, Jr. before his death last year. Associated with the South Indian bead industry, initially at Arikamedu, and made by specialized technology unique to this industry. these beads have been found, literally, from Bali to Mali, as Peter was fond of saying. The best documented early examples are those from Ban Don Ta Phet, discussed in Chapter 6, which date to the first half of the 4th century BCE, thus preceding the earliest levels at Arikamedu, where a rising water table prevented full excavation of the site. Possibly earlier drawn beads from both Taxila and Harappa suggest that production may not have originated at Arikamedu, but it appears to have found its fullest development there. By the 4th century, and most likely before, beadmakers at Mantai were producing drawn

FIGURE 7.7. Is this the face that launched a thousand ships? Probably not, but these may indeed be the beads. With the exception of the three larger orange beads, possibly ceramic, the others are Indo-Pacific drawn glass beads, of the type made in Mantai, Khlong Thom, or Oc-Eo. The small face bead is found only at Khlong Thom, Thailand, and remains a mystery; Face bead 1.1 cm.

beads with a similar appearance, now in the blue-green and orange colors found at Berenike, Egypt's southernmost Red Sea port. The thousands of Indo-Pacific beads from Khlong Thom in southern Thailand and Oc Eo in Vietnam, possibly a port for Funan, the first Southeast Asian state, suggest manufacture there as well, at least of beads, if not of glass. Suggested dates for both Khlong Thom and Oc Eo are from the 2nd to the 6th or 7th century, although the periods of bead production are less clear. The glass compositions at both Khlong Thom and Oc Eo may be distinct from those of Arikamedu, and marginally different from each other (Brill 1999: 337, 395, 397). One problem with any comparison is that Arikamedu may have been a beadmaker for over one thousand years, and comparing 12th century glass from Arikamedu with 3rd century glass from Khlong Thom may not be very instructive. The various chronologies for Indo-Pacific glass beadmaking may be most usefully approached by comparing well-dated beads from peripheral sites with those from the large centers, a task still in the preliminary stages (Glover and Henderson 1995: 141-170; Katsuhiko and Gupta

2002: 73-88; Lee 1997: 14-23; Francis 2002a: 210-220).

The small tabular face bead at 911a on this page is a mystery. It was found at Khlong Thom, as were the eleven additional examples, most showing the marked weathering consistent with age, in the Khlong Thom Museum. The total number of these beads is not known but may be less than one hundred, and possibly less than fifty. The face is always the same, as are the colors, suggesting the possible use of a single cane, and the beads have not been reported elsewhere. The three face beads at 553, Figure 7.0, are somewhat similar, and neither group has much in common with the stylized faces of the 1st century Roman beads. The three beads at 553, Figure 7.0, were said to have been found in Iran, near Shiraz, but both their origin and their authenticity have been questioned. There is no evidence for mosaic cane production at Arikamedu, although it will be very interesting to learn what types of mosaic beads were produced near Peshawar. Another mosaic bead found at Khlong Thom is a distinctive small oval collared tabular bead of turquoise glass, with a complex diagonal stripe in black, white,

FIGURE 7.8. Monochrome and striped Jatim glass beads, associated with far eastern Java. The dating for these beads has come down from the 19th century, to the 14th, to the Islamic period, and recently to the early 6th century, based on finds from Korea of a small green and yellow pelangi bead, along with several millefiori mosaic beads. Largest yellow/green bead below 927A, 3.7 cm.

and red mosaic glass. I was surprised to see an identical bead in the van der Sleen collection at the Allard Pierson Museum in Amsterdam, with van der Sleen's note that it had been found at Kausambi, an important beadmaking site in northern India. Perhaps our small face bead stares back at us just to remind us how little we understand.

More mystery beads: The monochrome, striped, and mosaic beads on this and the facing page are among the most instantly recognizable on our Timeline, yet very little is known about who made them or how, when, and where. They are associated with megalithic stone graves in East Java, but as early as 1898 Dutch excavators found that many of the graves had already been disturbed, and to my knowledge, there are no closely dated mosaic beads from Indonesian excavations (Adhyatman and Arifin 1996: 69). In

the absence of controlled excavation, unofficial reports that similar beads had been found with Tang Dynasty (618-906) ceramics are suggestive of a possible time period for at least some of the beads. Adyatman and Arifin, in their excellent book *Manik-manik di Indonesia*, propose the term Jatim for these beads, referring to their association with East Java, or Jawa Timur. Individual types of beads have their own Indonesian names, of which *pelangi*, or rainbow, refers to the multi-colored beads with dragged stripes shown at 927A, just visible on this page, and sometimes to the similar blue/white and green/yellow beads as well. The several proposed classification schemes for Jatim beads emphasize the difference between monochrome and polychrome beads, and among the latter, between striped beads and those with millefiori decoration over a monochrome core

(Francis 2002a: 135; Adhyatman and Arifin 1996: 60-68; Allen *unpublished*). Surface finds at Jatiagung, near Jember in far eastern Java, of partially melted beads similar to those at 930 opposite, and possibly to the large yellow and blue/white pelangi beads on this page, provide the only evidence for possible bead manufacturing (Francis 1993: 8). In recent years, truly remarkable reproductions of Jatim beads have been available to collectors, knowing or unknowing, and these also are said to be made in Jember (Bali 2002: *pers. comm.*).

Many of the monochrome beads appear to have been drawn, suggesting a possible link to the Indo-Pacific glass bead industry; the similarity in colors is also striking. On the other hand, the large hexagonal bicones in translucent blue and green (920 on this page) may have been folded and then marvered or lapidary worked (Allen 1998: 133). The usually small and sometimes squarish twisted stripe beads are quite similar to those of the Roman period (666, Figure 7.0) discussed earlier in this chapter, and both groups appear to be segmented drawn beads. Allen has proposed a convincing manufacturing sequence for the pelangi beads, in which the stripes on a twisted stripe cane are dragged into a festoon pattern before the canes are hot-pinched or segmented into individual beads (Allen 2003a: 6-7). The occasional doublet beads, shown at 927 on page 62, support this reconstruction.

While many of the Indonesian mosaic patterns are similar to those of supposed Egyptian or West Asian manufacture, the Jatim millefiori beads were also made by pinching or segmenting a tube of glass, in this case covered by a thin mosaic layer, a process not otherwise known from the Roman or Islamic periods, although small mosaic beads thought to be late Hellenistic, shown at 545, Figure 6, are also segmented beads with thin layers of mosaic cane. At least one end of each Jatim mosaic bead shows distorted cane segments pulled toward the perforation, which could only occur with a segmenting mechanism. The glass cores themselves are usually green or yellow and made from much rougher glass, with many large bubbles and inclusions. While the finished beads show a certain uniformity, the manufacturing methods vary considerably: Although many of the cores are drawn, some appear to have been wound; many, but far from all, of the beads have a characteristic central dilation in the perforation. If Jatim mosaic beads were made over a period of several hundred years, it would not be surprising to find such variation in technique; the absence of well-dated examples makes comparison difficult.

There is, however, some cause for optimism. By far the great majority of Jatim beads have been found in East Java, with a few beads from Johore, near Singapore, from the Philippines, and as heirloom beads from Palau. Malleret found several twisted stripe beads at Oc Eo, which look like the squarish Jatim striped beads (Ho Chi Minh City 2001; *pers. obs.*). Two recent reports find Jatim beads much further afield: a Jatim mosaic bead found on the surface at Berenike (Francis 2002c: 4), and several Jatim beads found in at least three different well-dated late-5th to early-6th century tombs in Korea, including one small green/yellow pelangi bead and several millefiori mosaic beads, each about 2 cm in diameter (Lankton 2002: 5; Lankton, Lee, and Allen 2003). Berenike was probably abandoned in the mid-6th century, with no subsequent

FIGURE 7.9. Jatim millefiori mosaic beads with some of the most common designs. The two outstanding characteristics of these beads are the thin layer of mosaic cane slices over a monochrome core, and the segmented or hot-pinched appearance of at least one of the ends, suggesting that several beads were prepared at one time. Largest bead 4.5 cm in diameter.

occupation, supporting a 6th century date for the surface finds; the Korean dates are important because they are not only the earliest but also the most reliable. Associated grave goods help to date the tombs, and in addition, the mounded wooden chamber tombs in which these beads were found were no longer used after the mid- to late-6th century.

The early megalithic cultures of Java and Bali, so-called because of large stone grave markers, are not well understood. Jatim beads have been found near Banyuwangi in East Java, directly across the 3 km wide Bali Strait from Gilimanuk, where archaeologists have found both Indian ceramics and Indo-Pacific beads, with glass compositions matching those from Arikamedu (Bellwood 1997: 294-5; Francis 2002a: 45) and dating to the first centuries CE. The Strait is shallow but with currents up to 7 knots; the Malays were known to be excellent sailors, and the possibility of a cultural connection between Gilimanuk, with its known outside trade links, and East Java seems

likely. The Indian goods at Gilimanuk and at Sembiran, on the north coast of Bali, hint strongly at early local involvement in the spice trade, perhaps with South India, Sri Lanka, or Oc Eo as an intermediary (Bellwood 1999: 133). The prevailing winds in eastern Indonesia worked to the advantage of traders based in East Java and Bali, and certainly by the 11th century East Javanese kingdoms controlled the important trade in cloves, nutmeg, and mace from the Molucca Islands (Hall 1999: 208-210). Although there has been little archaeological confirmation, it would appear that far eastern Java, the most likely source of Jatim beads, was well integrated into international trade well before the 6th century. Add to that the reported presence in 3rd century Oc Eo of Persian Gulf sailors from the Sasanian Empire (Hall 1999: 194), and the East Java production of mosaic glass beads with West Asian or Egyptian patterns does not seem so improbable. We will return to Jatim beads in Chapter 8, with a more com-

FIGURE 7.10. Three Korean *gokok* pendants, along with the dark blue Indo-Pacific beads most popular in Korea. The earliest well-documented *gokok* of the typical shape come from the far south of Korea in the 6th to 5th centuries BCE, with semi-lunar variations from the same period. Contemporaneous examples from Japan are known as *magatama*. Center pendant 4.9 cm.

prehensive discussion of 1st millennium mosaic glass.

Think of Korea as the California of the East, if not in terms of actual population movement, then certainly in terms of ideas and trade goods. Korea was the last stop, and in spite of a strong native culture, new ideas and objects played an important role. Chinese accounts of the Koreans' love of beads during the Proto-Three Kingdoms period of the first three centuries CE are supported by the wealth of imported glass and stone beads found in royal tombs. The earliest distinctively Korean ornaments are cylindrical gray-green jasper beads beginning as early as the 8th century BCE, followed by comma-shaped pendants known as *gokok*, identical

to the Japanese *magatama* developing at about the same time. The earliest *gokok* were made from amazonite, and a 6th to 5th century BCE workshop, complete with both drills and finished and unfinished amazonite *gokok*, has been excavated in the far south (Lee 2001: 326-329). High-lead glass Chinese beads from the 2nd century BCE indicate early trade, but by the 1st or 2nd century CE increasing numbers of Indo-Pacific beads, often in the dark blue shown on this page, are found in Korean graves (Lankton 2001: 5-7). Ceramic molds for making small glass beads suggest rapid local appropriation of at least some glass technology as well. Beautifully made carnelian and rock crystal beads have been excavated

from southern cemeteries near Busan, beginning in the 2nd century. These stone beads may be imported, possibly from South India, although the equally well-carved rock crystal *gokok* from the same period raise the question of Korean, or at least Korean-sponsored, work as well.

The earliest blue Indo-Pacific beads in Korea appear to have potassium as the main alkali, like at least some of those from Arikamedu, and the situation may be similar for Japan, where Indo-Pacific imports begin at about the same time, if not earlier (Gupta 1999:11). By the 3rd century, there is a marked shift to high sodium blue glass in Japan and in Korea as well, although the picture there is not so clear-cut. Arikamedu does not appear to have made very much, if any, high sodium blue glass (Francis 2002a: 213, although Gupta 2000: 8 finds both soda and potash blues), calling for a new source for the 3rd century blue Indo-Pacific beads traded to Korea and Japan. Both Khlong Thom and Oc Eo, and possibly Mantai (Brill 1999: 337, 395, 397), are good candidates, and may, in fact, have been stimulated to glass production by the ready-made markets to the east (Katshuiko and Gupta 2002: 77). If this 3rd century change in glass composition in Korea and Japan is substantiated by further research, it would provide a reasonable starting date for Indo-Pacific bead production in Southeast Asia. Analagous to the dating of Roman period beads by excavations in northern Europe, data from Japan and Korea may help provide a more accurate chronology for both Indo-Pacific and Jatim beads.

Like lapis lazuli in Mesopotamia, jade was the greatest treasure for the Olmec of Mexico, the Maya of Guatemala and

James W. Lankton

Mexico, and jade-using cultures of north-west Costa Rica (Thompson 1995: 52-55; Liu 1999b: 19). The green of jade was symbolic of water and of fertility (Pender-gast 1998-9:3-11), and even beyond symbol, jade was thought to be life-giving in itself, and one royal bead could be worth 100 pounds of gold (Francis 1997: 81). For Precolumbian people the color, and not the mineralogical properties of the the stones was paramount. The Olmec preferred translucent blue-green, while for the Maya bright apple green jadeite was a gift fit for the gods (Pender-gast 1998-99: 9).

Again similar to lapis lazuli, there was one main source of ancient jadeite, the most highly valued of the many stones treated as social jades (Pendergast 1998-99: 3), and it was located high in the mountains above the Rio Montagua in Guatemala, far from the Classic Maya cities of the Peten and Yucatan lowlands (Seitz et al 2001). Our pen-dant at 1327 on this page is jadeite, with Mohs' hardness between 6 and 7, while the larger pendant at 1328 may be serpentine. Even such high prestige objects as the jade mosaic masks found in royal Maya graves may include several different stones, all treasured for their green color (Guatemala 1998 *pers. obs.*).

Shell beads, particularly orange spondylus, were also important to many Native American cultures, with long-distance maritime trade routes extending 3800 km between West Mexico and Ecuador as early as 1500 BCE (Anawalt 1998:239).

FIGURE 7.11. Mixed green stone and spondylus shell ornaments, mainly from the Maya Classic Period (300-800). Jade, with its green color symbolizing water and fertility, was the most important natural material for the ancient Maya, who formed their pendants following the contours of the stone. The pendant at 1327 is jadeite. The large serpentine pendant is 5.0 cm in diameter.

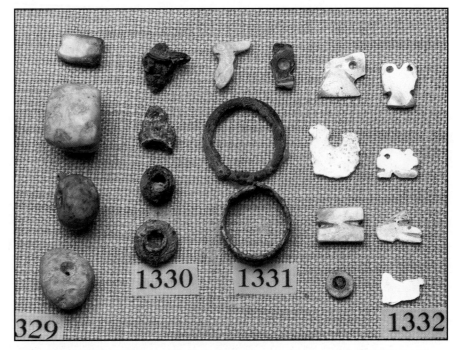

FIGURE 7.12. Copper alloy and mother-of-pearl ornaments from Ecuador and Peru. Andean metallurgy began in the 2nd millennium BCE, although these beads and rings are more associat-ed with the Tihuanaco culture near Lake Titicaca in Peru and Bolivia, with a Classic Period from 375-700 CE. The delicate shell pendants could be from Peru or Ecuador. The largest ring is 2.3 cm in diameter.

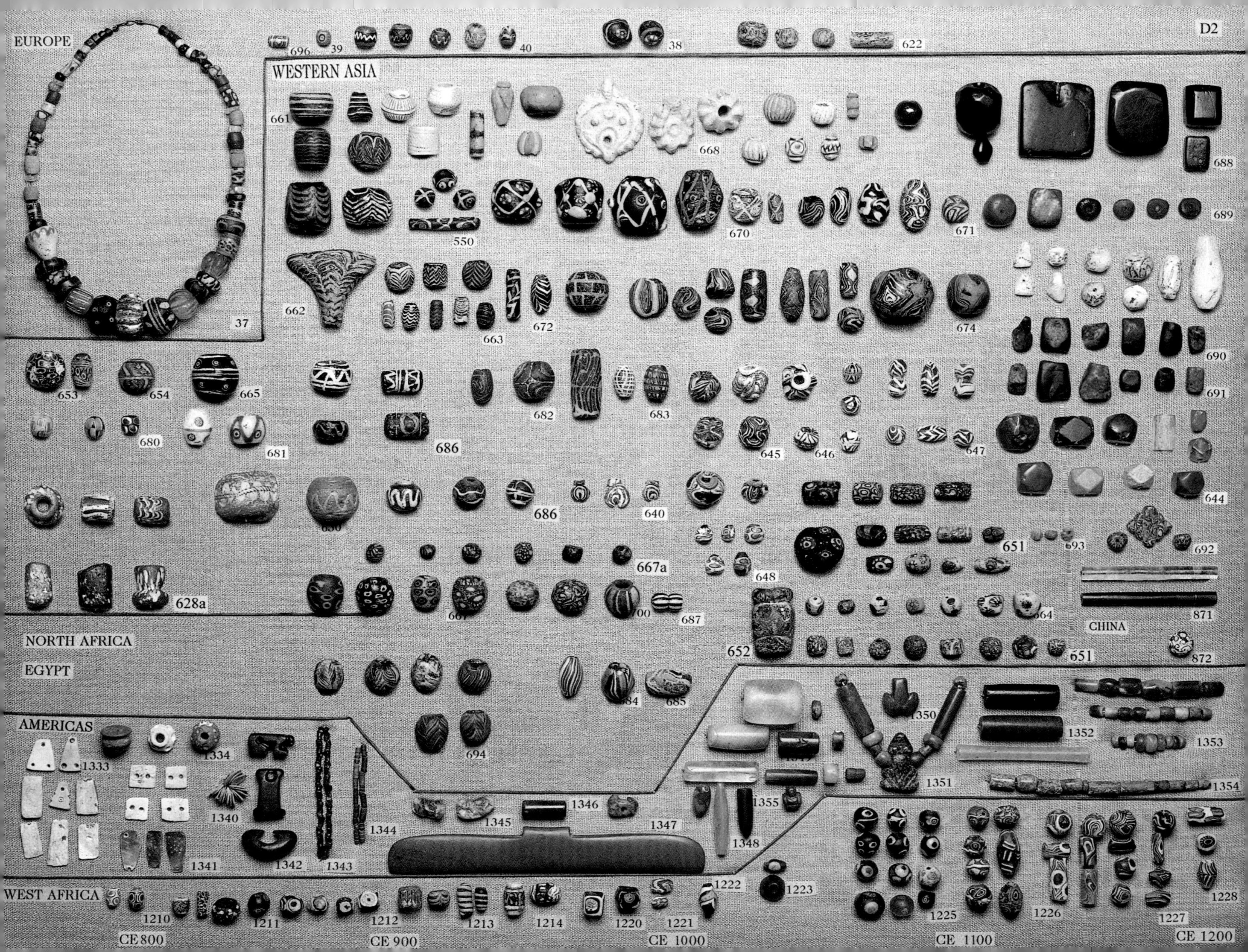

D2

EUROPE

WESTERN ASIA

CHINA

NORTH AFRICA

EGYPT

AMERICAS

WEST AFRICA

CE 1200

CE 1100

CE 1000

CE 900

CE 800

688
689
690
691
644
692
871
872
1353
1354
1228
1227
1352
651
1226
1225
622
671
674
647
651
64
1350
1351
668
670
646
1355
1223
645
648
652
1348
1222
38
683
640
667a
687
685
1347
1221
84
1346
1220
40
672
682
686
00
1345
1214
663
550
694
1213
686
67
1344
1212
39
696
661
662
690
681
1343
1211
37
665
628a
1342
1334
1340
1210
654
680
1341
653
1333

James W. Lankton

Figure 8.1 shows the only complete necklace on the Timeline, a remarkable collection of glass beads ranging in date from the 4th century BCE to the 10th century CE. Similar strands of beads, known as *Gougad-Pateraenneu*, or necklace of blessed beads, have long formed part of the Celtic culture of Morbihan, located in the Brittany region of France (Opper and Opper 1993b: 1-18). With origins in the Prechrisitian past, the healing powers of Gougad-Pateraenneu were recognized by the Church in the 12th century, and by the 19th century many of the necklaces formed part of church property, to be loaned or rented to parish-oners seeking the benefit of the beads. Eisen, writing in 1916, remarks that "to this day, the peasants of Brittany possess numerous (until lately innumerable) necklaces of antique beads preserved as heirlooms from remote centuries, which now pass hand to hand in the curing of various disease" (Eisen 1916:2). Each type of bead had its special virtues, and Gougad-Pateraenneu necklaces would be worn for a period of nine days to cure fever, diseases of the throat and eyes, colds and wounds, and to help mothers feed their children and the children to cut their teeth. The oldest beads on strands now in churches, museums, or private collections date to the Neolithic period, and amber and rock crystal were important as well. Phoenician and Egyptian glass beads reflect early trade, and these, along with Celtic, Merovingian, and imported

FIGURE 8.1. Gougad-Pateraenneu necklace with glass beads 4th century BCE to the 10th century. Heirloom strands of glass, crystal, and amber beads have been used in the Morbihan region of Brittany to cure a variety of ilnesses. Recognized by the Church since the 12th century, the original beliefs go deep into the Celtic past of this part of France. Central melon bead 2.6 cm diameter.

oriental beads, were transferred from generation to generation, passing to the oldest son, with the provision that he lend the Gougad-Pateraenneu to family members (Beck 1976: 33). The most immediately recognizable bead on our strand is also one of the oldest, the dark bead to the right of the center

melon bead. These 4th century BCE beads are known as Filottrano beads, after the Italian cemetery where they were first discovered (Stern 2001: 386). They are concentrated in the western Mediterranean area and were probably made in Carthage during the period of the great bearded head pendants. The

FIGURE 8.0. Beads and ornaments from the mid-8th century to 1200, roughly corresponding to the Early Islamic period in Egypt and West Asia. Following the Arab conquests of the mid-7th century, there were few changes in bead and glass technology until the development of distinctive Islamic period styles during the late-8th to 9th centuries, at such centers as Fustat, Samarra, and Nishapur. The period ends as the Fourth Crusaders sack Constantinople, and Chingis Khan begins the empire his successors will take to the doors of Europe. Tairona broadwing pendant 18.6 cm wide.

FIGURE 8.2. Mixed group of polychrome glass beads. The five drawn beads at 666 with spiral stripes date to the first half of the 1st millennium CE. Most of the rest of these beads are decorated with slices of mosaic cane, with or without an underlying core. The five lowest beads may be associated with 9th to 11th century Fustat, Egypt. The red mosaic bead at lower left is 2.1 cm in diameter.

large white bead with a blue zigzag design may be even older, and is similar to a 5th century BCE fig-shaped bead described by Eisen (Eisen 1930b: 1-7). There are four ring beads as well, best known from the late La Tène Celtic culture of the last two centuries BCE, with one at the 8 o'clock position, and the others between 3 and 5. The opaque orange beads, the cylindrical white bead with red eyes and blue-green trail, and several of the red-and-yellow beads are similar to those found in 6th century Merovingian graves. The most recent beads are the small cylinders with yellow central bands and red, white, and black mosaic ends, near 3 and 9 o'clock, which are found in Scandinavia in the 9th and 10th centuries and are thought to be imports from the east (Callmer 1977: 98).

Chapter 7 closed with the Arab capture of the primary and secondary glassworking

areas of West Asia and Egypt. The Umayyad Caliphate, with its capital at Damascus, brought a change in leadership but continuity in the types of glass vessels, and presumably beads, produced within its dominion. In 750, the Abbasids of eastern Iran defeated the Umayyad dynasty, now weakened by tribal feuding and the Shiite-Sunni conflict. The Abbasid caliphs founded a new capital, Madinat al-Salam, the City of Peace, soon to be known as Baghdad. Within forty years, Baghdad was probably the world's largest city and its cultural capital (Haywood 1998b: 3.14). Some of the greatest craftsmen from this, the largest empire the world had known, would come to Baghdad to create a distinctively Islamic art during the 300-year golden age of Arab and Islamic culture (Carboni 2001b: 4). We have some idea of the chronological sequence during this Early Islamic peri-

od, thanks to the fact that the Abbasid capital was twice moved, first to Raqqa in Syria from 796 to 808, and later to Samarra, north of Baghdad, from 836 to 892. Excavations at both sites have revealed primary and secondary glass industries, although no reports of beads (Henderson 1995a: 257 for a description of glass production at Raqqa). The palace at Samarra was decorated with glass mosaic tiles, fragments of which are on display in New York at the Metropolitan Museum of Art. These tiles were most likely made in Sarmarra, indicating a resurgent mosaic glass industry, and have not been found in any other excavations at Islamic period sites. Although there is no description of beadmaking at Samarra, mosaic glass beads, with patterns identical to some of the canes in these tiles, have been found in 9th and early 10th century graves in the Caucasus region of Russia (Kovalevskaya 2000: 93), strongly suggesting beadmaking associated with the mosaic glass industry.

Alexandria had been famous for the excellence of its glasswork for one thousand years, and the Arab conquest brought little change (Pinder-Wilson and Scanlon 1973: 16). At the same time, Fustat, the new Arab city along the Nile River, founded in 641 and now part of Cairo, was a center for both vessel and bead production. Fustat's period of greatest prosperity began in the 8th century, and continued into the 10th and 11th centuries under Fatimid rule. Excavations have revealed a surprisingly small number of beads, many of rather nondescript monochrome wound glass. There were at least two dark wound oblate beads with light-colored dragged trail decoration, one dated to the 8th or 9th century (Scanlon and Pinder-Wilson 2001: 122).

James W. Lankton

The most exciting find was seven barrel-shaped beads found together in an undisturbed area closely dated to 900 CE. The color illustration of these "Fustat fused rod beads" in Scanlon and Pinder-Wilson's 2001 report shows that three of the beads have mosaic eyes as well. Similar Timeline beads are on page 74 at 694. In addition, a short segment of glass cane with the same twisted stripe used for the beads was found in the fill from the area, along with 41 additional whole or fragmentary beads. Although no bead workshop was identified, the glass rod provides evidence for production of these beads in Fustat (Scanlon and Pinder-Wilson 2001: 121). Francis has suggested a manufacturing process for the beads (Francis 1989b: 29), while Spaer cautions that the large number of similar beads, primarily from the antiquities market, may indicate a production period from the 9th to the 11th century (Spaer 1993: 4). Similar beads have been excavated in Israel, Syria, Greece, Yugoslavia, and Russia, but not in Scandinavia; the mosaic beads from Birka mentioned as comparable by Scanlon are apparently not (Spaer 1993: 8). In addition, fused rod beads, including those with eyes, are found in Mauritania, where they are known as *morfia*, and have even been used as models for powder glass Kiffa beads. To complete the Fustat picture, Francis has reported on collections of unprovenanced beads from the Islamic Museum in Cairo, finding everything from drawn glass beads similar to those produced in Alexandria, to Chinese and Venetian examples (Francis 2002b: 12-31). The most intriguing observations are two beads from the Fouqi collection "made of concentric red and white mosaic canes without cores (Francis 1989b:

FIGURE 8.3. The pierced mosaic cane beads range from the 4th to the 9th century, with the third and sixth beads from the left, lower row, resembling early canes. The upper faceted mosaic beads with monochrome cores are more likely post-10th century. The small green Early Islamic vessel may be from West Asia or Iran. Large black bead with stripes and mosaic eyes is 2.7 cm in diameter.

29), and the suggestion of "mosaic beads formed without a core in the manner typical of the Early Islamic period" in a group of beads and wasters from Fustat now in the Allard Pierson Museum in Amsterdam (Francis 1996: 10). Unfortunately, without illustrations it is difficult to known what is intended, and Islamic period mosaic beads made entirely from red-and-white mosaic canes sound most unusual.

We saw a very early mosaic glass bead in Chapter 4, and noted the revival of the mosaic technique in the second half of the 1st millennium BCE, used first for beads, and then for vessels. We identified several mosaic beads on the Timeline as possibly Hellenistic, at 545 and 544 on page 54. One of these beads is an oval tabular bead made from fused canes, and several of the others are small oblates with a thin layer of cane over a monochrome base, with the ends suggesting

that the beads had been pinched or segmented. All of these beads have mosaic cane patterns of relatively small spirals, often in blue and white. The other pattern found in Hellenistic vessels is a 'daisy' pattern not found on beads (Grose 1989: 189-190 for a discussion of the vessels). Conventional wisdom is that both beads and vessels were made in Alexandria (Harden 1967: 35). At about the same time, small mosaic glass plaques in floral, star, and checkerboard design were being made in Egypt, with at least some from Gumaiyama in the 3rd century BCE (Grose 1989: 353-354). Similar mosaic plaques appear on beads, with examples on the Timeline at 600 and 602, also on page 54. The face beads at 603 are part of this same Egyptian industry.

Before the end of the 1st century BCE, glassworking had spread to Italy, and a number of mosaic glass cups, bowls, and

FIGURE 8.4. Glass and faience beads from the Early Islamic period (8th to 11th centuries). The large black beads with mosaic eyes and white trails may be from Syria, 10th century. Combed trail decoration was popular throughout the 1st millennium, with small examples excavated at Fustat, although additional production in West Asia is likely. Trailed "peacock tail" bead is 5.2 cm wide.

plates were produced, possibly in Rome itself, going into the 1st century CE. In contrast to the Hellenistic vessels, the Italian examples have a great variety of mosaic designs, more complex and diverse in color, construction, and design. Between three and five colors may be combined, all within a ground of contrasting color (Grose 1989: 243). None of these canes are found on beads from the period, and the spiral designs that are used are much larger than Hellenistic examples. The only exceptions are a few glass vessels with checkerboard mosaic design, one of which also incorporates face canes (Goldstein 1979: 186-187), and may have been found in Syria. If Syrian, these vessels may represent a different industry, perhaps with closer ties to Egypt.

There are three types of mosaic beads found in Europe as early as the 3rd century: those with an equatorial band of mosaic design, usually similar to Egyptian beads or inlays; small monochrome beads with an abstract flower mosaic inlay, not seen (or else very rare) in West Asia; and beads made entirely from mosaic cane slices, without an underlying base. This third group is illustrated by the checker mosaic beads at 596, Figure 7.0, with a number of very similar beads from the previously mentioned Danish cemetery at Skovegarde, dating generally from 210 to 260. The only other overall mosaic beads at Skovegarde were less common, and were made from slender blue-and-white canes with simple concentric patterns, somewhat similar to the blue-and-white mosaic bead at 673, Figure 7.0, but much smaller, with three or four registers of canes. Both the checkerboard and the blue-and-white beads may have been made by rolling a pad of mosaic glass around a mandrel, and then

smoothing the ends. There are a few similar beads from other European sites, some larger and in other colors (two examples at the British Museum from Gotland, Sweden, are dated 3rd to 4th century); they all appear to have been made with the same technique. Although checkerboard beads are found in Syria, the small blue-and-white beads appear to be rare, which could suggest production in Europe, perhaps near one or more of the Roman glasshouses established during the 1st century. Before the end of the 4th century, typical "Viking" beads with three registers of mosaic plaques, including checkerboards outlined in red alternating with floral patterns, can be found at such sites as Hvenekilde in Denmark, dated to 370 (Copenhagen 2002: pers. obs.). Even earlier examples from the Kragehul Bog may push production back into the 3rd century (Copenhagen 2002: pers. obs.); the example from Hvenekilde includes a floral cane similar to one found on 1st century Italian mosaic vessels, as do some of the later beads of the same type (Grose 1989:344, # 268). It seems even more likely that these beads were produced in Europe, although at least one example was reported by Alekseeva (Alekseeva 1982: Plate 49).

The mosaic glass vessel industry died out after the 4th century, with the last examples from late-4th century mosaic panels found in Greece (Whitehouse 2001: 147). Mosaic glass beads continued, particularly with checkerboard beads found in the Caucasus, Europe, and Scandinavia. Alekseeva illustrates overall mosaic, or millefiori, beads, and pierced cane beads, with dates from the 2nd to the 4th century. The pierced cane beads on the Timeline at 596, Figure 7.0, are similar to those illustrat-

James W. Lankton

FIGURE 8.5. Torus-folded beads from the 10th to 12th centuries. Complex folded beads were the great innovation of Islamic period bead-makers. Collared bead lower right 2.3 cm.

FIGURE 8.6. Early Islamic period folded beads, also called mirror beads. The large sizes and bright, opaque colors characterize many glass beads of this period, with likely production in a number of areas, including West Asia and the Volga-Bulgaria homeland in Russia. These beads were made by manipulating a pad of mosaic glass around an iron mandrel. Largest bead 3.7 cm in diameter.

ed (Alekseeva 1982: Plate 49, # 19-24). The cane design of a yellow eye surrounded by a thin red ring, all surrounded by alternating stripes of red and white, dating from the 2nd to 4th centuries, is quite unusual, but matches precisely one of the canes decorating our bead second from the left at 637, Figure 7.0 (Alekseeva 1982: Plate 49, # 20). The two beads at 637 are different from the other mosaic beads at 638 in that they were made of thin slices of mosaic cane over a green core, somewhat similar to the Hellenistic beads, but in this case not segmented. The use of a 4th century cane suggests that mosaic beads with and without cores may have been made during this period, perhaps representing different industries.

Early Islamic mosaic glass vessels began in the 9th century and continued into the 10th, but perhaps not beyond (Whitehouse 2001: 148-153).

Many, if not most, of the mosaic canes used for vessels were also used for beads. While some of these beads were simple pierced canes (Kovalevskaya 2000: 94), others are large, barrel-shaped beads made without a core, as shown on Figure 8.2, lowest row; the first and third beads from the right resemble known 9th century vessels, while the second bead from the right has both similar construction and a comparable date, with an example found at 10th to 11th century Sungai Mas, in Malaysia (Francis 2002a: color plate 23). Whether or not these beads resemble the Fustat material mentioned by Francis may be answered by further reporting on the Allard Pierson Museum collection. The barrel-shaped beads were made by rolling a prepared pad of mosaic canes around a mandrel, as illustrated by Allen (Allen 2003a: 1-3), and the large perforation, overall size

and shape, and method of construction are consistent with techniques used for Fustat fused rod beads.

Where do the Jatim mosaic beads, discussed in Chapter 7, fit into this picture? The early 6th century date for at least some of these beads, supported by the Korean finds, forces us to rethink prior ideas that Early Islamic mosaic beads, made without cores, inspired Jatim beads, made with cores. In fact, the Jatim beads come at least three hundred years before the Early Islamic mosaic beads, using 9th century Samarra for an early date. Possible precursors to Jatim beads would be the two Timeline mosaic beads with green cores at 637, Figure 8.0, particularly if the unusual red, white, and yellow cane proves to be limited to the 2nd to 4th centuries.

Between the 4th and the 8th century, there were at least two threads of mosaic bead manufacturing: One was concen-

FIGURE 8.7. Amber, glazed quartz, and lapis lazuli beads from the Islamic period. All three of these bead materials were excavated at 9th to 11th century Nishapur. Many Early Islamic beads, including these, provided protection against the evil eye. Largest glazed quartz bead is 4.5 cm long.

FIGURE 8.8. Rock crystal and glass beads from northern China, Liao Dynasty (907-1125). The revival of stone carving during the Song and Liao Dynasties brought new forms and increased use of stone ornaments, with rock crystal and agate particularly popular in the north. The precise drilling of these crystal beads reflects the excellence of Liao craftsmen. The etched or carved glass bead with a cloud pattern formed part of a Buddhist prayer strand. The crystal beads are 7.9 cm long.

trated in Europe and Scandinavia, making mosaic glass beads mostly without cores and primarily in checker or blue-and-white mosaic, when not of the better known "pre-Viking" style. The second thread is less certain. Both pierced cane and millefiori beads were found in the Black Sea area, dating to the 2nd and 3rd centuries (Alekseeva 1982: Plate 49. # 55-57); the method of manufacture is not clear from the drawings. The next well-dated examples from this second thread are the early-6th century beads found in Korea, representing a possibly early phase of Jatim mosaic glass bead production. It seems possible that our bead with a 2nd to 4th century cane pattern over a glass core could be an intermediate between the two. The productions site(s) for these late Roman period mosaic beads is not known, although Egypt would seem the most likely source for either the mosaic canes or the beads themselves. The stone molds excavated in Alexandria for making segmented beads are from this period, and the continuation of an earlier mosaic glass bead industry seems likely as well. Although the Sasanians controlled the sea routes in the 6th century, until then Egyptian Berenike seems to have remained an active port (Wild and Wild 2001: 211), providing an eastern trade route for Egyptian beads. Unfortunately, the one mosaic bead excavated at Berenike is a small tabular pierced cane from an earlier period. The segmented millefiori bead found on the surface at Berenike remains intriguing, but was it traveling from, or going to, the east?

The relationship between late Roman period mosaic glass beads and Early Islamic mosaic glass vessels is entirely unknown, and the same can be said

James W. Lankton

for the Early Islamic mosaic glass beads, which seem more closely related to vessel production, both stylistically and temporally. In the Early Islamic period the vessels and at least some of the beads began as pads of mosaic canes: The vessels were slumped over a mold, while the beads were rolled around a rod, but the techniques were analogous. At present, the only millefiori mosaic glass beads that we can identify as Early Islamic with any certainty are those closely resembling excavated examples such as reported by Callmer and Kovalevskaya, or from well-dated Southeast Asian sites; the beads with canes matching mosaic tiles or vessels; and possibly the barrel-shaped beads with large perforations but cane designs not yet found on Islamic period tiles or vessels. Late Roman beads, with or without cores, may be ancestral to the Islamic period beads, and likely are precursors to the Jatim beads. Further analysis of documented 4th to 6th century West Asian or Egyptian millefiori beads should help us decide whether we need a third thread of millefiori mosaic beadmaking: one starting in the 9th century, and related to such sites as Samarra, with its glass tile production. Early millefiori glass beads are both beautiful and fascinating, and again, the more we learn, the more fascinating they become.

Near the end of the 8th century, large numbers of glass beads were imported into Scandinavia, coming both through Europe and along trade routes leading north through the Black Sea and the Caucasus, then following river systems through the Ukraine (Callmer 1995:52). Similar beads are arranged along the top of Figure 8.0. Callmer relates the rise and fall of this trade with the changing fortunes of the Abbasid caliphate, and

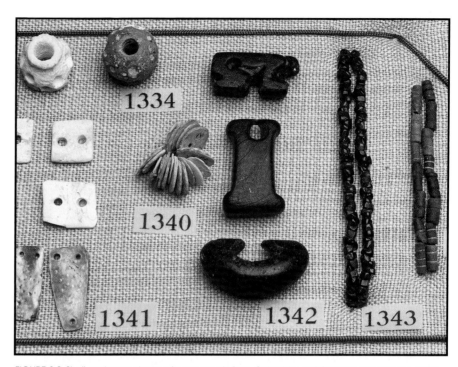

FIGURE 8.9. Shell, amber, and ceramic ornaments from Columbia and Ecuador. The terpene resins of trees related to the West Indian locust, found in the ancient jungles of the Dominican Republic, Mexico, Colombia, and Brazil, become polymerized over millions of years. This neotropical amber differs from the Baltic variety in lacking succinic acid, and may be classified as retinite (Armstrong 1993: 60). The larger ornaments and the very small amber beads were recovered in Colombia. The small green beads to the right are ceramic, possibly from Ecuador. The mother-of-pearl ornaments at 1341 are from Colombia, possibly Tairona culture. The amber nose pendant at 1342 is 3.2 cm wide.

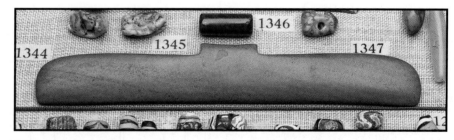

FIGURE 8.10. Broadwing pendants may be stylized representations of the bat, an animal important in many Precolumbian Central and South American cultures. Similar pendants are found in Colombia, Venezuela, Panama, Costa Rica, and Mexico. Jade examples from Costa Rica and Venezuela contrast with the softer stone pendants of the Tairona culture of northern Colombia (800-1500), the probable origin of this beautiful example (Liu 1985: 26). Pendant width 18.6 cm.

suggests that the beads could have been made within the caliphate. Late-10th century dark glass beads with mosaic eyes and a trailed design traded to Scandinavia, shown at 38, Figure 8.0, are similar to larger beads thought to be from Syria, shown at 670, Figure 8.0. The examples from Scandinavia were soon joined by distinctive orange millefiori beads, now formed over gray-green cores, shown at 622, Figure 8.0, with a design also found on at least one

FIGURE 8.11. Stone beads and pendants, Tairona culture (800-1500). Tairona craftsmen were particularly noted for their gold work, but were no less proficient in making beautiful ornaments from both soft and hard stone. The small frog pendant at 1351 may be serpentine (Mohs' hardness less than 4), while the more stylized version above is carnelian. The three beads at 1352 in jasper, carnelian, and rock crystal demonstrate the Tairona beadmakers' skill (Kessler and Kessler 1978: 2-5, 81-86). The 10th-11th century glass beads below have mosaic eye and trailed decorations, and may be found from Mali to eastern Java (Adhyatman and Arifin 1996: 10). Crystal bead 7.7 cm long.

Early Islamic vessel said to be from Nishapur in northeastern Iran (Callmer 2002: *oral presentation*).

The Early Islamic folded beads shown at 640, Figure 8.0, and in Figures 8.5 and 8.6, have been relatively common in the bead market, but are rare at excavated sites. Callmer illustrates one bead that looks as if it could be folded, dating from the second half of the 9th century (Callmer 1977: Taf 17, #A21). More certain examples from Russia (L'vova 1997: 258), and a possible production site in Volga-Bulgaria, a prosperous trading center in the middle Volga region (Valiulina 2002: *oral presentation*), provide dates from the 9th to 12th centuries, but primarily 11th and 12th. While it is not clear where else these beads might have been made — and the several styles suggest multiple sites — these are some of the best known Early

Islamic beads, and they represent the most important innovation in glass beadmaking since the Hellenistic period. While the method used to make these beads is not certain, Allen has proposed that beadmakers started with a pad of striped mosaic glass for the beads in Figure 8.6, and manipulated a donut of mosaic glass, with or without an underlying bead, for the torus-folded beads in Figure 8.5, a mechanism developed with Albert Summerfield (Allen 2003b: 1).

Along with Samarra and Fustat, the other great glassworking center of the Early Islamic period was Nishapur, in northeastern Iran. Nishapur was excavated during the 1930s and 1940s by teams from the Metropolitan Museum of Art in New York (Carboni 2001a: 19-20). During the 9th through 11th centuries, Nishapur, with the Silk Road going right through its center, prospered in

spite of changing political control. While only 53 glass beads were found, many beads in jet, faience, glazed quartz, and lapis lazuli suggest possible manufacture in the city (Francis 1988a: 78-93), and help us learn about some of the other bead materials from the Early Islamic period. Almost half of the beads found were jet, with some shapes similar to those at 688, Figure 8.1. Jet was worked in many ways at Nishapur, including cutting and engraving, and was used for seals as well as beads. The source of this jet is not known, although Anatolia is a possibility (Francis 1989b :24).

Faience was also produced at Nishapur, as both pendants and beads. Examples similar to those on display at the Metropolian Museum of Art are included in Figure 8.0 at 668. Faience beads far outnumber glass beads among the excavated examples, and suggest a very long history of faience production in Iran, going back at least to Parthian times, and apparently continuing into the present at the holy city of Qom, where large faience beads are made to protect animals against the evil eye.

The glazed quartz beads above 690 in Figure 8.8 are also typical for Nishapur production, described by Francis as crude oblates or pendants (Francis 1988a: 90). The second bead from the right is an uneven square bicone with four panels cut into the sides. None were found at Nishapur, and Francis suggests that they may be Sasanian, although the later date seems likely as well. Eight percent of the beads at Nishapur were lapis lazuli, and our beads at 691, Figure 8.8, illustrate some of the forms of Early Islamic lapis lazuli beads. Coral was also popular at many Islamic sites, and would have a Mediterranean source. Our coral beads

James W. Lankton

at 693, Figure 8.8, are particularly well-made, and consistent with an Early Islamic date. Amber continued to be popular, and the amber beads at 689 in Figure 8.8 would not be out of place.

Francis mentions that as many as 44% of the beads found at Nishapur could have served as amulets, most commonly against the evil eye (Francis 1988a: 84). Effective remedies would include anything blue, accounting for the popularity of lapis lazuli, faience, and glazed quartz; cowrie shells; stones such as carnelian and onyx; and anything with the dot-in-circle motif, common on bone spindle whorls found at many Islamic sites. Less obvious amuletic beads include large green jasper cornerless cubes, shown on the Timeline at 644, page 74, along with imitations in glass (Schienerl 1985: 8-9).

The three beads at 692 on Figure 8.0 may also have had amuletic power, and are made from a stone composed of the fossilized shells of sea worms. Known as *sang-i-Maryam,* or stone of Mary, this distinctive material was also imitated in glass.

Both Ptolemy, the great Roman geographer of the 2nd to 3rd centuries, and the anonymous author of the 1st century mariner's guide, *The Periplus of the Erythraean Sea*, mention the ivory-trading emporium of Rhapta, located in Azania, along the Swahili coast of East Africa. Recent excavations at Mkukutu in the Rufiji delta, Tanzania, have revealed the first evidence for Roman contact: four beads, including two dark blue melon shapes and one double-segment gold-glass bead (Chami 1999: 237), with associated radiocarbon dates from 200 to 400 CE. These correlate well with the early Indo-Pacific glass beads in West Africa, such as

FIGURE 8.12. Millefiori and folded glass beads, some with additional mosaic eye decoration. All of these beads were found in West Africa. The paucity of excavated examples makes it difficult to date these beads with precision, but possibly related finds suggest the 10th to 12th century. The green and white cylindrical bead without added eyes, to the right at 1226, is 2.4 cm long.

those from 4th to 7th century Iron Age sites near Kissi, in northeastern Burkina Faso (Magnavita 1999: 4-11).

By the mid-9th century, camel caravans crossing the Sahara brought salt and manufactured goods, including glass vessels and beads, to the developing kingdoms of West Africa. Excavations at Gao, along the Niger River in Mali, have revealed glass vessels, thought to be for local use, and glass beads, some of which were traded on, perhaps as far away as Igbo-Ikwu, in southeastern Nigeria (Insoll 1998: 77-78). The vessels have suggested sources in Egypt, West Asia, and Ifriqiya, corresponding to modern Tunisia. Many of the beads were imported, but at least some were made in Gao, with glassworking waste in ten colors, including multicolored canes (Roy and Insoll 1998: 4).

These encouraging recent reports help to narrow the gap between the archaeological evidence for glass beads and the large numbers of beads found in Mali and Mauritania. Beads with good 10th

century dates include the small checker mosaic bead with yellow caps at 1211, Figure 8.0, known also from 8th to 10th century sites of the Saltova culture north of the Black Sea, and the three beads at 1213, all known from Fustat (Scanlon and Pinder-Wilson 2001: 119). The folded beads shown in Figure 8.12 are similar in technique to beads found in West Asia and Afghanistan, but differ in shape and color. The use of translucent green in the African beads is particularly unusual. Allen has promoted a theory of Islamic glass technique dispersion, encompassing Northern Europe, West Africa, and Southeast Asia (Allen 2000: *pers. comm.*), which may help explain the similarities and differences. Were these beads the work of craftsmen in Africa using Middle Eastern techniques, or were they imported from some yet unknown beadmaking site, such as in the Fatimid homeland along the north coast of Africa? Perhaps by the time Volume II of our Timeline Catalog comes out, we will have the answer.

FIGURE 9.1. This early gold-glass bead is similar to one found among the rubble of a bead workshop from late 3rd century BCE Rhodes. See also page 55 for discussion. Length 2.1 cm.

FIGURE 9.2. Similar in shape to beads used in much earlier periods, these tourmaline beads may be as late as the 19th century. Tourmaline was particularly popular in Central Asia, with sources in the Ural Mountains, as well as in Sri Lanka. Nineteenth century jewelry from Bukhara combined gold or gold-washed silver with tourmaline beads and pendants. Largest bead 2.0 cm long.

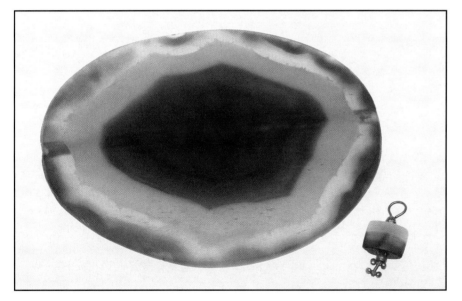

FIGURE 9.3. Unusually large tabular banded agate bead, cut to reveal the eye pattern of the stone, and associated with the Bactria Margiana Archaeological Complex (BMAC) of the early 2nd millennium BCE. Similar beads from the Royal Cemetery of Ur have a late 3rd millennium date. The small gold and agate earring includes a variant of the quadruple spiral design, and could also be from the 2nd millennium BCE. See p. 36 for discussion. Length 8.5 cm.

FIGURE 9.4. Massive bow-shaped banded agate bead. A very similar bead was excavated in a late 3rd century BCE Sarmatian grave near the northeast coast of the Black Sea (Beglova 2002: 304). The Greek historian Herodotus reported that the Sarmatians were said to be the offspring of Scythians who had mated with Amazons, and that Sarmatian women should not wed until they had killed a man in battle. Rich graves of armed female warriors support the story. Length 8 cm.

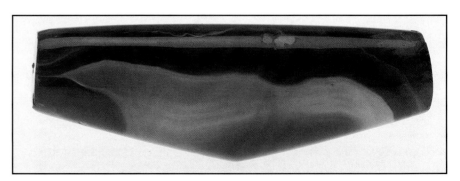

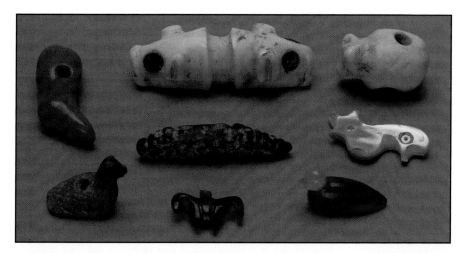

FIGURE 9.5. This group of small beads and pendants includes examples in shell, coral, lapis lazuli, mother-of-pearl, and carnelian. The double-headed shell pendant in the upper row (2.3 cm. long) may be as early as the 3rd millennium BCE, as could be the animal bead to its right. The small duck in the lower right corner, carved from one piece of stone, uses the natural color banding to great advantage.

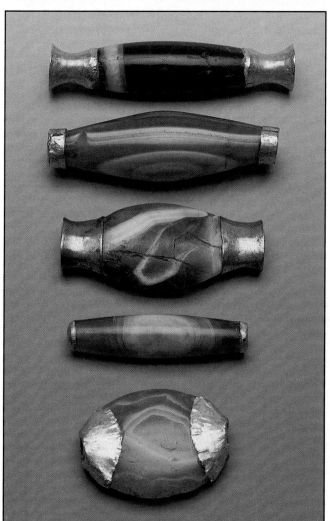

FIGURE 9.7. The combination of gold and banded agate begins in the Akkadian period (2350-2150 BCE) in Mesopotamia, producing richly set gems for the centerpiece of a necklace. Largest bead 4 cm.

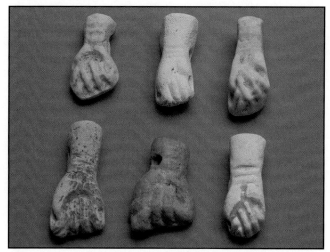

FIGURE 9.6. While Mesopotamian gold caps tend to fit closely to the stone, those from the Bactrian oases are more like hats than gloves, as shown in the upper and middle beads above. The gold caps on the lower two beads may be more recent replacements. Longest 5.7 cm.

FIGURE 9.8. The image of a closed fist with the thumb between the first two fingers, or *mano-fica*, was a common apotropaic symbol throughout the Roman empire. These faience amulets would protect the wearer against the harmful influence of the evil eye. Largest 1.5 cm.

Adhyatman, Sumarah and Redjeki Arifin 1996 *Manik-Manik di Indonesia,* 2nd ed. Jakarta: Djambatan. 10, 60-68, 69,

Alekseeva, E. M. 1975. Ancient Beads of the Northern Black Sea Littoral 1. *Archaeology of the USSR.* Moscow: Nayka. Plates 1-19.

—1978. Ancient Beads of the Northern Black Sea Littoral 2. *Archaeology of the USSR.* Moscow: Nayka. Plates 20-34.

—1982. Ancient Beads of the Northern Black Sea Littoral 3. *Archaeology of the USSR.* Moscow: Nayka. Plates 35-54.

Allard Pierson Museum 2002. *Personal observations* at the Allard Pierson Museum, Amsterdam, the Netherlands.

Allen, Jamey D. 1996. Bead arts: Kiffa beads. *Ornament* 20(1): 76-77.

—1998. *Magical Ancient Beads.* Singapore: Times Editions. 133.

—2000. *Personal communication,* September 2000. Washington, D.C.

—2002. Tibetan Zi beads: the current fascination with their nature and history. *Arts of Asia* 32(4): 72-91.

—2003a. *How millefiori beads have been made through time.* Article posted on National Bead Society Forum. http://www.nationalbeadsociety.com.

—2003b. *Reproductions of folded beads.* Message 927 to http://groups.yahoo.com/group/beadcollectors/message/927.

—2003c, d. *Personal communication, May, 2003.*

Amiet, Pierre 1966. *Elam. Auvers-sur-Oise.* Archée Editeur. 148.

Anawalt, Patricia R. 1998. They came to trade exquisite things: ancient West Mexican-Ecuadorian contacts. *In:* Townsend, Richard F. (ed.) *Ancient West Mexico: Art and Archaeology of the Unknown Past.* New York: Thames and Hudson. 233-250.

Andrews, Carol 1991. *Ancient Egyptian Jewelry.* New York: Harry N. Abrams. 208 p.

Armstrong, Wayne P. 1993. Neotropical amber. *Ornament* 17(1): 58-61, 108.

Bader, N.O. 1993. Summary of the earliest agriculturalists of Northern Mesopotamia. *In:* Yoffee, Norman and Jeffery J. Clark (eds.). *Early Stages in the Evolution of Mesopotamian Civilization: Soviet Excavations in Northern Iraq.* Tucson: University of Arizona Press. 63-72.

Bahn, Paul G. and Jean Vertut 1997. *Journey through the Ice Age.* Berkeley: University of California Press. 84-101.

Bali 2000. *Personal communication* with Bead dealers in Bali, *February, 2000.* Bali, Indonesia.

Ball, Warwick 2000. *Rome in the East. The Transformation of an Empire.* London: Routledge. 1-4, 28, 51, 130, 132, 397-398.

Bandaranayake, Senake, et al (eds.) 1990. *Sri Lanka and the Silk Road of the Sea.* Colombo: Sri Lanka National Commission for Unesco and the Central Cultural Fund. 291 p.

Bar-Yosef, O. 2002. The Upper Paleolithic revolution. *Annual Review of Anthropology* 31(1): 363-393.

Barthelemy de Saizieu, B. and A. Bouquillon 1995. Les matériaux utilises pour les parures à Mundigak (Afghanistan) de 4000 à 2500 av. J.-C. *In:* Tallon, Francoise (ed.). *Les pierres précieuses de l'Orient ancien des Sumériens aux Sassanides.* Paris: Réunion des Musees Nationaux: 47-50.

—2000. Emergence et évolution des matériaux vitrifiés dans la région de l'Indus du 5th au 3rd millénaire (Mehrgarh-Nausharo). *Paléorient* 26(2): 93-111.

Bass, G.F. 1991 Evidence of trade from Bronze Age shipwrecks. *In:* Gale, N.H. (ed.). Bronze Age Trade in the Mediterrranean. *Studies in Mediterranean Archaeology* 90. Jonsered, Sweden: Paul Astroms Forlag. 69-81.

—**C. Pulak, D. Collon and J. Weinstein** 1989 The Bronze Age Shipwreck at Ulu Burun: 1986 campaign. *American Journal of Archaeology* 93: 1-29.

Beck, Horace C. 1928. *Classification and Nomenclature of Beads and Pendants.* Reprinted 1981 by Shumway Publications, York, Penn.

—1941. The Beads from Taxila. Delhi, *Memoirs of the Archaeological Survey of India.*

—1976. The magical properties of beads. *The Bead Journal* 2(4): 32-39.

Becker, Andrea 1993. *Uruk. Kleinfunde I. Stein.* Mainz am Rhein: Verlag Philipp von Zarern: Taf I.

Beglova, Jelena 2002. Kopflos und gefesselt—Bestattungen der ganz anderen Art. *Antike Welt* 33(3): 297-304.

Bellwood, Peter 1997. *Prehistory of the Indo-Malaysian Archipelago,* Rev. ed. Honolulu: University of Hawai'i Press. 294-295.

—1999. Southeast Asia before history. *In:* Tarling, Nicholas (ed.). *The Cambridge History of Southeast Asia.* Vol. 1. Cambridge, U.K.: Cambridge University Press. 55-136.

Benea, Doina 1997. Die Glasperlenwerkstatten von *Tibiscum* und die Handelsbeziehungen mit dem Barbicum. *In:* von Freeden, Uta and Alfried Wieczorek (eds.), *Perlen.* Bonn: Rudolf Habett.

Berlin 2000. *Personal observation* at the Berlin Museum for Prehistory and Early History. Berlin, Germany.

Bertram, Marion 1995. *Merowingerzeit: Die Alterurmer im Museum fur Vor- und Fruhgeschichte.* Mainz: Verlag Philipp von Zabern. 115 p.

Bienkowski, Piotr and Alan Millard (eds.). 2000. *Dictionary of the Ancient Near East.* Philadelphia: University of Pennsylvania Press. 342 p.

Black, Jeremy and Anthony Green 1992. *Gods, Demons and Symbols of Ancient Mesopotamia: An Illustrated Dictionary.* Austin: University of Texas Press. 107-108. 115-116.

Boda, Yang 1994. *Chinese Archaic Jades From the Kwan Collection.* Hong Kong: Art Gallery, The Chinese University of Hong Kong. 163.

Bonatz, Dominik, Hartmut Kuhne, and As'ad Mahmoud 1998. *Rivers and Steppes: Cultural Heritage and Environment of the Syrian Jezireh.* Damascus: Ministry of Culture.

Boric, Dusan 2002. Apotropaism and the temporality of colours: colourful Mesolithic-Neolithic seasons in the Danube gorges. *In:* Jones, Andrew and Gavin MacGregor (eds.) *Colouring the Past: The Significance of Colour in Archaeological Research.* New York: Berg.

Braghin, Cecilia 1998. An archaeological investigation into ancient Chinese beads. *In:* Sciama, Lidia D. and Joanne B. Eicher (eds.). *Beads and Bead Makers: Gender, Material Culture and Meaning.* Oxford, U.K.: Berg. 273-293.

—2002. Polychrome and monochrome glass of the Warring States and Han periods. *In:* Braghin, Cecilia (ed.). *Chinese Glass: Archaeological Studies on the Uses and Social Context of Glass Artefacts form the Warring States to the Northern Song Period (fifth century BC to twelfth century AD).* Firenze: Leo S. Olschki Editore. 3-45.

Brill, Robert H. 1999. *Chemical Analyses of Early Glasses.* Volume 2. Corning, NY: Corning Museum of Glass. 337, 395, 397.

—2001. Chemical analysis of some glasses from the collection of Simon Kwan. *In:* Kwan, Simon 2001. *Early Chinese Glass.* Hong Kong: Art Museum, The Chinese University of Hong Kong. 450.

—**Robert D. Vocke, Jr., Wang Shixiong, and Zhang Fukang** 1991. A note on lead-isotope analyses of faience beads from China. *Journal of Glass Studies* 33: 116-118.

Bunker, Emma C. 1995. Chinese luxury goods enhanced: Fifth century B.C.- first century A.D. *In:* So, Jenny F. and Emma C. Bunker (eds.). *Traders and Raiders on China's Northern Frontier.* Washington, D.C.: Arthur M. Sackler Gallery, Smithsonian Institution. 69-75.

Callmer, Johan 1977. Trade Beads and Bead Trade in Scandinavia ca. 800-1000 AD. *Acta Archaeologica Lundensia.* Lund: CWK Gleerup. 98.

—1995. The influx of oriental beads into Europe during the 8th century AD. *In:* Rasmussen, Marianne, Ulla L. Hansen, and Ulf Nasman (eds.). *Glass Beads: Cultural History, Technology, Experiment and Analogy.* Studies in Technology and Culture 2. Lejre: Historical-Archaeological Experimental Centre. 49-54.

—2002. *After the big wave: some Oriental millefiori beads in Northern and Eastern Europe of the late tenth and early eleventh centuries.* Presented at the 2nd Nordic Glass Bead Symposium, August, 2002. Copenhagen.

Cambridge 2001. *Personal observation* at the Harvard Semitic Museum. Cambridge, Mass.

Cameron, Averil 1985. *Procopius and the Sixth Century.* Berkeley: University of California Press. 66.

Carboni, Stefano 2001a. *Glass from Islamic Lands.* New York: Thames and Hudson. 15-17, 19-20, 29

—2001b. Glass production in the Islamic world: a historical overview. *In*: Carboni, Stefano and David Whitehouse. *Glass of the Sultans.* New York: Metropolitan Museum of Art. 3-7.

Casanova, Michele 2000. Le lapis-lazuli de l'Asie centrale à la Syrie au Chalcolithique et à l'âge du Bronze: traits communs et particularités régionales. *In*: Matthiae, Paolo, Alessandra Enea, Luca Peyronel, and Frances Pinnock (eds.). *Proceedings of the First International Congress on the Archaeology of the Ancient Near East.* Rome, May 18th-23rd, 1998. Rome: Dipartimento di Scienze Storiche, Archeologiche e Antropologiche Dell'antichità. 171-183.

Cauvin, Jacques 2000. *The Birth of the Gods and the Origins of Agriculture.* Cambridge: Cambridge University Press. xviii,1-8.

Chakrabarti, Dilip K. 1990. *The External Trade of the Indus Civilization.* New Delhi: Munshiram Manoharial Publishers. 183 p.

Chami, Felix A. 1999. Roman beads from the Rufiji Delta, Tanzania: first incontrovertible archaeological link with the Periplus. *Current Anthropology* 40(2): 237-241.

Childs-Johnson, Elizabeth 2001. *Enduring Art of Jade Age China: Chinese Jades of Late Neolithic through Han Periods.* New York: Throckmorton Fine Art. 13-18.

Chung, Tang (ed.) 1998. *East Asian Jade: Symbol of Excellence.* Hong Kong: Chinese University of Hong Kong.

Collon, Dominique 1996. Mesopotamia and the Indus: the evidence of the seals. *In*: Reade, Julian (ed.). *The Indian Ocean in Antiquity.* London: Kegan Paul. 209-225.

—2001. How seals were worn and carried: The archaeological and iconographic evidence. *In*: Hallo, William W. and Irene J. Winter (eds.) *Seals and Seal Impressions.* Bethesda, MD: CDL Press. 15-30

Copenhagen 2002. *Personal observation* at the National Museum, August 2002. Copenhagen, Denmark.

Damerji, Muayad S.B. 1999. Graber Assyrischer Koniginnen aus Nimrud. Mainz: *Jahrbuch des Romisch-Germanischen Zentralmuseums* 45. Abb. 25,30.

Dixon, J.E., J.R. Cann and Colin Renfrew 1998. Obsidian and the origins of trade. *In*: Reprint. Fagan, Brian M. (ed.). *Avenues to Antiquity.* Readings from *Scientific American*. San Francisco: W.H. Freeman, 1975.

Doyel, David E. 1991. Hohokam exchange and interaction. Crown, Patricia L. and W. James Judge (eds.). *Chaco & Hohokam: Prehistoric Regional Systems in the American Southwest.* Santa Fe: School of American Research Press. 225-252.

Douglas, Janet, Blythe McCarthy and Insook Lee 2002. Gokok. Korean stone and glass comma-shaped beads at the Freer Gallery of Art. *Ornament* 25(4): 34-39.

Dubin, Lois S. 1987. *The History of Beads from 30,000 BC to the Present.* London: Thames and Hudson. 364 p.

Dussubieux, Laure and Bernard Gratuze 2001. Analysis of glass from the Indian world and from Southeast Asia. *BSTN* 37: 8-9.

Eisen, Gustavus A. 1916. The characteristics of eye beads from the earliest times to the present. *Journal of the Archaeological Institute of America* 20(1): 1-27.

—1930a. Lotus and melon beads. *American Journal of Archaeology* 34(1): 20-43.

—1930b. Antique fig-beads. *American Journal of Archaeology* 34(2): 1-7.

—and Fahim Kouchakji 1927. *Glass: Its Origin, History, Chronology, Technic and Classification to the Sixteenth Century.* Volume I. New York: William Rudge.

Erickson, Bruce 1998. Special objects: glass, bone artifacts, terracotta jewelry. *In*: Carter, Joseph C. (ed.) *The Chora of Metaponto: the Necropoleis.* Austin: University of Texas Press. 835-838.

Ethelberg, Per 1995. The glass beads from the Skovgarde cemetery. *In*: Rasmussen, Marianne, Ulla L. Hansen, and Ulf Nasman (eds.). *Glass Beads: Cultural History, Technology, Experiment and Analogy. Studies in Technology and Culture 2.* Lejre: Historical-Archaeological Experimental Centre. 91-94.

— 2000. Skovgarde: Ein Bestattungsplatz mit reichen Frauengrabern des 3.Jhs. n.Chr. auf Seeland. Kobenhavn: *Det Knogelige Nordiske Oldskriftselskab:* 246, 284.

Fiandra, Enrica 2000. Before Seals. *In*: Matthiae, Paolo, Alessandra Enea, Luca Peyronel, and Frances Pinnock (eds.) *Proceedings of the First International Congress on the Archaeology of the Ancient Near East. Rome, May 18th-23rd, 1998.* Rome: Dipartimento di Scienze Storiche, Archeologiche e Antropologiche Dell'Antichita. Figure 4.

Fischer, Alysia and W. Patrick McCray 1999. Glass production activities as practised at Sepphoris, Israel (37 BC-AD 1516). *Journal of Archaeological Science* 26: 893-905.

Foglini, Laura and Massimo Vidale 2000. Reconsidering the lapis-lazuli working areas of Sharh-i Sokhta. *In*: Matthiae, Paolo, Alessandra Enea, Luca Peyronel, and Frances Pinnock (eds.) *Proceedings of the First International Congress on the Archaeology of the Ancient Near East. Rome, May 18th-23rd, 1998.* Rome: Dipartimento di Scienze Storiche, Archeologiche e Antropologiche Dell'Antichita. 471-479.

Forsyth, Angus 1995. Neolithic Chinese jades. *In*: Keverne, Roger (ed.) *Jade.* London: Lorenz Books. 53-87.

Fortin, Michel 1999. *Syria: Land of Civilizations.* Quebec: Les Editions de L'Homme. 94, 152.

Francis, Peter Jr. 1980. Bead report II: etched beads in Iran. *Ornament* 4(3): 24-28.

—1988a. Nishapur: an Early Islamic city of Iran. *Ornament* 12(2): 78-93.

—1988b. Some news about old beads. *Ornament* 11(4): 34-35, 70-76.

—1989a. Mantai: Bead crossroads of the Medieval world. *Ornament* 12 (3): 82-91.

—1989b. Beads of the Early Islamic period. *Beads* 1: 21-39.

—1990. Beadmaking in Islam: the African trade and the rise of Hebron. *Beads* 2: 15-28.

—1993. Southeast Asian glass beads and the western connection. *The Margaretologist* 6(2): 7-9.

—1996. Some notes on articles in Beads: Beads of the Early Islamic period. *Bead Forum* 28: 10.

—1997. Ancient Mexican burials. *Ornament* 20(3): 80-81.

—1999. Middle Eastern glass beads: A new paradigm. *The Margaretologist* 12(2): 2-11.

—2000-1. The stone bead industry of southern India. *Beads* 2000-2001: 46-62.

—2002a. *Asia's Maritime Bead Trade.* Honolulu: University of Hawai'i Press. 45, 135, 210-220,

—2002b. Beads. *In*: Bacharach, Jere L. Fustat Finds: *Beads, Coins, Medical Instruments, Textiles, and Other Artifacts from the Awad Collection.* Cairo: The American University in Cairo Press. 12-31.

—2002c. *The bead trade in the Indian Ocean, with special reference to Berenike, Egypt* (Pt.3). www.thebeadsite.com/ABM-RIO3.html.

Francis 2002. *Personal communication,* September, 2002. Washington DC.

Frape, Christopher J. (ed.) 2000. *Burnished Beauty: The Art of Stone in Early Southeast Asia.* Bangkok: Orchid Press. 35.

Fukai, Shinji 1985. *Persian Glass Beads.* Tokyo: Tankosha. (in Japanese). Plate 18.

Fukang, Zhang 1991. Scientific studies of early glasses excavated in China.

In: Brill, Robert H. and John H. Martin (eds.) *Scientific Research in Early Chinese Glass*. Corning: The Corning Museum of Glass. 157-162.

Gale, N.H. (ed.). 1991. Bronze Age Trade in the Mediterranean. *Studies in Mediterranean Archaeology* 90. Papers presented at the conference held at Rawley House, Oxford, in December 1989. Jonsered, Sweden: Paul Astroms Forlag. 402 p.

Gessler, Trisha 1988. Precolumbian Jewelry from Peru. *Ornament* 11(3): 50-55.

Glover, Ian C. 1990. Ban Don Ta Phet: the 1984-85 excavation. *In*: Glover, Ian C. and E. Glover (eds.) *Southeast Asian Archaeology 1986*: 139-83.

—1996. The archeological evidence for early trade between South and Southeast Asia. *In*: Reade, Julian (ed.). *The Indian Ocean in Antiquity*. London, New York: Kegan Paul International. 365-400.

—**and Julian Henderson** 1995. Early glass in South and South East Asia and China. *In*: Scott, R. and J. Guy (eds.) *China and Southeast Asia: Art, Commerce and Interaction*. London: Percival David Foundation of Chinese Art. 141-170.

Goldstein, Sidney M. 1979. *Pre-Roman and Early Roman Glass in The Corning Museum of Glass*. Corning, NY: The Corning Museum of Glass. 47-48, 112, 114, 186-187, 269, 270.

Gore, Rick 1984. The dead do tell tales at Vesuvius. *National Geographic* 165(5): 557-613.

Gorin-Rosen, Yael 2000. The ancient glass industry in Israel: summary of the finds and new discoveries. *In*: Nenna, Marie-Dominique (ed.). *La Route du Verre*. Lyon: Maison del'Orient méditerranéen.; Paris: Boccard. 49-63.

Green, Peter 1991. *Alexander of Macedon, 356-323 BC: A Historical Biography*. Berkeley: University of California Press. 386

Grose, David F. 1989. *The Toledo Museum of Art: Early Ancient Glass*. New York: Hudson Hills Press. 48, 58-59, 78, 88-92, 110, 189-190, 257-260, 346, 353.

Guatemala 1998. *Personal observation* at the National Museum of Archeology and Ethnology. Guatemala City.

Guido, Margaret 1978. *The Glass Beads of the Prehistoric and Roman Periods in Britain and Ireland: A Preliminary Visual Classification of the More Definitive and Diagnostic Types*. Reports of the Research Committee of the Society of Antiquaries of London No. 35. London: The Society of Antiquaries. 250 p.

—1999. *The Glass Beads of Anglo-Saxon England: c. AD 400-700*. 72, 78, 79,

Gupta, Sunil 1999. Indo-Pacific beads in Japan. *BSTN* 34: 11-14.

—2000. New analyses of Indo-Pacific beads and glass waste from Arikamedu, India. *BSTN* 35: 8-9.

Gwinnett, A. John and Leonard Gorelick 1989. Evidence for mass production polishing in ancient bead manufacture. *Archeomaterials* 3(2): 163-168.

—1993. Beads, scarabs, and amulets: Methods of manufacture in ancient Egypt. *Journal of the American Research Center in Egypt* 30: 125-132.

—1998-1999. A brief history of drills and drilling. *Beads* 10-11: 49-56.

Haevernick, Thea E. 1987. *Glasperlen der Vorromischen Eisenzeit II: Ringaugenperlen und Verwandte Perlengruppen*. Marburg: Dr. Wolfram Hitzeroth Verlag. 23, 25.

Hajime, Inagaki 2001. Ancient glass in China. *In: Miho Museum: Catalogue of Ancient Glass*. Shiga Prefecture: Miho Museum. 217 p.

Hall, Kenneth R. 1999. Economic history of early Southeast Asia. *In*: Tarling, Nicholas *The Cambridge History of Southeast Asia*. Cambridge: Cambridge University Press. 183-275.

Hansen, Donald P. 1998. Art of the Royal Tombs of Ur. a brief interpretation. *In*: Zettler, Richard L. and Lee Horne (eds.). *Treasures of the Royal Tombs of Ur*. Philadelphia: University of Pennsylvania Museum of Archeology and Anthropology. 42-47.

Harden, D.B. 1967. Some aspects of Pre-Roman mosaic glass. *Annales du 4e*

Congres de l'Association Internationale pour l'Histoire du Verre. Liege: AIHV. 29-38.

Hayden, Brian 1995. The emergence of prestige technologies and pottery. *In*: Barnett, William K. and John W. Hoopes (eds.) *The Emergence of Pottery*. Washington: Smithsonian Institution Press. 257-265.

Haywood, John 1998a. *Historical Atlas of the Classical World: 500 BC- AD 600*. Reprinted 2001: New York: Barnes and Noble. 2.14.

— 1998b. *Historical Atlas of the Medieval World: AD 600-1492*. Reprinted 2001: New York: Barnes and Noble. 3.14.

Heck, M. and H. Hoffmann 2000. Coloured opaque glass beads of the Merovingians. *Archaeometry* 42(2): 341-357.

Hedge, K.T.M., R.V. Karanth, and S.P. Sychanthavong 1982. On the composition and technology of Harappan microbeads. *In*: Possehl, G.L. (ed.) *Harappan Civilization*. New Delhi: Oxford and IBH Publishing Co. 239-244.

Hencken, Hugh 1978. *Mecklenburg Collection, Part II: The Iron Age Cemetery of Magdalenska gora in Slovenia*. Cambridge, MA: Peabody Museum of Archaeology and Ethnology. 125, 182.

Henderson, Julian 1995a. Glass production in Raqqa, Syria. New evidence for an interim assessment. *Annales du 13e Congres de l'Association Internationale pour l'Histoire du Verre*. Lochem: AIHV. 257-268.

—1995b. The scientific analysis of glass beads. *In*: Rasmussen, Marianne, Ulla L. Hansen, and Ulf Nasman (eds.). *Glass Beads: Cultural History, Technology, Experiment and Analogy. Studies in Technology and Culture 2*. Lejre: Historical-Archaeological Experimental Centre. 67-73.

Henshilwood, C.S. (in press). *The Origins of Modern Human Behaviour: Exploring Alternatives*. Volume in honour of Randi Haaland. BAR series. Bergen, Norway: University of Bergen.

—**F.E. d'Errico, C.W. Marean, R.G. Milo and R. Yates** 2001. An early bone tool industry from the Middle Stone Age at Blombos Cave, South Africa: implications for the origins of modern human behaviour, symbolism and language. *Journal of Human Evolution* 41: 631-678.

Hiebert, Fredrik T. 1994. *Origins of the Bronze Age Oasis Civilization in Central Asia*. Cambridge, MA: Peabody Museum of Archaeology and Ethnology. 139, 148.

Higham, Charles and Rachanie Thosarat 1998. *Prehistoric Thailand: From Early Settlement to Sukhothai*. Bangkok: River Books. 78-89.

Ho Chi Minh City 2001. *Personal observation*, Ho Chi Minh City History Museum. These beads were on display at the Museum, but are not illustrated in Malleret's publication of the excavations. Ho Chi Minh City, Vietnam.

Holder, Ian 1982 *Symbols in Action: Ethnological Studies of Material Culture*. Cambridge, U.K.: Cambridge University Press. 244 p.

—1997. *On the Surface. Catalhoyuk 1993-1995*. Cambridge, U.K.: McDonald Institute for Archaeological Research.

Horicht, Lucia A.S. 1989. *I Monili di Ercolano*. Roma: "L'Erma" di Bretschneider. 94.

Horton, M.C. 1996 Early maritime trade and settlement along the coasts of eastern Africa. In: Reade, Julian (ed.). *The Indian Ocean in Antiquity*. London: Kegan Paul International. 439-459.

Huot, J.L., V. Pardo, and A. Rougeulle 1980. A propos de la perle L76.5 de Larsa: les perles a quatre spirales. *Iraq* 42(2): 121-129.

Insoll, Timothy 1996. Islam, Archaeology and History: Gao Region (Mali) ca. AD 900-1250. *Cambridge Monographs in African Archaeology* 39. Oxford: BAR.

—1998. Islamic glass from Gao, Mali. *Journal of Glass Studies* 40: 77-88.

Jernigan, E. Wesley 1978. *Jewelry of the Prehistoric Southwest*. School of American Research, Santa Fe. Albuquerque: university of New Mexico Press. 260 p.

Katsuhiko, Oga and Sunil Gupta 2000. The Far East, Southeast and South Asia: Indo-Pacific beads from Yayoi tombs as indicators of early maritime exchange. *South Asian Studies* 16: 73-88.

Kenoyer, Jonathan M. 1986. The Indus bead industry: contributions to bead technology. *Ornament* 10(1): 18-23.

—1992. Lapis lazuli beadmaking in Afghanistan and Pakistan. *Ornament* 15(3): 71-73, 86.

—1997. Trade and technology of the Indus Valley: new insights from Harappa, Pakistan. *World Archaeology* 29(2): 262-280.

—1998. *Ancient Cities of the Indus Valley Civilization.* Karachi: Oxford University Press; Islamabad: American Institute of Pakistan Studies. 262 p.

—in press. Bead technologies at Harappa, 3300-1900 BC: A comparative summary. *In*: Jarrige, C. and Vincent Lefevre (eds.) *South Asian Archaeology 2001.*

—and M. Vidale 1992. A new look at stone drills of the Indus Valley tradition. *In*: Vandiver, P. et al (eds.) *Materials Issues in Art and archaeology, III.* Pittsburgh: Materials Research Society. 495-518.

—M. Vidale, and K.K. Bhan 1991. Contemporary stone bead making in Khambhat, India: patterns of craft specialization and organization of production as reflected in the archaeological record. *World Archaeology* 23(1): 44-63.

Kessler, Earl and Shari Kessler 1978. Beads of the Tairona. *The Bead Journal* 3(3/4): 2-5, 81-86.

Koch, U. 1997. Polychrome Perlen in Württemberg/Nordbaden. *In*: Freeden, Uta von and Alfried Wieczorek (eds.) *Perlen: Archäologie, Techniken, Analysen. Akten des Internationalen Perlensymposiums in Mannheim vom 11. bis 14. November 1994.* Bonn: Dr. Rudolf Habelt GmbH. Tafel 5.

Kovalevskaya, Vera B. 2000. *Komputernaya Obrabotka Massovovo Archeologicheskovo Materiala iz Rannesrednevekovik Pamyatikov Evrazi.* Moscow: Russian Academy Archaeological Institute. 93, 94,

Kröger, Jens 1995. *Nishapur: Glass of the Early Islamic Period.* New York: Metropolitan Museum of Art. 1-37, 191-201.

Kuhn, Steven L., Mary C. Stiner, David S. Reese, and Erksin Gulec 2001. Ornaments of the earliest Upper Paleolithic: New insights from the Levant. *Proceedings of the National Academy of Science* 98(13): 7641-7646.

Kwan, Simon 2001. *Early Chinese Glass.* Hong Kong: Art Museum, Chinese University of Hong Kong. 117-121, 188-193.

Kwan 2001. *Personal communication* from Dr. Simon Kwan. Hong Kong.

Kyiv 2000 *Personal observation* at the National Museum of Ukrainian History. Kyiv, Ukraine.

Lankton, James W. 2001. Early beads in Korean national museums, part 1. *BSTN* 38: 3-7.

—2002. Early beads in Korean national museums, part 2. *BSTN* 40: 3-6.

—2004 *A new look at the glass beads from Nuzi.*(In preparation).

—**In-Sook Lee, and Jamey D. Allen** 2003. *Indonesian (Jatim) glass beads in early sixth century Korean tombs.* Poster presentation at AIHV 2003. London, September 2003.

Lee, In-Sook 1997. Early glass in Korean archaeological sites. *Korean and Korean American Studies Bulletin* 8(1/2): 14-23.

—2001. Academic Investigation Report Volume 14. *Nam-Gang Dam Reservoir Area Excavation Report* No. 8. (in Korean). 326-329.

Lee, Yun K. and Naicheng Zhu 2002. Social integration of religion and ritual in prehistoric China. *Antiquity* 76: 715-723.

Leiden 2002 *Personal observation* at the National Museum of Antiquities. Leiden, Netherlands.

Lilyquist, C. and R.H. Brill 1993. *Studies in Early Egyptian Glass.* New York: Metropolitan Museum of Art. 80 p.

Liu, Robert K. 1975. Ancient Chinese glass beads. *The Bead Journal* 2(2): 11.

—1985. Identification: broadwing pendants. *Ornament* 9(2): 26-27.

—1995. *Collectible Beads. A Universal Aesthetic.* Vista, CA: Ornament. 256 p.

—1996-1997. Ancient Chinese Glass Ornaments. Research, Looting and

Collecting. *Jewelry* 1: 25-39, Pl. 2.

—1997. The Beaded Universe: Strands of Culture. *Ornament* 20(3): 58-59.

—1999a. Bead Report: Breast beads. *Ornament* 23(2): 70-71, 73.

—1999b. Exhibition review: Jade in ancient Costa Rica. *Ornament* 22(4): 19.

—1999c. Collectible beads: Leech beads.*Ornament* 22(4): 8-10.

—2000a. Comparisons of ancient faience ornaments. *Ornament* 23(3): 56-61.

—2000b. Ancient Arts. Precolumbian greenstone beads. *Ornament* 24(1): 28-29.

—2002. Ancient arts. Slit-ring earrings. *Ornament* 26(1): 38-39.

Lothal 1999. *Personal observation* at the Lothal Museum. Lothal, India.

Lordkipanidze, O. 2002. The "Akhalgori Hoard": an attempt at dating and historical interpretation. *Archaeologische Mitteilungen aus Iran und Turan* 33: 143-190. 151.

Lucas, A. and J.R. Harris 1962. *Ancient Egyptian Materials and Industries* (4th ed. revised). Mineola, NY: Dover Publications, Inc., reprint 1999.

Lugalbanda 2003. *Lugalbanda and the Anzu bird.* www.gatewaystobabylon.com/myths/texts/classic/lugalanzu.htm

L'vova, Zlata 1997. A rare group of 11th century glass beads from the southern part of Russia. *In*: Freeden, Uta von and Alfried Wieczorek (eds.) *Perlen: Archaologie, Techniken, Analysen. Akten des Internationalen Perlensymposiums in Mannheim vom 11. bis 14. November 1994.* Bonn: Dr. Rudolf Habelt GmbH. 252-258.

Mackay, E. 1933. Bead making in ancient Sind. *Journal of the American Oriental Society* 57: 1-15.

Magnavita, Sonja 1999. Beads from the Iron Age graves of Kissi, NE Burkina Faso. *Bead Forum* 35: 4-11.

Masson, V.M. and T.P. Kiiatkina 1981. Man at the dawn of civilization. *In*: Kohl, Philip L. (ed.) *The Bronze Age Civilization of Central Asia: Recent Soviet Discoveries.* Armonk, NY: M.E. Sharpe, Inc. 123.

Matabaev, B. Ch. 1998. Fruhmittelalterliche Brabstatten im nordlichen Fergana-Tal, Uzbekistan. *Archaeologische Mitteilungen aus Iran und Turan* 30: 269-306.

Maxwell-Hyslop, K.R. 1971. *Western Asiatic Jewellery c. 3000-612 BC.* London: Methuen and Co. Ltd. 194,

McCray, Patrick (ed.) 1998. *The Prehistory and History of Glassmaking Technology.* Westerville, OH: American Ceramic Society.

Meconcelli Notarianni, Gioia 1999. *Vetri Antichi: Arte e Tecnica.* Bologna: Museo Civico Archeologico. 6,

Mellaart, J. 1967. *Catal Huyuk: A Neolithic Town in Anatolia.* London: Thames & Hudson.

Merpert, N. Ya and R.M. Munchaev 1993a. Yarim Tepe I: The Lower Hassuna levels. *In*: Yoffe, Norman and Jeffery J. Clark (eds.) *Early Stages in the Evolution of Mesopotamian Civilization: Soviet Excavations in Northern Iraq.* Tucson: University of Arizona Press. 113.

—1993b. Yarim Tepe II: The Halaf levels. *In*: Yoffe, Norman and Jeffery J. Clark (eds.) *Early Stages in the Evolution of Mesopotamian Civilization: Soviet Excavations in Northern Iraq.* Tucson: University of Arizona Press. 128-163.

Moore, A.M.T., G.C. Hillman, and A.J. Legge 2000. *Village on the Euphrates: From Foraging to Farming at Abu Hureyra.* Oxford: Oxford University Press. 258-259, 286-292, 478.

Moorey, P.R.S. 1994. *Ancient Mesopotamian Materials and Industries: The Archaeological Evidence.* Oxford: Clarendon Press. 83, 168-171.

Musche, Brigitte 1992. *Vorderasiatischer Schmuck von den Anfangen bis zur Zeit der Achaemeniden (ca. 10,000-330 v.Chr).* Leiden: E.J. Brill. Taf. LXIII,

Naples 1998. *Personal observation,* Archaeological Museum of Naples. Naples, Italy.

Negahban, Ezat O. 1998. Suggestions on the origin and background of the Marlik culture. *Iranica Antiqua* 33: 43-55.

Nenna, Marie-Dominique 1999. *Les verres.* Athens: Ecole Française d'Athenes: 216 p.

— Maurice Picon, and Michèle Vichy 2000. *Ateliers primaires et secondaires en Egypte à l'époque Gréco-Romaine*. *In*: Nenna, Marie-Dominique (ed.) *La route du verre*. Lyon: Maison de l'Orient méditerranéen; Paris: Boccard. 97-112.

New York 2002. *Personal observation* of beads on display at the Metropolitan Museum of Art. New York City.

Nicholson, Paul T. and Ian Shaw (eds.) 2000. *Ancient Egyptian Materials* and *Technology*. Cambridge: Cambridge University Press.

Oakley, Kenneth 1965. Folklore of Fossils. *Antiquity* 39: 9-18, 117-125.

Oates, David, Joan Oates, and Helen McDonald 1997. *Excavations at Tell Brak. Vol.1: The Mitanni and Old Babylonian Periods*. Cambridge: McDonald Institute for Archaeological Research. 246-247.

Odessa 1999. *Personal observation* at the Odessa Archaeological Museum. Odessa, Ukraine.

Opper, Marie-Jose 2003. Sea urchin beads. *Bead Bulletin. Newsletter of the Bead Museum and the Bead Society of Greater Washington*. 20(1): 10.

—**and Howard Opper** 1993a. Powdered-glass beads and bead trade in Mauritania. *Beads* 5: 33-44.

—1993b. *Gougad-Pateraenneu: Old Talisman Necklaces from Brittany, France*. Washington DC: Bead Society of Greater Washington. 1-18.

Pendergast, David M. 1998-99. Dressed to kill: jade beads and pendants in the Maya lowlands. *Beads* 10-11: 3-12.

Pettinato, Giovanni 1991. *Ebla: A New Look at History*. Baltimore: Johns Hopkins University Press. 113.

Pfeiffer, John E. 1982. *The Creative Explosion: An Inquiry into the Origins of Art and Religion*. New York: Harper & Row. 270 p.

Pinder-Wilson, R.H. and George T. Scanlon 1973. Glass finds from Fustat: 1964-71. *Journal of Glass Studies* 15: 12-30.

—1987. Glass finds from Fustat: 1972-80. *Journal of Glass Studies* 29: 61-71.

Pittman, Holly 1998. Jewelry. *In*: Zettler, Richard L. and Lee Horne (eds.) *Treasures from the Royal Tombs of Ur*. Philadelphia: University of Pennsylvania Museum. 114, 118.

Possehl, Gregory L. 1996. Meluhha. *In*: Reade, Julian (ed.). *The Indian Ocean in Antiquity*. London: Kegan Paul International. 133-208.

—2002. *The Indus Civilization: A Contemporary Perspective*. Walnut Creek, Calif.: Altamira Press. 215-218.

Price, Jennifer 1998. The social context of glass production in Roman Britain. *In*: McCray, Patrick (ed.) *The Prehistory and History of Glassmaking Technology*. Westerville, OH: American Ceramic Society. 331-348.

Puttock, Sonia 2002. Ritual Significance of Personal Ornament in Roman Britain. *BAR British Series* 327. London: BAR. 94-97.

Reade, Julian (ed.) 1996. *The Indian Ocean in Antiquity*. London; New York: Kegan Paul International in association with the British Museum, London: distributed by Columbia University Press. 523 p.

Renfrew, Colin and Paul Bahn 2000. *Archaeology: Theories, Methods, and Practice*. New York: Thames and Hudson. 175.

Rice, Patty C. 1993. *Amber. The Golden Gem of the Ages*. New York: The Kosciuszko Foundation. 3rd Printing, with revisions. Originally published by Van Nostrand Reinhold 1980.

Rodziewicz, M. 1984. *Alexandrie III: Les habitations romaines tardives d'Alexandrie a la lumiere des fouilles polonaises a Kom el-Dikka*. Warsaw.

Rose, Lois R. 2002 *Deciphering King Solomon's Knot: Beadwork Symbol Supreme*. Bead Expo 2002.

Rothman, Mitchell S. 2002. *Tepe Gawra: The Evolution of a Small, Prehistoric Center in Northern Iraq*. Philadelphia: University of Pennsylvania, Museum of Archaeology and Anthropology. 8, Plates 29, 37, 56.

Roualt, Olivier and Maria G. Masetti-Roualt 1993. *L'Eufrate e il tempo: Le civilta del medio Eufrate e della Gezira siriana*. Milano: Electa.

Roy, B. and Timothy Insoll 1998. *BSTN* 32: 4-7.

Saldern, Axel von 1980. *Ancient and Byzantine Glass from Sardis*. Cambridge, MA: Harvard University Press. Plate 19, # 847.

Scanlon, George T. and Ralph Pinder-Wilson 2001. *Fustat Glass of the Early Islamic Period*. London: Altajir World of Islam Trust. 118-123.

Schienerl, Peter W. 1985. Cornerless cube stone beads in Egypt and Palestine. *The Bead Forum* (7): 8-9.

Schmandt-Besserat, Denise 1992. *Before Writing. Volume I: From Counting to Cuneiform*. Austin: University of Texas Press. 184, 195-199.

Schwartz, Glenn M. 2001. Syria and the Uruk Expansion. *In*: Rothman, Mitchell S. (ed.) *Uruk Mesopotamia and its Neighbors: Cross-Cultural Interactions in the Era of State Formation*. Santa Fe: School of American Research Press. 255.

Sciama, Lidia D. and Joanne B. Eicher 1998. *Beads and Bead Makers: Gender, Material Culture and Meaning*. Oxford: Berg. 317 pages.

Seefried, Monique 1979. Glass core pendants found in the Mediterranean area. *Journal of Glass Studies* 21: 17-26.

—1982. *Les pendentifs en verre sur noyau des pays de la Méditerranée antique*. Collection de l'Ecole Française de Rome 57. 186 p.

Seitz, R., G.E. Harlow, V.B. Sisson and K.E. Taube 2001. 'Olmec Blue' and Formative jade sources: new discoveries in Guatemala. *Antiquity* 75(289).

Seligman, C. G. and H. C. Beck 1938. Far eastern glass: some western origins. *Bulletin of the Museum of Far Eastern Antiquities* 10: 1-64.

Sen, S.N. and Mamata Chaudhuri 1985. *Ancient Glass and India*. New Delhi: Indian National Science Academy. 201 p.

Sherratt, A. and S. Sherratt 1991. From luxuries to commodities: the nature of Bronze Age trading systems. *In*: Gale, N.H. (ed.) *Bronze Age Trade in the Mediterranean*. Jonsered: Paul Astroms Forlag. 351-386.

Shixiong, Wang 1991. Some glasses from Zhou Dynasty tombs in Fufeng County and Baoji, Shaanxi. *In*: Brill, Robert H. and John H. Martin (eds.) *Scientific Research in Early Chinese Glass*. Corning: The Corning Museum of Glass. 151-156.

Siegmund, Frank 1995. Merovingian beads on the lower Rhine. *Beads* 7: 37-53.

Spaer, Maud 1993. Some observations on "Fustat beads". *Bead Forum* 22: 4-11.

—2001. *Ancient Glass in the Israel Museum: Beads and Other Small Objects*. Jerusalem: The Israel Museum.

—2002. Some ubiquitous glass ornaments of the early centuries of the first millennium BC. *In*: Kordas, George (ed.) *Hyalos =Vitrum = Glass: History, Technology, and Conservation of Glass and Vitreous Materials in the Hellenic World*. Athens: Glasnet Publications. 56.

Squadrone, Filomena F. 2000. Metals for the dead. Metal finds from the Birecik Dam Early Bronze Age cemetery in the Middle Euphrates area, near Carchemish (Turkey). *In*: Matthiae, Paolo, Alessandra Enea, Luca Peyronel, and Frances Pinnock (eds.) *Proceedings of the First International Congress on the Archaeology of the Ancient Near East. Rome, May 18th-23rd, 1998*. Rome: Dipartimento di Scienze Storiche, Archeologiche e Antropologiche Dell'Antichita: 1541-1556.

Stern, E. Marianne 2001. *Roman, Byzantine, and Early Medieval Glass. Ernesto Wolf Collection*. Ostfildern-Ruit: Hatje Cantz. 386, 388.

—**and Birgit Schlick-Nolte** 1994. *Early Glass of the Ancient World. 1600 BC-AD 50. Ernesto Wolf Collection*. Ostfildern-Ruit: Dr. Cantz'sche Druckerei. 128-129.

Stout, Ann M. 1986. The archaeological context of Late Roman period mosaic glass face beads. *Ornament* 9(4): 58-61,76-77.

Talalay, Lauren E. 2000. Review Article: Cultural biographies of the Great Goddess. *American Journal of Archaeology* 104: 789-792.

Tallon, Francoise (ed.) 1995. Les pierres precieuses de l'Orient ancien des Sumeriens aux Sassanides. Paris: Reunion des Musees Nationaux. 80, 96,

Tatton-Brown, Veronica 1995. Some Greek and Roman pendants and beads in the British Museum. *In*: Rasmussen, Marianne, Ulla L. Hansen, and Ulf Nasman (eds.). *Glass Beads: Cultural History, Technology, Experiment and Analogy. Studies in Technology and Culture 2.* Lejre: Historical-Archaeological Experimental Centre. 37-43.

Theunisson, Robert 1998. Agate and carnelian ornaments from Noen U-Loke, Northeast Thailand: some thoughts on their social function and 'value'. *BSTN* 32: 8-10.

Thompson, Deidre M. 1995. Ancient Costa Rican Jade. *Ornament* 18(3): 52-55.

Toll, H. Wolcott 1991. Material distributions and excahnge in the Chaco system. *In*: Crown, Patricia L. and W. James Judge (eds.). *Chaco & Hohokam: Prehistoric Regional Systems in the American Southwest.* Santa Fe: School of American Research Press. 77-107.

Torbrugge, Walter 1968. *Prehistoric European Art.* New York: Harry N. Abrams.

Triantafyllidis, Pavlos 2002. *Rhodian Glassware I. The Luxury Hot-formed Transparent Vessels of the Classical and Early Hellenistic Period.* Athens.

Valiulina, Svetlana 2002. *The glass beads of pre-Mongolian Volga-Bulgaria.* Presented at the 2nd Nordic Glass Bead Symposium, August, 2002. Copenhagen.

Vandiver, Pamela B. 1983. Glass technology at the mid-second-millennium BC Hurrian site of Nuzi. *Journal of Glass Studies* 25: 236-247.

— and **W. David Kingery** 1986. Egyptian faience: the first high-tech ceramic. *In*: Kingery, W.D. and Esther Lense. *High Technology Ceramics: Past, Present, and Future.* Proceedings of the 88th Annual Meeting of the American Ceramic Society, held on Aril 29 and 30, 1986, in Chicago, Illinois. Westerville, OH: American Ceramic Society. 19-34.

— **McGuire Gibson, and Augusta Mc Mahon** 1995. Glass manufacture in the late third millennium BC at Nippur in Iraq. *In*: Vincenzini, P. (ed.) The Ceramics Cultural Heritage: *Proceedings of the International Symposium The Ceramics Heritage of the 8th CIMTEC-World Ceramics Congress and Forum on New Materials.* Faenza: Techna. 331-341.

Venclova, Natalie 1983. Prehistoric eye beads in Central Europe. *Journal of Glass Studies* 25: 11-17.

Vidale, Massimo 1995. Early beadmakers of the Indus tradition: the manufacturing sequence of talc beads at Mehrgarh in the 5th millennium BC. *East and West* 45(1-4): 45-80.

Vogt, Burkhard 1996. Bronze Age maritime trade in the Indian Ocean: Harappan traits on the Oman peninsula. *In*: Reade, Julian (ed.). *The Indian Ocean in Antiquity.* London: Kegan Paul International. 107-132.

Warmington, E.H. 1974. *The Commerce Between the Roman Empire and India.* 2nd ed., rev. and enl. Dehhi: Vikas Pub. House. 417 p.

Wegewitz, Willi 1994. *Das Abenteuer der Archäologie.* Oldenburg: Isensee Verlag. 339-341. (Excellent photograph of 8th-9th century beads from cemetery near Issendorf).

Weinberg, Gladys Davidson 1969. Glass manufacture in Hellenistic Rhodes. *Archaiologikon Deltion* 24: 143-151, Plates 76-88.

Welch, Martin 1999. Glass beads in early Anglo-Saxon contexts. *In*: Guido, Margaret. *The Glass Beads of Anglo-Saxon England c. AD 400-700.* London: Society of Antiquaries. 1-10.

White, Randall 1995. Ivory personal ornaments of Aurignacian age: technological, social and symbolic perspectives. *In*: Menu, M. P.Walter, and F Widemann (eds.) *Le Travail et l 'Usage de l'Ivoire au Paléolithique Supérieur.* Centre Universitaire Européen pour les Biens Culturels. Ravello, Italy. Also available at: www. insticeagestudies.com/Library/Ivory/ivory4.html.

—2003. *Prehistoric Art: The Symbolic Journey of Humankind.* New York: Harry N. Abrams.

Whitehouse, David 1997. *Roman Glass in The Corning Museum of Glass.* Volume One. Corning: The Corning Museum of Glass. 283-285.

—2001. Mosaic glass. *In*: Carboni, Stefano and David Whitehouse. *Glass of the Sultans.* New York: Metropolitan Museum of Art. 147-154.

Wild, Felicity C. and John P. Wild 2001. Sails from the Roman port at Berenike, Egypt. *The International Journal of Nautical Archaeology* 30(2): 211-220.

Wilford, John Noble 1993. New finds suggest even earlier trade on fabled Silk Road. *New York Times*, B5 March 16 March, 1993.

—2002. Of early writing and a king of legend. *New York Times*, April 16, å2002. Also: www.nytimes.com/22002/04/16/science/social/16SCOR.html.

Woolley, Leonard 1982. *Ur 'of the Chaldees': The Final Account, Excavations at Ur,* Revised and Updated by P.R.S. Moorey. London: The Herbert Press. 172.

Wright, Henry T. and E.A.S. Ripley 2001. Calibrated radiocarbon age determinations of Uruk-related assemblages. *In*: Rothman, Mitchell S. (ed.) *Uruk Mesopotamia and Its Neighbors: Cross-Cultural Interactions in the Era of State Formation.* Santa Fe: School of American Research Press. 100-119.

Wright, P.W.M. 1982. The bow drill and the drilling of beads. Kabul, 1981. *Afghan Studies* 384: 95-101.

Yoffe, Norman and Jeffery J. Clark (eds.) 1993. *Early Stages in the Evolution of Mesopotamian Civilization: Soviet Excavations in Northern Iraq.* Tucson: University of Arizona Press.

Zepezauer, Maria A. 1997. Chronological and cultural aspects of Late Celtic glass beads. *In*: Freeden, Uta von and Alfried Wieczorek (eds.) *Perlen: Archäologie, Techniken, Analysen. Akten des Internationalen Perlensymposiums in Mannheim vom 11. bis 14. November 1994.* Bonn: Dr. Rudolf Habelt GmbH. 61.

Zettler, Richard L. and Lee Horne (eds.) 1998. *Treasures from the Royal Tombs of Ur.* Philadelphia: University of Pennsylvania Museum of Archaeology and Anthropology. 195 pages.

Zurins, Juris 1996. Obsidian in the larger context of Predynastic/Archaic Egyptian Red Sea trade. In: Reade, Julian (ed.). *The Indian Ocean in Antiquity.* London: Kegan Paul International.

Numbers in bold refer to figures.

abrasives, 10, **15**, 16-18, 26, 29, 35
Abu Hureyra (Syria), 22 23
Afghanistan, 21, 27, 32, 36, 83
Africa, 17, 28
agate, 11-13, **15**, 16-18, **19**, 39, 42, **45**, **56**
    banded, **14**, 15, **15**, 18, 27, **31**, 35-37, 41, 55, 60, **84**, **85**
    bow-shaped, 35, 42
    dyed, **14**
    moss, **14**
    tabular, 41
agate glass, 53, **53**, 55, **55**, 58, **58**
Al Mina (Syria), 49
alabaster, 28, 33, 36, 43
Alexandria (Egypt), 13, 53, 58, 63, 67-68, 76-77, 80
alkali, 19, 26, 34, 41, 50, 58, 69, 72
Allard Pierson Museum (Amsterdam), 37, 70, 77, 79
Amarna, 43
amazonite, 27, 72
amber, 9, 13, 47, 64, 75, **80**, 83
American Southwest, 16
amethyst, 13, **14**
amulets, 9, 12, 23, **31**, **42**, 43, 64-65, 83
Anatolia, 11, 13, 37, 39-40, 42, 48, 63, 82
animal beads and pendants, 28, **28**, 34, 36, 49-50, **85**
Antioch (Syria), 65, 68
antler, 11
Aratta (Iran), 34
Arikamedu (India), 13, 60-61, 68-69, 71-72
Assyria, 47
Athens (Greece), 53
atificial colors, stone, 18
aventurine, **14**
azurite, 19
Babylon, 33, 39, 42-43, 46-47
Bactria Margiana Archaeological Complex, 36
Bahrain, 33
Bali (Indonesia), 69, 71
Baltic, 13, 47, 67
Baltic Sea, 9
Ban Chiang (Thailand), **53**, 60-61
Ban Don Ta Phet (Thailand), 60-61, 69
banded agate
    See: agate, banded
Banyuwangi (East Java), 71
barium, 50-51
barrel, 16, 36, 61, 68, 79
basalt, 14, **14**
bead blanks, **15**, 16
    See also: roughouts
bead caps, 35, 37, 55, 57
Bead Museum, Prescott AZ, 4
Bead Museum, Washington DC, **2**, 4, 6
bead research, 8, 19, 47, 72
Bead Society of Greater Washington, 2
bead symbolism
    See: symbolism, beads
bead timeline, **2**, 4, 6-7, 14, 18-19, 21, 26-27, 33, 36, 75
Bead Timeline Exibition: #30, 48; #38, 81; #94, 50;
    #201, 21; #202, 21; #203, 21; #204, 22; #205, 22;
    #209, 22; #210, 23; #229, 43; #230, 43; #232, 27;
    #234, 26; #240, 28; #241, 28; #243, 28; #246, 27,
    35; #260, 27; #261, 28; #262, 28; #264, 26; #284,
    28; #285, 28; #288, 34; #289, 34; #303, 35; #309,
    33; #320, 33; #332, 36; #344, 35; #354, 35; #361,
    36; #362, 37; #364, 35; #368, 37; #373, 40; #374,
    41; #380, 40; #381, 37, 41; #385, 41; #386, 40;
    #386a, 40; #387, 42; #389, 42; #390, 41; #391,
    41; #392, 41; #395, 41; #396, 41; #403, 42; #404,
    41; #414, 46; #421-422, 46; #430, 48; #452-455,
    45; #470-474, 46; #480, 46; #483, 48; #489, 47;
    #492, 50; #500, 50; #502, 50; #503, 49; #506, 50;
    #507, 49; #508, 50; #509, 49; #510, 50; #521, 55;
    #525, 53; #527, 53; #528, 53; #529, 53; #544, 77;
#545, 70, 77; #553, 69; #570, 64; #572, 65; #575,
45; #584, 58; #588, 55; #592-594, 58; #593, 58;
#596, 67, 78; #600, 57, 77; #602-603, 77; #605,
65; #606, 64; #607, 65; #609, 68; #610, 65; #613,
65, 66; #622, 81; #623-624, 66; #628, 66; #637,
79; #640, 82; #644, 83; #666, 70; #668, 82; #669,
81; #673, 78; #688, 82; #689, 83; #690, 82; #691,
82; #692, 83; #693, 83; #694, 77; #696, 58; #800,
29; #812, 29; #831, 50; #846, 51; #847, 60; #848,
51; #849-850, 59; #850a, 51; #851, 51; #852, 51;
#855, 51; #856, 59; #900-902, 60; #903, 61;
#904, 60; #910, 69; #911a, 69; #920, 70; #927,
70; #927a, 70; #930, 70; #1211, 83; #1213, 83;
#1327-1328, 73; #1604-1607, 35; #1610, 61
beaded clothing
    See: clothing, beaded
beadmaking, 14-15, 19, 32, 35
    agate, 36
    faience, 37, 43, 46, 82
    glass, 39-40, 43, 46-48, 51, 53-58, 61, 63-67, 69-
    71, 76-77, 79-83
    Habuba Kabira, 26
    ivory, Paleolithic, 10
    jade, 29
    lapis lazuli, 32
    metal, 37, 42
    Neolithic, 23
    stone, 15, **15**, 16-19, 22, 26-27, 29, 32-33,
    35, 60, 82
beads in museums
    See: museums, bead collections; individual muse-
    ums
beadstringing, 12, 26, 41, 64
Beck, Horace, 42-43, 61, 68
Berenike (Egypt), 53, 71, 80
beryl, 65
Bet Eli'ezer (Israel), 63
Beth Shean (Israel), 49
bicone, 12-13, 16, 18, 31, 34, 50, 60, 70
Black Sea, 48-50, 57-58, 65-67, 80-81, 83
bloodstone, **14**
bone, 9-11, 21, **21**, 33, 83
    Early Bronze Age, **31**
    spacer beads, **32**
British Museum (London), 78
Brittany (France), 75
broad collar, 8, 45
broadwing pendant, **81**
    Tairona, **75**
bronze, 12-13, 37, **37**, 58
Bronze Age, 9, 31-33, 33-34, 37, 39-40, 42, 45-46, 49, 60
burials, 10-12, 21-22, 29, 31, 36, 42, 47-48, 50, **56**, 57,
    60-61, 64, 72, 76, 78
Burkina Faso, 83
butterfly bead, **21**, 22, **23**
Byblos, 12, 47
Cairo (Egypt), 31, 63, 65, 76
calcite, **14**, 27, **31**, 33, **33**
Cambay, 17
    See also: Khambhat
Camiros (Rhodes), 48
cane, 76, 78-79, 83
    flat, 55
    floral, 67, 78
    glass, 77
    millefiori, 80
    mosaic, 56-58, 67, 69, 71, 80-81
    pierced, 79-80
    twisted stripe, 77
cane beads, pierced, 78
carnelian, 11-13, **14**, 15, **15**, 16-17, **17**, 18, **19**, 23, **25**,
    26-27, 31, **31**, 33-36, 39, 64, 69, 72, 83, **85**
    bleached, **19**
    etched, 19, **19**, 34, 68, **68**, 69
    long beads, 35
    long bicones, **35**

spacer beads, **32**
Carthage (North Africa), 48-50, 75
casting, 39
casts, silicon rubber, **16**, **17**
Catalhoyuk, 11-12
Caucasus, 76, 78, 81
Celtic, 48-49, 54, 75-76
Central Asia, 23, 32-33, 35-37, 41
Central Europe, 9, 48, 54
Chagai Hills (Pakistan/Afghanistan), 32
chalcedony, 13, **14**, 15, 23, 27, **31**, **32**, 35
Chanhudaro (Pakistan), 17, 35
chank shell, Indian Ocean, 33
checker mosaic, 57, 67, 78, 80, 83
chert, 15, 17-18, 36
China, 9, 13, 21, 25, 29, 31, 50, 72
chlorite, 14, 27-28, 36
chronology, 6, 31, 51, 58, 69, 72, 76
chrysocolla, 33
citrine, 18
clay, 25, 33
clothing, beaded, 10-11, 23
cobalt, 61
collared beads, 41, 69, **79**
Colombia, 81
color enhancement, 15, 18
columella of *Turbinella pyrum*, 33
combed, 41, 47, 66, **78**
comma-shaped, 61
compound stratified eye beads
    See: eye beads
concentric patterns, 78
Constantinople, 63, 67
conus shell, 60, **60**
copper, 11-13, 19, 32, 36-37, 39, 45, 50
coral, 9, 11, 13, **14**, 22, 82, **85**
core-formed, 53, 66
cornerless cube, 61, 64, 83
Corning Museum of Glass (Corning NY), 50, 54
corundum, 17-18, 35
Costa Rica, 72, 81
cowrie shells, 11, 83
craft specialization, 12, 22, 25-26
Crete, 13
cristobalite, 19
crumb decoration, 66
crystal, 14-15
    See also: rock crystal
cuneiform, 25, 43, 45
cutting, 82
cylinder seals
    See: seals, cylinder
cylindrical beads, 45, 50
Cyprus, 13, 53
Damascus (Syria), 76
date beads, 59
Deccan Plateau (India), 27
Delos, 55
Denmark, 47, 57, 67, 78
Dentalium, 11, 13, 21
diamond, 18
diorite, 22
disk shape, 13, 16, 27, 40, 42, 45, 61
dot-in-circle design, **31**, 33, 83
double-axe beads, 22, **23**
doublet bead, 48, 70
dragon, 29, 36
drawn bead, 43, 53-54, 61, 71, **76**, 77
drilling, 11-17, **16**, **17**, 18, 23, 26, 28, 33, 35, 37, 60, 72
drum polisher, **19**
dZi, see: Zi
Early Islamic beads, **75**, **80**, 82
East Java, 70-71
Ebla (Syria), 31-34, 39
ebony, 13
Ecuador, 73

Penelope Diamanti de Widt and Pat Diamanti

Egypt, 12-13, 19, 23, 25, 28, 31, 37, 39-41, 43, 45-46, 48-49, 53, 55, 57-59, 63, 65, 67-68, 70-71, 75-80, 83
electrum, 12
emerald, 14, 18, 64
emery, 16, 35
endless knot pattern, 36
engraving, 82
etching, 19, 69
Etruscan, 47-48
Europe, 22, 25, 45-46, 48, 50, 54, 57, 72, 81, 83
    See also: Central Europe; individual countries
evil eye, 33, 51, 58, 80, 82-83
eye beads, 41-43, **43**, 48-49, **49**, 50-51, **51**, 53, **55**, 56, 58
    agate, 41, **41**, 42, 55
    composite, 51, **51**
    compound, 50
    stratified, 48, **49**, 51, **51**, 53, **55**, 59, **59**
    tabular, 41
    Warring States, 51, **51**
face beads, 57, **57**, 58, 69, **69**, 70, 78
faceted, 18, 35, 68, 77
faience, 12-13, 19, 37, **37**, 39, **39**, 41-43, 45-46, **46**, 50-51, 65, 82-83
    amulets, **85**
    Chinese, 50
    Early Islamic period, **78**
    Egyptian, 29, 50
    figures, **56**
fakes
    See: imitations
feather decoration
    See: combed
feldspar, 27
female figures, 9, 33, 40
fig-shaped beads, 76
Filottrano beads, 75
flint, 27
floral designs, 41, 45, 57
flux, 19
fly pendant, 46
folded beads, 48, 53, 55, 59, 61, **61**, **64**, 65, 65, 78-79, **79**, 81-83, **83**
fossils, 22-23, 83
France, 9-10, 47
Francis, Peter Jr., 8, 13, 55, 58, 63, 68-69, 77, 79, 82-83
Frattesina (Italy), 46
frit, 43, 45
furnace-wound, 65
fused rod beads, 77, 79
Fustat (Egypt), 75-76, 79, 82-83
Gao (Mali), 83
garnet, 17
Gdansk (Poland), 67
Germany, 65
Gimbutas, Marija, 33
Giza (Egypt), 31
glass, 12-13, 19, 33, 39, **39**, 40, **40**, 41, 43, 45-47, **45**, **46**, 51, 56, 58, **58**, 60-61, 64, 72, 75-76, **78**, **80**, 83
glass colors, 46-48, 54-55, 64-66, 69-70, 78
glass ingots, 43, 45, 54
glazing, 28, 39, 45-46
    See also: steatite, glazed
Glycyneris shell, 13
goddess, 9, 33, 40, 42
gokok, 72, **72**
gold, 12-13, 32, 35, 39, 41-42, 45, 50, 56, 64, 73, 82
gold-capped beads, **85**
gold-glass beads, 54, **54**, 55, 67, **67**, 83, **84**
Gotland (Sweden), 78
Gougad-Pateraenneu, 75, **75**
grave goods, 10-12, 21-23, 25, 28, 31-33, 35-36, 42, 45, 47-48, 50-51, 57, 59-60, 64-67, 70-72, 75-76, 78
Greece, 13, 47-48, 53, 77-78
greenstone, 27, 43
grinding, 14, 16, 18

Guatemala, 72-73
Gujarat (India), 17, 33, 42, 68
Gumaiyama (Egypt), 57
gypsum, 26
Habuba Kabira (Syria), 25-28, 31, 37
Hallstatt culture, 48, 65
Hao (China), 50
Harappa, 12, 35-36, 69
hardstone, 9, 17
Harvard Semitic Museum (Cambridge MA), 40
Hasanlu (Iran), 47
Hauterive-Chanpreveyres (Switzerland), 46
head beads & pendants, 49-50, 75
heat treatment, 15, 18-19, 22, 26-27, 37, 45
heirloom beads, 71, 75
heishi, 16
Hellenistic, 13, 53, **53**, 55, 79, 82
hematite, 10, 13, 18
Herculanium (Italy), 57
Hohookam, 13
Hongshan (China), 29
hot-pinched, 71
Hvenekilde (Denmark), 78
Igbo-Ikwu (Nigeria), 83
imitations, 10, 14, **19**, 35, 40-41, **41**, 42, 45-46, 55, **55**, 56, 59, 65, 69-70, 83
Inanna, 34
India, 9, 13, 17, 27, 33, 35, 42, 55, 60-61, 63, 65, 68-72
Indo-Pacific beads, 13, 60-61, 68, **69**, 70-72, **72**, 83
Indus Valley, 17, 19, 21, 26, 31, 33-35, **35**, 36, 39, 45
Inner Mongolia, 29
inverse indirect percussion, 15, **15**
Iran, 23, 27, 32-36, 40, 42, 46-47, 50, 68-69, 82
Iraq, 22-23, 28, 32-33, 40, 42, 47, 76
Ireland, 47
iridescent, 41, 55, 65
iron, 18, 27
Ishtar, 33, 40-42, 46
Islamic Museum (Cairo, Egypt), 77
Islamic period, 57, 66, 77, **79**
Israel, 21, 63, 65, 77
Italy, 46-48, 54, 57-58, 64-65, 75, 77
ivory, 9-13, 17, 45, 68, 83
    mammoth, 10, 21
    Paleolithic beadmaking, 10
jade, **14**, 15, 22, **25**, **27**, 29, 31, 51, 60, **63**, 72-73, 81
Jade Age ornaments, Hongshan culture, **29**
jadeite, 14-15, 29, 73
jasper, 13, **14**, 15, 17, 27, **34**, 35, 72, 83
Jatiagung (Java, Indonesia), 70
Jatim beads, 70, **70**, 71, **71**, 72, 79-81
Java (Indonesia), 71, 82
Java, East
    See: East Java
Jerusalem, 68
jet, 9, 82
jewelry, 12-13, 26, 31-32, 37, 42, 45-46, 61, 64, 67, 75
Jordan, 21, 37
Kandahar (Afghanistan), 27, 32
Karaguhul Bog, 78
Kausambi (India), 70
Khambhat (India), **17**
Khlong Thom (Thailand), 69, 72
Khlong Thom Museum (Thailand), 69
Khuzistan (Iran), 27
Kiffa beads, 77
Kirkuk (Iraq), 40
Kissi (Burkina Faso), 83
Kopet Daj Mountains (Turkmenistan), 36
Korea, 13, 71-72, 79-80
Kwan Museum, 51
La Tene, 48-49, 76
lapidary, 12, 14-18, 22-23, 26-29, 32, 35, 55, 61, 70
lapidary worked glass, **55**
lapis lazuli, 12, 14, **14**, 15-17, **25**, 27, **28**, 31, **31**, 32-34, 39-40, 45-46, 64, 66, 72-73, **80**, 82-83, **85**

lead, 32, **37**, 50-51
Lebanon, 21
leech beads, 42
lentil shape, 13, 36
Levant, 12-13, 21, 39, 63, 65-67
Liangzhu (China), 29
Liaoning Province, 29
limestone, 9, **14**, 14, 17, 36
literacy, 26
    See also: cuneiform; writing
lost-wax casting, 37
Lothal (India), 33, 42
lotus blossom design, 57
luxury goods, 12-13, 21, 32, 36, 45-48, 51, 60, 64, 66
magatama, 72
malachite, **14**
Malaysia, 79
Mali (West Africa), 23, 69, 82-83
manganese, 41
mano-fica, closed fist bead, **85**
Mantai (Sri Lanka), 58, 69, 72
marble, 14, 22-23, 28, 32
Mari (Syria), 31, 34
Marlik (Iran), 35, 46-47
marvering, 70
masks, 29, 49-50
materials, 8-12, 14, **14**, 15, 19, 21-23, 26, 32, 40, 56, 60, 82
    See also: individual materials: bone; stone; *etc.*
Mauritania, 58, 77, 83
Maya, 72-73
Mediterranean, 9, 11-13, 17, 21, 36, 39-40, 47-50, 53-54, 63-64, 66, 75
Mehrgarh (Afghanistan), 21, 27, 32, 45
melon beads, 31, **31**, 33, 41-42, 64-66, 83
Merovingian beads, 51, 64, 75-76
Mesopotamia, 13, 19, 22-23, 25-28, 31-37, 39, 42-43, 45-48, 72
metallurgy, 11, 34, 37, 39, 41, 46, 60, 73
Metropolitan Museum of Art (New York, NY), 7, 49, 82
Mexico, 72-73
microbeads, **15**, 16
Middle Asian Interaction Sphere, 36
millefiori, 53, **53**, 57, 70, **70**, 78, 80-81, **83**
    See also: mosaic
mining, 14-15, 23, 32, 42
mirror beads, 79
Mitanni kingdom, 40
Mkukutu (Tanzania), 83
Mohenjo-daro, 35
Mohs' hardness, 14-15, 23, 27, 29, 33, 35, 73, 82
molds, 40, 50, 58, 67, 72, 80
morfia, 77
mosaic, **40**, 41, 53, **53**, 55, **55**, 56, **56**, 57-58, 64, **64**, 65, 69-71, 76, **76**, 77, **77**, 78, **78**, 79-81, **83**
    See also: millefiori
mother-of-pearl, 9-11, **32**, **85**
Mumbaqa (Syria), 41
Mundigak (Afghanistan), 27, 32
Musee Guimet (Paris, France), 27
museums, bead collections, 26, 27, 33, 35, 37, 40-41, 49, 50-51, 64, 69-70, 77-79, 82
    See also: individual museums
mythology, 34, 36
Nagar, 31, 39
Nassarius, 21
Native American, 73
natron, 58
Neolithic, 9, 17, 21, **21**, 23, **23**, 29
nephrite, 14-15, 29, **29**
Nigeria, 83
Nile Valley, 25, 28
Nimrud (Iraq), 42
Nippur (Mesopotamia), 39
Nishapur (Iran), 75, 80, 82

Niuheliang (Inner Mongolia), 29
Noen U-Loke (Thailand), 60
Nubia, 28
Nuzi (Iraq), 40-41, 46, 65
oblate, 41, 45
obsidian, 11, 14-15
Oc Eo (Vietnam), 69, 71-72
Olmec, 73
onyx, **14**, 18, 83
ornaments, 10, 13, 16, 21, 23, 25-27, 35, 37, 39-40, 46, 50-51, 60, **73**
ostrich eggshell, 9, 13
Pakistan, 17, 21, 23, 27, 32, 35, 37, 61, 67
Paleolithic, 8-11, 22, 47
Palestine, 43, 58, 68
Panama, 81
peacock tail bead, **78**
pearls, 13, 64, 68
pecking, 16
pelangi (rainbow), 70, **70**
pendants, 10-13, 25, 27, 29, 33, **39**, 40-41, 43, **49**, 55, 58, 60, **60**, 65, **65**, 66, 68, 72, **73**, 82
perforation, 10, 12, 16, **16**, 17, **17**, 18, 23, 26, 29, **29**, 33, 40-41, 46, 60, 71, 79, 81
Persian Gulf, 33, 36, 68, 71
Peru, 73
Peshawar (Pakistan), 17, 67, 69
Peten, 73
Petrie Museum, 41
phallic imagery, 56, **56**, 58
Philippines, 71
Phoenicia, 12-13, 40, 47-48, 57, 75
pinching, 77
polishing, 10, 14-15, 18, **19**
    bag, 18, **19**
Pompeii (Italy), 57, 65
potassium, 50, 72
powder glass, 77
pyrite, 14
pyrotechnology, 19
Qom, 82
quadruple spiral, **39**, 42, **84**
quartz, 13, 15-16, 23, 26-27, 35
    glazed, 19, **80**, 82-83
quartzite, 18, 22
Queen Puabi, 12, 32, 35-36
radiocarbon dating, 7
Rhapta (East Africa), 83
Rhodes, 13, 48, 53, 55, 64, 66
Ribe (Denmark), 57, 67
ring beads, 76
Rio Montagua (Guatemala), 73
rock crystal, 11, **14**, 18, 22, 26-27, **31**, 33-34, 64, 72, 75, **80**
Roman, 9, 13, 18, 47, 55, 58, 63-66, 68, 70, 72, 78, 80
Roman period beads, **53, 56, 58, 63**
rose quartz, **14**
Rosen Collection, 4, **84-85**
roughouts, 15-16, 35
    See also: bead blanks
Royal Cemetery of Ur, 12, 31-32, 35, 41
ruby, 14, **14**, 18
Russia, 9-10, 21, 76-77, 79, 82
Sahara, 13, 83
Samarra (Iraq), 75-76, 79, 82
sand-blasting, 60
sang-i-Maryam, 83
sapphire, 14
Sar-i Sang (Afghanistan), 32
Sarazm (Central Asia), 32
Sardis, 48
sardonyx, **14**, 18
Sasanian Empire, 19, 68, 71

sawing, **15**, 16
Scandinavia, 13, 58, 76-77, 81
Scanning Electron Microscope, 16, **16**
scarabs, 12-13
Scythian, 50, 65
seals, 12-13, 19, 22, 25, 31, 33, 35, 41, 82
    cylinder, 25, 28, 31, 33, 39, **39**, 41
    stamp, 25, 28, 36, 65
segmented beads, **54**, 55, 58, 67, 70-71, 77, 79
Sepphoris (Israel), 63
serpentine, 9, 14, **14**, 15, 22, 27, 73, **73**
Shandong-Longshan (China), 29
Shanghai (China), 29
Shanxi Province (China), 50
shapes, 12, 16, 21, 23, 26, 28-29, 31, 33-37, 40-42, 45, 48-49, 51, 55, 65, 68, 76-77, 79
    See also: individual shapes: binone; bow; *etc.*
shaping, 15-16
Sharh-i Sokhta (Iran), 32, 35
shell, 8-11, 13, 17, 21, **21**, **28**, **31**, 32, **32**, 33-35, 46, 60, 73, **85**
Shiraz (Iran), 69
Shortughai (Central Asia), 32
Sidon, 39, 47
silica, 18-19, 41, 45-46
Silk Road, 13, 48, 82
silver, 12-13, 32, 42
silver-glass beads, 67
Sinai Peninsula, 23
Skovegarde (Denmark), 78
slit rings, 60
smoky quartz, **14**
soapstone, 14-15, 19, 22
social jade, **27**, 73
social stratification, 10-12, 18, 21-23, 25, 28, 31-33, 37, 45, 65
sodalite, **14**
sodium, 50, 72
Solomon's knot design, 66
South Asia, 19, **21**, 36
Southeast Asia, 13, 61, 83
spacer beads, 13, **32**, 33, 40-41
spidle whorls, 83
spiral, 77-78
spondylus, 73
Sri Lanka, 71
steatite, 13-14, **14**, 15, 17, 19, 22-23, **25**, 26, **26**, 27-28, 36-37, 43
    glazed, 19, 27, 37
stone, 9, 16, 21, 33
    Central Asian, **31**
    Early Bronze Age, **31**
    tubular bead, **60**
Sumarians, 12, 31-32, 34
Sungir (Russia), 10, 21
surface decoration, 9, 14, 22, 28-29, 33, 40-41, 47-48, 50-51, 53, 55-57, 59, 66, 68, 76-77
    See also: combed; etched; *etc.*
surface modification, 18-19, 28-29, 33, 68
Susa (Iran), 27, 34-35
Switzerland, 46
symbolism, bead, 8, 10-12, 21-22, 25, 31-33, 39, 42-43, 46, 51, 65, 67, 72-73, 75, 83
Syria, 21-23, 26, 31, 34-35, 37, 39, 41-43, 45-46, 49-50, 67-68, 76-78, 81
tabular, 26, **31**, 41, **54**, 55, **84**
Tairona (Colombia), 81, **82**
talc, 9, 14, **14**, 15, 19, 22
Tall-i Malyan (Iran), 34
Tanzania, 83
Taurus Mountains (Anatolia), 39
Taxila (Pakistan), 61, 69
technology, 9-12, 14, 19, 22, 25-26, 31, 34, 37, 39, 41,

45-46, 53, 69
faience, 39, 45-46, 50
glass, 41, 43, 45-48, 53-55, 63, 66, 72, 75-76, 78, 80-82
teeth, 8-11, 13, 21, **21**
Tel Sotto (Syria), 32
Tell Brak (Syria), 31, 34, 41-42, 46, 54
Tell el-'Ajull (Palestine), 42
Tell Kashkashok (Syria), 23
Tell Sabi Abyad (Syria), 22
Tepe Gawra (Iraq), 27-28, 32
Tepe Hissar (Iran), 32, 42
terra cotta, 35, 51
Thailand, 58, 60-61, 68-69, 72
thunderstones, 23
Tibiscum (Romania), 57, 64-65, 67
Tihuanaco (Peru), 73
timeline
    See: bead timeline
tin, 13
tokens, 12, 22, 25
tombs
    See: burials; grave goods
tools, 10-11, 13-14, 16, 21, 46, 68
torus-folded beads, **79**, 82
tourmaline beads, **84**
trade, 9, 11-13, 21-23, 25-27, 32-33, 35-36, 39-40, 42, 45-48, 50, 53, 55, 58, 60, 63-64, 67, 71-72, 75, 80
trade routes, 33-34, 47, 50, 67-68, 73, 80-81, 83
trailed decoration, 55, **55**, 66, 76, 81
Trier, 64
Troy, 42
tumbling, 18
Tunisia, 83
Turkey, 21, 45
Turkmenistan, 27, 36
turquoise, 11, **14**, 15, 17, 23, 27, 33, 39, 45-46
Tyre, 12, 39, 47-48, 63
Ubaid culture, 26
Ugarit, 39
Ukraine, 48, **56**, 57, 81
Uluburun shipwreck, 13, 45, 54
Ur, 12, 19, 31-32, 35-36, 39, 41
urbanization, 12, 21-22, 25, 28, 31, 35-36, 53
Urkesh (Syria), 31
Uruk, 26, 26, 31, 34, 43
Uzbekistan, 68
vertebrae, 9
Vietnam, 60, 71-72
Viking, 13, 67, 78
Warring States, 50, **51**, 59, **59**, 60
wasters, 77
wave design, 48, **55**, 56
weathering, 41, **46**, **47**, 51, 59, 65, 69
West Africa, 23, 83
West Asia, 21-22, 45-48, 70-71, 78-79, 83
workshops, 12, 17, 32, 35, 48, 50, 53-54, 58, 65-67, 72, 77-78, 83
wound bead, 41, 48-49, 57, 71, 76
writing, 22, 25, 28, 34
Xinjiang Province (China), 29
Xinlongwa (Inner Mongolia), 29
Yarim Tepe, 22, 27, 33
Yucatan, 73
Yugoslavia, 77
Zawi Chemi Shanidar (Iraq), 23, 33
zhulong, **29**
Zi, 19, 61

Deborah K. Zinn

Learning about Beads online: You can continue your study of the beads in this catalog on the World Wide Web, the Internet. Use these tips to get you started, if you are new to the Web, or to get more from the Web, if you are already online: **Tip 1:** Use ALL tips together to get the best learning experience and have the most fun! **Tip 2:** Use Search Engines. **Tip 3:** Go to reputable websites. **Tip 4:** Join online Discussion Groups. **Tip 5:** Join a Bead Society with an informative and active website.

Using Search Engines: The World Wide Web is the home to billions of websites. Using a Search Engine allows you to find information of interest to you in a matter of seconds. It just takes a little practice. There are many different Search Engines. However, learn to use one Search Engine well and then you can learn to use others easily. Google is one of the best Search Engines; their website address is: http://www.google.com/ First, try searching for pictures of beads. Click on Images from the Google menu. Then type "faience beads" and click Google Search. You will see wonderful images of beads. By clicking and selecting a thumbnail (small picture) you will be taken to the webpage that hosts the picture. Usually these websites will have text that describes the images. You will find by looking at the website addresses of the images that these bead pictures may be from the recommended websites below. Then you know the information is as accurate as it is possible to be. Second, click on Web from the Google menu. This gives you a list of websites with written information about the beads of interest in this example, faience beads. Google Image Search, shows you pictures; Google Web Search gives you a list of websites (a combination of text and pictures). To learn more about how to search with Google, use the online help provided. On Google, look for a menu item on the top or right of your computer screen called: Advanced Image Search or Search Tips or Advanced Search and just click. Caution: On the Internet, as with all media, you must learn to evaluate all the information that you read. Use your own common sense. If you find information of interest, share it with a Discussion Group, then you will benefit others and learn, too.

Go to reputable websites: There are many, many bead websites. If you know the website address, you do not have to use a Search Engine. Just type the website address into your Web browser. Below are a handful of websites that you can count on for accurate information about beads and their history: For more information about The Bead Museum DC Timeline and future exhibits, visit our website at

http://beadmuseumdc.org/ The website of The Bead Museum in Glendale, Arizona features exhibits and educational information: http://www.beadmuseumaz.org/ A wonderful Timeline of Art History is available at the Metropolitan Museum of Art and beads are featured throughout on http:// www.metmuseum.org/toah/splash.htm

The Cambridge University Museum of Archaeology and Anthropology, in conjunction with the Bead Study Trust, document the collection of Horace Beck, bead research pioneer on http://www.beadstudytrust.org.uk/ and http://museum-server.archanth.cam.ac.uk/

Download Bead Bibliographies recommended by the late Peter Francis, Jr, Stefany Tomalin, Gabrielle Liese, Karlis Karklins and other members of Beads-L at http:// home.attbi.com/~judvan/Beads_LBibliographies2.pdf

Join online Discussion Groups: All groups mentioned welcome new members from newbies to experts. For each group of the following, you will find instructions on how to join at their website address. Beads-L (L for list) includes many of the world's leading bead and beadwork researchers and authors as well as bead enthusiasts. Deborah Zinn is the founder and co-moderates with Stefany Tomalin on http://home.attbi.com/~judvan/ Jamey Allen moderates Bead Collector's Corner and Trade Bead Talk on Yahoo at http:// groups.yahoo.com/group/beadcollectors/ and http://groups.yahoo.com/group/tradebeads/ National Bead Society hosts a free-wheeling discussion group at http://nationalbeadsociety.com/page1.html

Join a Bead Society with an informative and active website: The Bead Society of Greater Washington hosts the website of The Bead Museum DC, http://beadmuseumdc.org/ The Bead Society of the Great Britain welcomes new members from all parts of the globe at http://www.beadsociety.freeserve.co.uk/ The International Society of Glass Beadmakers uses http://www.isgb.org/index.shtml To find a list of Bead Societies use Google or go to the link below. Caution: As with all information on the Web, contact details may be outdated or inaccurate so you may need to also check with a Discussion Group to find current information. See Bead Society and Guild Listings at the Bead Bugle, http://www.nfobase.com/html/organizations.htm

In conclusion, learning about beads is an enjoyable life-long activity. The World Wide Web, the Internet, brings the knowledge and expertise of bead enthusiasts and researchers from around the world into your home with a few keystrokes.